The Trial of Billy the Kid

First Edition

David G. Thomas

Mesilla Valley History Series, Vol 7

Doc45 Publishing, P. O. Box 5044, Las Cruces, N. M. 88003
books@doc45.com

To obtain books, visit:
doc45.com

YouTube Channel
youtube.com/c/Doc45Publications

Cover artwork by Dusan Arsenic.

ISBN 978-1-952580-02-4

000

DOC45 PUBLISHING

Dedicated To

Joseph E. Lopez

Friend, artist, and historian. You left this world too early.

DEATH SENTENCE of Billy the Kid Mesilla. 1881.

Mesilla Valley History Series

La Posta – From the Founding of Mesilla, to Corn Exchange Hotel, to Billy the Kid Museum, to Famous Landmark – by David G. Thomas

Giovanni Maria de Agostini, Wonder of The Century – The Astonishing World Traveler Who Was A Hermit – by David G. Thomas

Screen with a Voice – A History of Moving Pictures in Las Cruces, New Mexico – by David G. Thomas

Billy the Kid's Grave – A History of the Wild West's Most Famous Death Marker – by David G. Thomas

Killing Garrett, The Wild West's Most Famous Lawman – Murder or Self-Defense? – by David G. Thomas

The Stolen Pinkerton Reports of Colonel Albert J. Fountain Investigation – David G. Thomas, Editor

The Trial of Billy the Kid – by David G. Thomas

Mesilla Valley Reprints

When New Mexico Was Young – by Harry H. Bailey

Doc 45

Buenas noches boys,
A social call no doubt –
Do we talk it over,
Or do we shoot it out?

I'm Doc 45,
Toughest man alive.
Hand over those golden bills
Or I'll dose you up with dirty leaden pills.

Contents

Acknowledgments

I thank Richard Weddle for permission to use the tintype image of Billy the Kid on the cover and in the text. I thank Sally Kading and Karla Steen for permission to use the tintype image of Pat Garrett in the text.

I thank Mary Chastain, Dan Aranda, Dan Crow, Lucinda Allshouse, Karla Steen, and Josh Slatten for proofing the manuscript and making corrections and suggestions.

Special thanks to the many who sought out source materials and provided invaluable help in my research efforts: Dennis Daily, Elizabeth Villa, and Teddie Moreno, Library Archives & Special Collections, NMSU; Evan Davies, Institute of Historical Survey Foundation; Rick Hendricks, New Mexico State Records Administrator; Judy Pate, E. A. Arnim Archives & Museum of Flatonia, Texas; Claudia Rivers and Abbie H. Weiser, C. L. Sonnichsen Special Collections, UTEP; Daniel Kosharek and Catie Carl, Palace of the Governors Photo Archives, New Mexico History Museum; Tomas Jaehn, Special Collections, UNM; and Dena Hunt, State Archives of New Mexico.

For photographs and permission to use them, I thank Sidney L. Gardner, Beth Wilson, Bernice Letourneau, and Bob Gamboa.

Unattributed photos are from the author's collection.

List of Images

Introduction

This book is about Billy the Kid's trial for murder, and the events leading to that trial. The result of Billy's trial sealed his fate. And yet Billy's trial is the least written about, and until this book, the least known event of Billy's adult life.

Billy's real name was William Henry McCarty. Most historians believe he was born in New York in 1859, although no records documenting his birth or his paternal parentage have been found. His mother may not have been married. Billy, his younger brother Joseph, and his mother Catherine McCarty left New York in 1872 for Wichita, Kansas. There they lived with William H. Antrim, a farmer, who later would become Billy's stepfather. Catherine and her sons were probably taken on by Antrim as a charity case, and as free labor.[1] Within a few months, Antrim and his three wards left Kansas for New Mexico, where Antrim married Catherine in Santa Fe on March 1, 1873. [2]

Shortly after the marriage, the family moved to Silver City, New Mexico.[3] There, on September 16, 1874, Catherine died of tuberculosis. One year after his mother's death, Billy was arrested and jailed for concealing stolen property. Billy was manipulated into hiding the purloined items by George Schafer, a much older tough known around Silver City as "Sombrero Jack." [4] Billy escaped from the jail by shinnying up a fireplace chimney in the corner of his cell. Following his escape, Billy fled Silver City, beginning his now famous life as an adult.

During his life, in court records, Billy was referred to as William Bonney, alias "Kid,' alias William Antrim. It is unknown why Billy began calling himself Bonney. It is possible that his birth father's surname was Bonney. Billy went by Henry Antrim while growing up in Silver City. In letters, Billy signed his name as W. H. Bonney, or occasionally, W. Bonney.[5]

The best eye-witness description of Billy in his last year appeared in the December 28, 1880, issue of the *Las Vegas Gazette*. The author, an unnamed reporter, interviewed Billy just as he was being locked up in the Las Vegas jail.

> *"He is about five feet eight or nine inches tall, slightly built and lithe, weighing about 140; a frank open countenance, looking like a school boy, with the traditional silky fuzz on his upper lip; clear blue eyes, with a rougish [roughish] snap about them; light hair and complexion."* [6]

As Billy was being unshackled from the other prisoners who had been captured with him (Dave Rudabaugh, Billy Wilson, and Thomas Pickett), the four men were surprised by a gift of new clothes by Michael Cosgrove (not known to be a close friend). This is one of the three times that a public act of kindness appears in Billy's story. Dave Rudabaugh was notorious for not ever changing his clothes – his nickname was "Dirty Dave" Rudabaugh. He likely reeked from body odor. Probably the other three had also not changed their clothes for a long time.[7]

A second act of public kindness occurred when Billy was jailed in Mesilla. Before his trial began, he was given a new suit and shoes by the Sisters of the Loretto Academy.[8]

The third act of public kindness occurred after Billy's death. Pat Garrett paid for Billy's body to be dressed in new clothes for his burial. Garrett paid for *"a beige suit, a shirt, an undershirt, shorts, and a pair of stockings."* [9]

This book begins with the event that initiated the chain of events that led to Billy's trial – Billy's capture by Patrick Floyd Garrett. After detailing the consequences of that happening, which led to Billy being incarcerated in the jail in Mesilla, the book flashes back to the actions that produced the criminal charges against Billy. That flashback begins with Chapter Three and lasts four chapters. An extended flashback is unusual in a history book, but, in my mind, it is the best way to tell the story of Billy's trial.

I consider Billy's trial the most important event in Billy's life. You may respond that his death is more important – it is in anyone's life! That is true, in an existential sense, but the events that lead to one's death at a particular place and time, the cause of one's death, override the importance of one's actual death. Those events are determinative. Without those events, one does not die then and there. If Billy had escaped death on July 14, 1881, and went on to live out more of his life, that escape and not his trial would probably be the most important event of Billy's life.

Chapter Eight ends the flashback. The remainder of the book details the events of the trial and its aftermath.

Prior biographies have provided extensive – and fascinating – details on Billy's life, but they supply only a few paragraphs on Billy's trial. Just the bare facts: time, place, names, result.

The information presented here has been unknown until now. This book makes it possible to answer these previously unanswerable questions:

- Was there a trial transcript and what happened to it?
- What kind of defense did Billy present?
- Did Billy testify in his own defense?
- Did Billy have witnesses standing for him?
- Who testified against him for the prosecution?
- What was the jury like?
- What action by the trial judge virtually guaranteed his conviction?
- What legal grounds did he have to appeal his verdict?
- Was the trial fair?

Appendix A gives the story behind the locating and marking of the spot where John Henry Tunstall was murdered, the event which triggered the Lincoln County War. Appendix B gives the story behind the locating and marking of the graves of Richard M. Brewer and Andrew "Buckshot" Roberts. Appendix C gives biographies of 116 men and women who have important roles in the events covered in this book. Providing this information in an appendix makes it possible to avoid interrupting the flow of the narrative with repeated biographical asides.

All places not otherwise identified are in New Mexico. See the publisher's website doc45.com for a bibliography.

First generation scan of the Billy the Kid tintype. Courtesy Richard Weddle.

Prior Page: A first generation scan of the only authenticated photo of Billy the Kid, taken in 1879 or 1880 at Fort Sumner. My most profound thanks to Richard Weddle for his gracious permission to reproduce this image. Richard made an extensive study of the original tintype, including examining it microscopically. His deductions include that Billy's sweater is homemade; his pull-over workshirt bears an emblem of a nautical anchor entwined by three dolphins; his vest is of the type sold then by Reed Brothers & Co; his cartridge belt is leather belted with a riveted buckle; his left vest pocket holds something, likely a deck of cards or tobacco; and the ring on his left little finger has a mirrored surface, a type of ring often worn by card gamblers of the time, designed to help the wearer see the cards of other players.[10]

His pistol is a Colt model 1873 single action revolver. His rifle is a Winchester model 1873 carbine. Both used .44-40 cartridges, meaning Billy only had to carry one size of ammunition.[11] These are the same model weapons taken off of Billy Wilson when he was captured with Billy at Stinking Springs on December 23, 1880 (see Chapter 1).

Billy's unknown photographer used a four lens multiplying camera that enabled him to make four images on one plate, which were cut apart to make four tintype photographs. This image was the upper, left image. The images produced by a tintype camera are "mirror images," images with the left and right sides reversed. As a result, the tintype made it appear that Billy was wearing his Colt pistol on his left side. The image on page 3 has been reversed, showing Billy as he actually looked.

One of four tintypes was obtained by Pat Garrett, probably taken from Billy when he was captured at Stinking Springs. This tintype was used to make the image of Billy reproduced in the January 8, 1881, issue of *"The Illustrated Police News, Law Courts and Weekly Record."* That publication was shown to Billy while he was in jail in Santa Fe (see page 41). This tintype was also used to make the image of Billy reproduced in Garrett's book *"The Authentic Life of Billy, the Kid, the Noted Desperado of the Southwest, Whose Deeds of Daring Have Made His Name a Terror in New Mexico, Arizona, and Northern Mexico,"* published in 1882. Garrett still owned the tintype when he was killed February 29, 1908. His daughter Pauline loaned the tintype to author John Milton Scanland, who reproduced it on the back cover of his *"The Life of Pat F. Garrett and the Taming of the Border Outlaw,"* published in late 1908.[12] There is no further record of this tintype. It apparently was never returned to the Garrett family and is lost.

A second tintype was given to a Patrick McGraw, a White Oaks merchant (not a known friend of Billy). [13] This tintype is also lost.

A third tintype was given to Deluvina Maxwell. This tintype was copied in 1904 by author Emerson Hough and is the source of the images of Billy that have since been universally reproduced in books and on the internet. Paulita Maxwell told Hough:

"The Kid gave her his only photograph which he had carried around in his pocket. He could have given Deluvina nothing she would have prized more."

"My mother kept the picture in a cedar chest for years, and finally my sister, Odila, give it to John Legg, a Fort Sumner saloon keeper and friend of the family. Legg was shot and killed and Charlie Foor, as executor of his estate, came into possession of the picture. When Foor's house burned down, the original was destroyed...." [14]

The fourth tintype was given to Billy's friend Daniel C. Dedrick. It remained in the possession of Dedrick's descendants until 2011 when it was sold at auction to a collector for 2.3 million dollars. The image on page 3 is copied from that tintype. It is reproduced courtesy of Richard Weddle.

BILLY THE KID.—[From a Photograph.]

Engraving of Billy used as the frontispiece in Garrett's 1882 book. The engraving was copied from the tintype that Garrett took from Billy at Fort Sumner. The image was not reversed, which led many early writers to assert that Billy was left-handed.

Patrick Floyd Garrett, tintype, undated. Courtesy Sally Kading and Karla Steen.

Chapter 1 | Capture

Billy the Kid was betrayed by a snitch – Manuel Silvestre Brazil.

That finking would cost Billy his freedom. Two hundred and three days later, Brazil would snitch on Billy a second time. That finking would cost Billy his life.[1]

Hunting Billy the Kid

The sheriff's posse that began to hunt Billy and his companions in early December, 1880, consisted of men drawn from two different jurisdictional localities – the Territory of New Mexico and the State of Texas – with two different rationales for joining the hunt.

The leader of the New Mexico posse, the person who afforded the posse its legal authority, was Patrick Floyd Garrett. Garrett was deputy sheriff of Lincoln County, New Mexico, and the sheriff-elect of the county. He had been backed for the sheriff position by an influential group of community leaders, including cattleman John Simpson Chisum and Roswell merchant Captain Joseph Charles Lea, for one reason – to combat the violence and lawlessness that was endemic in Lincoln County.[2]

Several months earlier, the *Santa Fe New Mexican* newspaper had deplored the sorry *"state of affairs"* in Lincoln, reporting that *"it would appear that another reign of terror has been inaugurated there, and that the pistol supersedes the law and mob violence rules supreme."* [3] The *Las Vegas Gazette* countered by noting that the rampaging lawlessness was bigger than Lincoln County – it encompassed also the adjoining counties of Valencia and San Miguel:

> *"The bivouac of the desperadoes is on what may be termed disputed territory. Living on or near the boundaries of Valencia, Lincoln, and San Miguel counties, it is yet held by many that it is included within the limits of the former county. From this very uncertainty, officials of the three counties have made it an excuse for hesitating about raiding them, each claiming that it is outside of their jurisdiction."* [4]

One gang, primarily, said the *Gazette*, was responsible for all the lawlessness:

> *"The gang includes from forty to fifty men, all bad characters, the off-scouring of society, fugitives from justice, and desperadoes by profession. Among them are men with whose names and deeds the people of Las Vegas are perfectly familiar, such as 'Billy the Kid,' Dave Rudabaugh, Charlie Boudre [Bowdre], and others of equally unsavory reputation...."*

> *"The gang is under the leadership of 'Billy the Kid,' a desperate cuss, who is eligible to the post of captain of any crowd, no matter how mean and lawless."* [5]

At least one person vehemently disagreed with that assessment. Billy responded to the *Gazette* article with a letter to Territorial Governor Lew Wallace, in which he said in part:

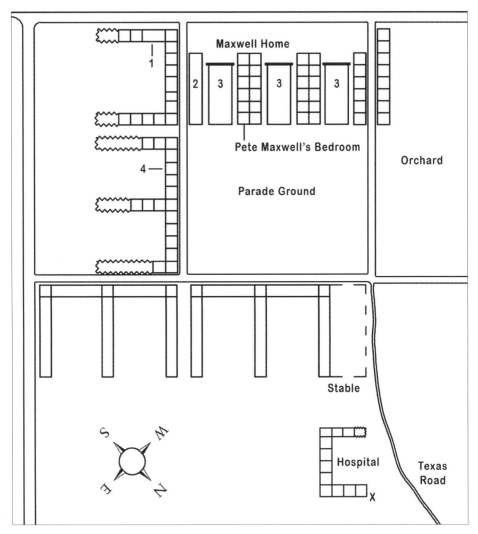

Fort Sumner, based on the October, 1881, map drawn by Charlie Foor. (1) Beaver Smith's saloon/store, (2) Dance hall, (3) Flower gardens, (4) Home of Sabal and Celsa (Martinez) Gutierrez, (x) Spot where Tom O'Folliard was shot. Pete Maxwell's bedroom was located in the southeast corner of the Maxwell home. The June, 1880, census shows Billy, Charles and Manuela Bowdre, A. B. Bennet, and Wilis Pruitt living in one room of the Hospital Building. Also living at Fort Sumner at the time according to the 1880 census are Barney Mason and his 17-year-old wife Juana María.

"I noticed in the Las Vegas Gazette a piece which stated that Billy 'the' Kid, the name by which I am known in the country, was the Captain of a Band of Outlaws who hold forth at the Portales. There is no such Organization in Existence. So the Gentlemen must have drawn very heavily on his imagination...."

"I have been at [Fort] Sumner Since I left Lincoln making my living gambling.... J. S. Chisum is the man who got me into Trouble, and was benefited Thousands by it and is now doing all he can against me. There is no Doubt but what there is a great deal of Stealing going on in the territory and a great deal of the Property is taken across the Plains as it is a good outlet but so far as my being at the head of a Band there is nothing of it...." [6]

In 1880, Fort Sumner was no longer a government fort. The fort and an adjoining million-acre reservation for Mescalero Apache and Navajo Native Americans had been authorized in October, 1862, during the second year of the Civil War. The fort was named after Major General Edwin Vose Sumner. The reservation was called Bosque Redondo (round woods), the Spanish name for the dense scrub-brush lining the Pecos River where the reservation and fort were established.[7]

With the reservation abandoned, there was little purpose in maintaining Fort Sumner, so it was ordered sold by the Federal Government. On October, 17, 1870, Lucien Bonaparte Maxwell bought the grounds and buildings of the fort, less the cemetery burial ground, for $5,000. He had earlier offered $700 for the property, which was rejected.[8]

Accompanying Lucien Maxwell in his move to Fort Sumner were about two hundred persons: relatives, employees, tenant farmers – and their families – who had lived with or worked for Maxwell.[9]

In December, 1880, when Billy was residing at Fort Sumner, he was living on property owned by Pete Maxwell, Lucien Maxwell's son. Pete had inherited the property when Lucien died on July 25, 1875.

In late September, 1880, the U.S. Treasury Department dispatched Secret Service Agent Azariah F. Wild to Lincoln County to investigate counterfeit hundred-dollar bills being circulated in the area.[10] Wild soon obtained circumstantial evidence that one member of Billy's "gang," Billy Wilson, had passed at least two of the counterfeit bank notes.[11] The Eastern press picked up the sensational story of the phony bills and the "Kid" outlaw and reported:

"Government officials are now interested in the campaign [against Billy and his companions], for, in addition to their other crimes, the outlaws have put into circulation a large quantity of counterfeit money manufactured by William Brockway, the forger." [12]

Wild approached Territorial Marshal John Sherman about pursuing the counterfeiters and was told, *"I prefer not to do so."* [13] Wild then approached Garrett, who said he was willing to form a posse to go after Billy and his gang, and would do so without (extra) pay.[14]

Garrett's legal justifications for hunting and apprehending Billy were two arrest warrants for murder. The first was for the murder of Lincoln County Sheriff William Brady on April 1, 1878; the second was for the murder of Andrew "Buckshot" Roberts

Left: Louis Philip "The Animal" Bousman, 1938 photo. Courtesy *Amarillo Sunday News-Globe*. Right: Frank Stewart, real name John W. Green, undated photo. Courtesy Bernice Letourneau.

on April 4, 1878 (see Chapter 4 for details on these charges).[15]

The "boys" from Texas were after Billy and his companions for rustling.

In July, 1880, the cattlemen of the Texas Panhandle formed the Panhandle Cattleman's Association for the purpose of combating cattle stealing.[16] One of the Association's first actions was to hire Frank Stewart as a range detective.[17] Frank Stewart's real name was John W. Green.[18] Sometime in mid-November, Stewart led several men into New Mexico with the goal of recovering stolen Texas cattle. The foray was a failure; the men returned with no retrieved cattle.[19]

Frank "Big Foot Wallace" Clifford, real name John Menham Wightman, undated painting.

Stewart's cattle-recovery failure made LX Ranch foreman Bill Moore so mad *"he concluded to rig up an outfit of his own and send them over after the cattle."* [20] However, one of the participants in the second Texas expedition, James Henry East, said that Moore's motives were not all that philanthropic, as Moore was himself guilty of secretly rustling cattle.

It was called *"sleeper work."* During round-ups, Moore had his cowhands mark un-branded cattle *"as much by ear work as by brand."* [21]

> *"Later on, these were found on the range, the boys branded and changed the mark easily, and they belonged to that outfit. All the time Moore was doing this, he was posing as taking a strong stand against cattle stealing. He made quite a bit of talk bout men who stole ought to be strung up. It was part of his game."* [22]

The second Texas expedition consisted of men from the LX, LIT, and EXE (E-cross-E) Ranches.

The LX Ranch sent James Henry East, Louis "The Animal" Philip Bousman, Lee Hall, Alonso "Lon" Chambers, Calvin "Cal" W. Polk, and a driver-cook known only as Francisco under the command of Charles A. Siringo. The LIT Ranch sent Thomas "Poker Tom" Emory, Bob Williams, and an unnamed driver-cook under the command of Bob Robinson. The EXE Ranch sent Frank "Big Foot Wallace" Clifford. Both the LX and the LIT Ranches consigned a mess wagon with their group. Clifford rode with the LX group.[23] Siringo was given $500 to cover the expenses of the posse.[24]

The men armed themselves well:

Thomas "Poker Tom" Emory and wife Ada, real name William Oscar Arnim. 1898
Wedding Photo. Courtesy E. A. Arnim Archives and Museum.

"We all had 2 belts full of cartridges a peace [piece] around us and was armed to the teeth with six shooters Bowie knives and Winchesters on our saddles." [25]

Besides their weapons, four members of the posse were packing "riding names" to hide their true identities. Frank "Big Foot Wallace" Clifford's real name was John Menham Wightman.[26] Tom Emory's real name was William Oscar Arnim.[27] Bob Robinson's real name was William T. Hughes.[28] Lee Hall's real name was Lee Hall Smith.[29]

Moore had a report that Billy the Kid was at or near White Oaks, New Mexico, with a herd of stolen Texas cattle, so he sent the posse there. Polk says they left on November 22, 1880, which could be off by a few days.[30] It was a harsh winter and the snow was *"6 to 12 inches deep."* The first night was spent in Tascosa, Texas, where the men stocked up on grub.[31] At Tascosa, Frank Stewart left the party and struck out on his own for Las Vegas, New Mexico, with the goal of raising additional men for the posse.[32]

When the posse reached Anton Chico, Siringo left the party.

"Charles [Siringo] said, 'Now I'll go on to Las Vegas, buy some grub, and you fellows go straight across to Anton Chico and wait until I get back....' [The rest of us] went over to Anton Chico and spent all our money buying whiskey, playing, and betting on rooster fights and horse racing and going to 'baile' [dances] with Mexican girls. We spent all our money thinking Charlie would soon be in with the grub." [33]

Anton Chico is a tiny community located along the Pecos River, 200 miles directly west of Tascosa. It was founded in 1822 as a Mexican Land Grant.[34] (Garrett married Apolinaria Gutierrez in the Anton Chico Catholic Church on January 14, 1880. There was no church in Fort Sumner. For details on that marriage and a debunking of the often repeated claim that Apolinaria was the sister of Garrett's first wife, who died in November, 1879, see Chapter 9.)

Siringo, in his account of his visit to Las Vegas, says:

"I found Las Vegas to be a swift dance-hall town, and the first night of my arrival I went broke playing monte.... I blew in all my expense money, about three hundred dollars, which Bob Roberson [Robinson] had given me to buy ammunition and grub." [35]

Garrett and Texans Join Forces

The Texans spent 10 days waiting for Siringo. When he finally showed up, he *"'fessed up."*

"All we [could] do was to tighten up our bits a little and postpone a few meals." [36]

The next morning the men left for White Oaks:

"...it was snowing. There was already about five inches of snow on the ground. By the time we stopped at noon, snow was from eight to ten inches deep. We made a dry camp and melted snow to water our horses. Before we could get started again, Pat Garrett... and Frank Stewart... and another man (Barney Mason) rode into camp." [37]

A. Nelson & Co. General Store, Anton Chico. 1875-1906 photo. Courtesy Palace of the Governors Photo Archives (NMHM/DCA), 091340.

Stewart had joined Garrett at Las Vegas, and when they received word that the Texas posse was at Anton Chico, they left to join them. Garrett took Barney Mason, a friend, with him as deputy sheriff. (The two had married their wives on the same day in the Anton Chico Catholic Church. [38]) Mason lived in Fort Sumner and knew Billy well.[39]

A few days before the meeting with the Texas posse, Mason killed John Farris:

> *"In a shooting affray at Fort Sumner on the 29th ultimo John Farris was shot and killed by Barney Mason. Farris shot three times at Mason without any provocation, when the latter went off, got a pistol and returning to the store where Farris was, shot him twice in the breast."* [40] (Farris was buried in the Fort Sumner cemetery.)

Mason was also working as a spy for Secret Service Agent Wild for two dollars a day and expenses. He was required to furnish his own horse.[41]

The day before Garrett and his party left for White Oaks, Charles Bowdre, Billy's good friend and companion, who fought alongside him in the Lincoln County War, arranged a meeting with Garrett in which he sought his advice about avoiding capture. Garrett told him to *"leave the country... and stay awhile; then come back when this thing is over."* [42] Bowdre, who was living with his young wife Manuela Herrera at Fort Sumner, chose to ignore the eminently sensible advice that he flee immediately. Instead, he wrote a letter to the Territorial Governor saying he would surrender to authorities:

> *"...upon the condition that the indictments against him for the murder of Roberts in the Lincoln Co. War, and his other offences be abolished."* [43]

At the "dry camp," Garrett and the Texans argued over how to proceed. The Texans' goal was the recovery of Texas cattle. Billy's capture would be a satisfying extra. Garrett's goal, even though he would be pleased to recover Texas cattle, was to capture Billy and his companions. Siringo wrote:

White Oaks after it became a ghost town. 1935 photo. Courtesy Center for
Southwest Research and Special Collections, UNM.

*"...our orders were strictly to get the cattle first, and then if we could assist
in the capture of the 'Kid' to do so."* [44]

The discussion became heated. Texas posse leaders Robinson and Siringo *"demeaned
[Garrett] and didn't mince words...."* Finally:

*"Bob and Charlie agreed to leave it to their men personally to decide who
would go with Pat. We split up exactly even, seven went, and seven wouldn't
go."* [45]

The incentive for the Texas men who joined Garrett was the expectation that there
would be a reward for capturing Billy. That expectation was met when Territorial
Governor Lew Wallace offered a $500 reward for Billy – and the press quickly responded
that $500 was *"too small."* [46]

*"What should be done by the people of this and neighboring counties is
to raise a purse of $5,000 to be paid the men engaged in this campaign...."* [47]

Knowing they faced a serious fight ahead, Garrett sent to Las Vegas for ammunition.

*"Deputy Sheriff Pat Garrett of Lincoln county sent in yesterday for a large
supply of ammunition to be poured into the gang of desperadoes should they be
foolish enough to resist his posse of determined men.... Our latest advices state
that the worst members of 'the Kid's' band are still at large but their capture is
merely a question of time."* [48]

Garrett told the posse that Billy was at Fort Sumner and *"by a forced march we
might catch [him]."*

*"We left our camp at daylight, rode all day without anything to eat, rode
all that night, and the next day to about 5 o'clock and got to Punta [Puerto]*

Puerto de Luna, Grzelachowski store/residence. The man wearing the derby hat (second from right) is believed to be Grzelachowski. Circa 1878. Courtesy Library of Congress.

Grzelachowski store/residence today. 2009 Photo.

de Luna.... We spent the night there. The horses were very tired as we often rode them that long with no feed. We slept in a house that night, as it was very cold." [49]

The house where the posse spent the night was the territorial-style, L-shaped store/residence of Puerto De Luna merchant Alexander "Alejandro" Grzelachowski. Grzelachowski was born in Poland in 1824. He came to New Mexico in 1851 and to Puerto de Luna in 1873.

When Grzelachowski arrived in the United States, he was a practicing Catholic priest. He served as a priest from his arrival in the U.S. in 1850 to 1862. In February, 1862, he joined the 2nd Regiment of the New Mexico Volunteers as a chaplain. The Volunteers were a Union force raised to fight the Confederate troops that invaded and occupied Southern New Mexico in July, 1861. After participating in the Battles of Glorieta Pass and Valverde, Grzelachowski left the priesthood and became a shopkeeper, first in Las Vegas, then in Puerto de Luna. [50]

Puerto de Luna, when Garrett and his posse arrived, was a tiny village of about 400 persons situated along both sides of the Pecos River. The community was founded by 13 settlers in 1862. A few years later the settlement was given its name by Don José Luna, who homesteaded in the pass just south of the settlement. He called his homestead Puerto de Luna (Gateway or Port of the Moon, a pun on his name), and within a few years, the community itself acquired that name. [51]

At Puerto de Luna, Garrett hired José Roibal to sneak into Fort Sumner and determine if Billy and his "gang" were there. At Fort Sumner, José was detained and *"rigorously"* questioned by two of Billy's companions *"as to his purpose in the village."* José justified his presence by claiming that he was just a simple sheepherder looking for strays. [52]

While José was away, Garrett attempted to recruit additional posse members from among the citizens of Puerto de Luna. The only person who agreed to join the posse was Juan Roibal, José's brother. [53]

When José returned with the news that Billy was at Fort Sumner, the posse left for:

"...John Gayheart's [Gerhardt's] ranch, eighteen miles below Puerto de Luna and twenty five above Fort Sumner. We reached here about nine o'clock in the night of December 17th in a terrible snow storm from the northwest." [54]

At Gerhardt's, two more men from Puerto de Luna, Charles Frederick Rudolph and George Wilson, joined the posse. After some food and a short rest, the posse pushed on:

"We got to [Fort] Sumner a little before daylight. We went to Beaver Smith's store. He was supposed to be friendly to us. Smith was the man the Kid and his gang branded. He was down in Lincoln County and supposed to be unfriendly to Kid's side. Billy and his bunch caught him one time, pulled his trousers down and put a brand on him. Beavers wanted to get even." [55]

Interrogated, Beaver Smith said he thought Billy and friends were in a vacant house across the plaza. (The well-known tintype of Billy is said to have been taken in Henry A. "Beaver" Smith's saloon by an itinerant photographer in late 1879 or early 1880. [56]) The "branding" story was a myth.

Ad for Con Cosgrove Mail Line, January 18, 1880. *Las Vegas Daily Gazette.*

The posse approached the house and observed a fire burning in the fireplace:

> *"Garrett pushed the door open and we all jumped in [in] unison. We found that it was the mail carrier. He said, 'Very good. Don't shoot boys.' We came mighty near shooting him, not knowing who he was and not having much light."* [57]

The mail carrier was Michael Cosgrove, who was living at Fort Sumner. His brother Con Cosgrove owned the stage line that ran once a week between Las Vegas and Las Cruces. Con had the government contract for mail delivery between those two towns, and Michael supervised the operation for his brother.[58]

Leaving Michael Cosgrove to his refuge, the posse took shelter in the Fort's old hospital building, a U-shaped adobe structure partitioned into numerous small rooms. The building nearest to it was the horse stable. It was only a few yards from the "Texas road" that connected Fort Sumner and Colorado City, Texas (see map page 8). Charles and Manuela Bowdre lived in one room of the building.[59]

The posse put their horses in the stable and spent the night in the building.

> *"As soon as anyone was stirring in the plaza of Fort Sumner on the morning of the 18th, I left our party, except Mason, in concealment and started out to take observations. I met a Mexican named Iginio Garcia in my rounds, who I*

Wilcox-Brazil Ranch House. Undated photo. Courtesy Maurice G. Fulton Papers, Special Collections, UA.

knew to be a tool of the Kid's, and spoke to him. I warned him not to betray my presence to any of the gang and not to leave the plaza." [60]

Garcia replied:

"...that his wife and baby were at home and had no milk for the baby. He said that his cow had gone down toward some Springs and [he] wanted permission to get her; he said he would be right back." [61]

Garcia is shown living with his 24-year old wife Maximiana and their six-month-old son Hilario in the 1880 Fort Sumner census.[62]

The "springs" where Garcia's cow had wandered was Brazil Springs, the site of the Wilcox-Brazil ranch. Garrett, who learned that Billy and his companions were at that ranch (in the existing deadly weather conditions, there were few places of shelter), negotiated a deal with Garcia. He would allow Garcia to go to the ranch, even pay him, to carry the information to Billy that he (Garrett) and Mason – and no one else – were in Fort Sumner. Clifford says that Garrett paid Garcia one hundred dollars. It was certainly less. As the rest of the posse was sheltering inside their hospital sanctuary, Garcia did not know they were there.[63]

Death of Thomas O'Folliard

Billy responded to the information that Garrett was in Fort Sumner by sending Thomas Wilcox's 16-year old stepson Juan Gallegos to Fort Sumner to verify the account, and to confirm that Garrett did not have a large posse with him.[64]

Juan attempted to fulfill his mission without being caught, but Garrett spotted him when he crossed the parade ground (plaza):

"I suspected his errand, accosted him, and found my surmise was correct. After a little conversation, I concluded that I would fully trust him. I made

Thomas "Tom" O'Folliard. Killed by Garrett's posse at Fort Sumner December 19, 1880. Buried in the Fort Sumner cemetery. Undated photo. Courtesy Maurice G. Fulton Papers, Special Collections, UA.

known my business to him, he promised to faithfully follow my instructions, and I believed him." [65]

Garrett also caught José Valdez, a known friend of Billy's, sneaking into town. Valdez told him he had seen Iginio Garcia in the distance during Garcia's trek to the Wilcox-Brazil ranch, but had not spoken with him. But when Garrett asked Juan, he said Garcia had indeed told Valdez about Garrett, and, further, Valdez had passed the information on to Billy.

Garrett forced Valdez to:

"...write a note to the Kid saying that I and all of my party had gone to Roswell and there was no danger. I then wrote a note to Wilcox and Brazil stating that I was at Fort Sumner with thirteen men, that I was on the trail of the Kid and gang, and that I would never let up until I got them, or ran them out of the country, and asking them to cooperate with me." [66]

Garrett gave the two notes to Juan, *"warning him not to get them mixed"* up.

As Garrett expected, when Billy received the Valdez note from Juan, he decided to come to Fort Sumner:

"The Kid's idea was... to slip in and steal the horses, put us afoot, and [leave us] on foot in that town, helpless." [67]

That evening, December 19, Billy and his "gang," Tom O'Folliard, Charles Bowdre, Tom Pickett, Billy Wilson, and Dave Rudabaugh, galloped into Fort Sumner on the Texas road. Garrett was prepared. He placed Chambers on guard outside the hospital building. Inside, cozy next to the warm fireplace, Garrett, Barney Mason, Tom Emory, and Bob Williams were playing poker. James East was trying to get a little sleep in anticipation of taking guard duty later in the night.[68]

Suddenly, Chambers:

"...slipped up to the door and said, 'Get your guns, boys; they're coming.' He had heard them. The boys threw down their chips and cards, got their guns, and we ran out. Just then they turned around the end of the hospital. The only light we had was from the snow. Garrett hollered at the bunch to throw up their hands. They jirked [sic] their six-shooters, and the fight commenced." [69]

"They was about 40 shots fired." [70]

Everyone in Billy's party *"whirled"* their horses and fled – with the exception of the person riding the lead horse – O'Folliard. His horse *"ran in a circle and came back."* [71]

East described the events that followed:

"Garrett said, 'Throw up your hands, or we'll shoot you down.' [O'Folliard] said, 'Don't shoot any more, Pat, I'm dying....'" He was shot through the heart. We took him inside and laid him down on my blanket. The boys went back to playing poker and I sat down by the fire."

"'Tom, in a low voice, cussed Garret, saying 'God damn you Pat, I hope to meet you in hell.' Pat said, 'I wouldn't talk that way Tom, you're going to die

Rock House at Stinking Springs built by Alejandro Perea. To the left of the building you can see the remains of a "summer porch," an outdoor workspace. In 1884, Lon Reed visited the rock house and saw the "bleached skeleton" of the horse Garrett shot still lying in the doorway. Undated photo. Courtesy Bosque Redondo Memorial Monument

Rock House site today. 2020 photo.

in a few minutes,' and then [Tom] said, 'and go to Hell, you longlegged S-- of B--.'"

"The game went on and blood began running inside Tom, gurgling. He asked me to get him a drink of water. I did and he drank a little, laid back, shuddered, and was dead. The poker-playing went on. It was a thing to get their mind off the fight, and to keep the men from growing weary." [72] [Intense thirst is a symptom of heavy bleeding – satisfying it invariably quickens death.]

In the exchange of gunfire, a bullet hit Rudabaugh's horse. Rudabaugh was able to ride the horse for twelve miles before it died; he then doubled up behind Billy Wilson.[73]

None of the existing first-person accounts of O'Folliard's killing mention the reaction of Manuela, Bowdre's wife. She was in the hospital building when O'Folliard was tortuously dying, which took an agonizing 45 minutes according to Garrett.[74] Manuela must have been confined to her room by Garrett. Nor is there any mention of any reactions to the shooting, happening just across the plaza from their residence, by Pete Maxwell and his family.

O'Folliard was buried the next morning in the frigid, snow-covered Fort Sumner cemetery. He was 32 years old. A resident was paid to build a wooden box for his body. [75] It is possible that Garrett paid for new clothes for O'Folliard to be buried in – he would do that for Charles Bowdre, and – 207 days later – for Billy himself.[76]

Stinking Springs (Ojo Hediondo)

The day of O'Folliard's burial, Manuel Brazil came to Fort Sumner. He was dispatched by Billy to determine if Garrett remained at Fort Sumner.

Brazil was born June 12, 1850, in Rosais, Sao Jorge Island, then as now a Portuguese colony in the Azores Archipelago. The name Brazil is common on the island. He came to the United States about 1865, and to the Fort Sumner area about 1871. He began ranching at a spring that became known subsequently as Brazil Springs, and he soon formed a ranching partnership with Thomas Wilcox.[77]

Billy's trust in Brazil was fatal. On arriving in Fort Sumner, Brazil immediately sought out Garrett. Brazil agreed to return to his ranch and tell Billy that Garrett was *"considerably scared"* and intended to leave for Roswell. He instructed Brazil that if Billy was at his ranch, he was to remain there; if Billy was not at his ranch, Brazil was to return to Fort Sumner.[78]

At his ranch, Brazil found Billy and his companions gone. Brazil promptly turned around and made the hard trek back to Fort Sumner, reaching Fort Sumner about midnight:

"There was snow on the ground, it was desperately cold, and Brazil's beard was full of icicles." [79]

Garrett ordered his men to saddle up. It was snowing heavily. Garrett planned to take a *"circuitous route"* to the ranch. Brazil was ordered to ride directly to his ranch and determine whether Billy had returned. A dozen miles from the Fort, the posse spotted *"a dead horse, the one Dave Rudabaugh had ridden to death."* The corpse was frozen and was shot *"through the entrails."* [80]

Manuel Silvestre Brazil, undated photo.

Three miles from the Wilcox-Brazil ranch, the posse met Brazil. Brazil had been to his ranch already, determined Billy was not there, and learned where he was. Billy and his companions had left for an abandoned – and now infamous – "rock house" at Stinking Springs.[81]

Brazil pointed to a line of horse tracks in the snow – it was Billy's trail, he told Garrett. That act was the determinative betrayal of Billy by Brazil. Garrett emphasized in his book that Brazil had always been Billy's *"faithful friend"* before this secret double-cross.[82]

Brazil made extraordinary efforts to get Billy captured or killed. To supply Garrett with intelligence on Billy, in a 36-hour period, he made two round trips in horrendous winter weather and six-inch deep snow between his ranch and Fort Sumner. And, then, he waited outside in the cold for perhaps hours for Garrett to turn up.

Garrett says Brazil rendered him the *"invaluable assistance"* that he did, because he was a *"law-abiding citizen,"* and because Billy would have killed Brazil *"without compunction"* if necessary.[83] Neither of these explanations is convincing. One cannot be killed for betrayal if there is no betrayal.

Unmentioned by Garrett is the reason the Texas posse was with him – he had promised them a share of the reward money. Also unmentioned is the money Garrett gave Garcia for his intelligence, and he undoubtedly promised or gave money to Gallegos and Valdez for their help and information.

In the author's opinion, Brazil's clear motive for betraying Billy was money.

The posse spurred their tired horses and began trailing the frozen tracks:

> *"The snow was pretty deep, and we had to travel slowly."* [84]

> *"We rode on there trail until about 2 o'clock in the morning. When we come in sight of there horses tide in front of a little house that had been a ranch, but was vacant. We got down tide our horses and left too men with them. The balance of us sliped up to a little spring branch which ran along in front about 20 steps from the door. There they all stoped except me [Polk] and Jim East. We crauld up and went all around the little house to see if they was any port holes in it."* (Spelling uncorrected) [85]

The *"little house"* was built about 1870 by Alejandro Perea. Perea appears in the 1870 Census living at Rio Colorado, just south of Puerto de Luna. The community no longer exists. Perea, 22 in 1870, was the second richest man in Rio Colorado. His net

Wilcox-Brazil Ranch House site today. 2020 photo.

worth was $4,756. Perea was a sheep raiser and the house was likely built for sheltering his sheepherders and storing forage.[86] It was constructed from sandstone blocks and had no windows or back door.[87]

Garrett continues the account:

> *"When within about four hundred yards, we divided our party and left Juan Roibal in charge of the horses. Finding a dry arroyo, we took its bed and were able to approach the house pretty close.... There were three horses tied to projecting rafters of the house, and, knowing that there were five of the gang, and that they were all mounted when they left Wilcox's, we concluded that they had led two horses inside."* [88]

Polk says:

> *"They horses was tide to a pole that stuck out over the door. We could hear them snoring in side the wall.... We then went back to the craud at the branch and told them how every thing was shaped up. We put some blankets down on the snow under the brow of the hill and lay down on them."* [89]

Cold it was – and Garrett's intentions were just as cold:

> *"Shivering with cold, we awaited daylight or a movement from the inmates of the house. I had a perfect description of the Kid's dress, especially his hat. I had told all the posse that, should the Kid make his appearance, it was my intention to kill him, and the rest would surrender.... [I] told my men when I brought up my gun, to all raise and fire."* [90]

As the sun broke over the snow on that December 23, a man carrying a morral (nosebag) stepped out of the house to feed his horse. Garrett, thinking it was the Billy:

Charles and Manuela (Herrera) Bowdre. This photo is one of two taken at the same time. The other photo is said to have traces of blood on it. Undated photo. Courtesy Arizona Historical Society.

"...gave the signal by bringing my gun up to my shoulder, my men raised, and seven bullets sped on their errand of death." [91]

The man was hit by three bullets, *"one in the leg and too (sic) in the body."* [92]

But the mortally wounded man wasn't Billy – it was Charles Bowdre. Garrett, so certain he could recognize Billy by his clothes and hat, had made an appalling mistake.

It was discovered later *"that [Bowdre] had been shot through the right breast, the ball coming out in the neck."* [93]

Bowdre fell back *"with his head back in the house."* [94] The men inside dragged him out of gunfire range:

"[Inside] we could hear them talk. Kid said, 'Charles, you're going to die anyway, so go on out to see if you can't get more of them.' He came out but we could see he was staggering along. He had a six-shooter in his hand, but was not able to cock it. The bank was about 2 1/2 feet high. Lee Hall and I [East] were lying together, and he fell over on Lee. We took his six-shooter which was useless to him, as he was dead." [95]

Garrett saw that someone inside was trying to lead one the horses tethered outside into the house. Seeing that the tether to the horse was *"shaking"* too much to shoot it, he shot the horse dead, *"just as the horse was fairly in the opening."*

"To prevent another attempt of this kind, I shot the ropes in two which held the other two horses, and they walked away." [96]

East made this comment on Garrett's shooting feat:

"A good deal has been said of the wonderful workmanship [shooting]. We were only about 30 feet away, and it wasn't a hard bit-rope with winter. At that distance it took two or three shots to cut the ropes." [97]

The felled horse obstructed the entrance, forestalling any attempt to make a wild break for freedom on Billy's racing mare, *"celebrated for speed, bottom, and beauty,"* one of the two horses confined inside the house.[98]

Garrett shouted for Billy to surrender; Billy refused. In the banter that followed, Garrett made it clear to Billy – *"to drop on the fact"* – that he was betrayed by Brazil. After a bit:

"We heard some pecking on the other side of the house, and Garrett sent Tom Emory and me [East] to stop that. We fired a shot or two at the place and it stopped.... [We] fired a shot or two at the door once in a while to pass the time away." [99]

"They was 2 boys went up on a little hill and commence shooting at the house. The horses in side got scard and was a bout to run over Billy and his men, so they turned them loose and out they come over the dead horse." [100]

In 1884, Lon Reed visited the rock house and saw the *"bleached skeleton"* of the horse Garrett shot still lying in the doorway.[101]

In the extreme cold, Charles Rudolph suffered frostbite:

Tom Pickett, undated photo. Courtesy Palace of the Governors Photo Archives (NMHM/DCA), 089720.

"My stomach was growling with hunger since we had had nothing to eat all day. I soon realized it was the least of my worries when I found out that my feet were almost frozen; I could feel nothing in my toes." [102]

About three in the afternoon, Garrett led half the posse to the Wilcox-Brazil ranch, returning with food, firewood, and forage:

"I did not know how long the outlaws might hold out, and I concluded I would make it as comfortable as possible for myself and the boys. We built a rousing fire and went to cooking." [103]

Debating their situation, recognizing the inevitable, and, as they later admitted, impelled by the enticing aroma of sizzling bacon, the "gang" resolved to surrender. Rudabaugh thrust out a stick with a white rag tied to it.

"We asked what he wanted and he said Billy said he wanted to surrender. He wanted to surrender under the conditions that we would give thim safe conduct to Santa Fe. Garrett promised the Kid safe conduct through Las Vegas."

"Kid and his men came out with their hands up. Barney Mason said, 'Kill him, he's [slippery] and may get away....' He leveled his gun and Lee Hall and I [East] threw our guns down on Mason and said, 'If you fire a shot, we'll kill you.'" [104]

Surrendering with Billy were Dave Rudabaugh, Thomas Pickett, and Billy Wilson.

Rudabaugh was an escaped, indicted murderer, facing a probable death sentence. Eight months earlier, he and John "Jack" Allen had endeavored to break John J. Webb out of the Las Vegas jail (Webb chose to decline Rudabaugh and Allen's unsolicited offer of liberty). During the break out attempt, Allen shot and killed jailor Antonio Lino Valdez. Rudabaugh was indicted in absentia for accessory to the murder of Valdez. It was while he was running from that charge that he hooked up with Billy. [105]

Thomas Pickett was the least likely person to be riding with Billy. He came from a religious family, was an ex-Texas Ranger, ex-merchant policeman at Las Vegas, and ex-assistant marshal at White Oaks. After quitting his White Oaks marshal job, Pickett began riding with Billy. The only criminal charge in his past was one for stealing horses, for which he had paid a $300 fine and had been released. [106]

Billy Wilson was the man that Secret Service Agent Wild desperately wanted Garrett to capture. Wild had recovered counterfeit bank notes that Wilson had spent with several Lincoln County merchants. But Wilson was a victim of the phony bills, not the perpetrator. He had received the counterfeit bills from W. H. West, who gave him $500 in the bills as payment for his (Wilson's) ranch.[107]

Wilson was wanted also for robbing the U.S. Mail. On October 16, 1880, three men held up mail carrier Fred Weston. Weston was one of Con Cosgrove's transport drivers. Weston was riding the route from Las Vegas to Fort Sumner when he was held up four miles north of Fort Sumner:

Charles Frederick Rudolph, undated photo. Courtesy Center for Southwest Research and Special Collections, UNM.

> "Three men stopped the buckboard and robbed [Weston] and Mrs. Deolatere, who was the only passenger he had, of all the money they had and also cut open and rifled two mail bags.... Only one man approached the buck board. He was on horseback, and two other men who remained a little off from the road were backing him. All three men were masked and the two who staid back wore only their underclothes." [108]

Taking one's clothes off for a disguise suggests that one has only one set of clothes, and those clothes are quite well known by everyone in the area.

The robbers took $22 from Weston and $15 from Mrs. Deolatere.[109]

Although Wild was convinced that Billy and Billy Wilson were two of the three robbers, both Weston and Mrs. Deolatere were tried for the robbery under the theory that they faked it. They were acquitted, and Wilson was later indicted for the crime. Billy and Wilson's motive for the crime was supposedly to read the reports that Secret Service Agent Wild was mailing to his superiors in Washington D.C. Rudabaugh later confessed that he, Wilson, and Pickett held up that stage. Billy was not involved.[110]

Following their decision to surrender:

> "...the boys came on out and left the arms in the house. When they got to us they all shuck hands with every man then sat down and [ate] supper. After supper we all mounted our horses. I took Billy the Kid up behind me while the other boys doubled up on ther horses and we started to Wilcoxes ranch...." [111]

> "The Kid and Rudabaugh were cheerful and gay during the trip. Wilson seemed dejected, and Pickett was frightened." [112]

Inside the Grzelachowski residence looking into the back room where tradition says Billy, Dave Rudabaugh, Thomas Pickett, and Billy Wilson were held prisoner on Christmas Day, December 25, 1880, by James East. 2007 photo.

Dining room, Grzelachowski residence. 2007 photo.

On arrival at the Wilcox-Brazil ranch, Garrett dispatched Brazil, Mason, and Rudolph back to the rock house with a wagon to recover the arms abandoned in the house and to retrieve Bowdre's now-frozen corpse.

> *"Billy made me [Polk] a present of his Winchester and Frank Stewart took his fine Bay mare."* [113]

> *"Stewart now has the pleasure of owning the fleetest horse in the territory."* [114]

Garrett took a *"Winchester 1873 saddle ring carbine and a Colt Frontier six-shooter"* from Billy Wilson. Both weapons fired a .44 Winchester cartridge, a huge advantage as both weapons could be carried without requiring two kinds of ammunition. Garrett would use that pistol to kill Billy 203 days later. (For more details on these two weapons, and the lawsuit that Garrett's widow filed to recover the weapons in 1933, see *"Killing Pat Garrett, The Wild West's Most Famous Lawman – Murder or Self-Defense?"*) [115]

At the Wilcox-Brazil ranch, *"Wilcox's wife fixed some supper and we took turns guarding them, two of us at time."* [116] Next morning, posse and prisoners left for Fort Sumner. They *"had a wagon and put the prisoners in it while the other boys rode horse back."* [117]

> *"When we were getting right at Fort Sumner, Bowdre's wife came out to meet us in the snow. We whipped up the horses when we passed her and ran right up to the door, and I [Bousman] and Jim East grabbed the body and took it in and put it on the table. We didn't stop when we met her because we did not want to hear her abuse. She cussed Pat Garrett out. He told her to go over and pick out a suit of clothes to bury her husband in and he would pay for it. He also had the grave dug."* [118]

María "Manuela" Bowdre was born April 20, 1866. Her maiden name was Herrera. When she married Bowdre is unknown, but she was only 14 when he was killed. Manuela married three times after Charles' death: to José Portillo, Maximiano Corona, and James Salsberry. [119]

While at Fort Sumner, Garrett was asked by María Luz Maxwell, Lucien Maxwell's widow, to permit her daughter Paulita to speak with Billy:

> *"...so she could bid him good-by. So Garrett detailed Lee Hall and I [East] to guard Billy over – he being shackled to Dave Rudebaugh [sic]. The mother asked Lee and I to unlock Billy from Dave and let Paulita go into another room with him for an affectionate farewell, but of course we had to refuse – altho all the world loves a lover."* [120]

For more on Billy's relationship with Paulita Maxwell, see Chapter 9.

Christmas at Puerto de Luna

Garrett left Fort Sumner that evening with the prisoners, taking only Frank Stewart, Jim East, Tom Emory and Barney Mason as guards. After a short layover at Gerhardt's ranch, the party reached Grzelachowski's residence at Puerto de Luna at 2 p.m. It was December 25, 1880 – Christmas Day. [121]

All but East enjoyed a celebratory Christmas dinner with the Grzelachowski family:

"I was put on guard by myself with a long adobe room and a fireplace in one end and a door in the other. They put me in there and locked us all in. We had Rudabaugh and Kid chained together. I sat down on a pile of wood by the door and the prisoners were in the other end."

"After we sat there awhile, Billy said. 'Jim, do you have anything to smoke?'"

"I said, 'Yes, I have some tobacco.' He said he had some papers. I said, 'Billy I'll throw you the tobacco.'"

He said, 'No I'll come and get it,' and he started across the room toward me."

"I said, 'Hold on Billy; if you come any farther, I'm going to shoot you.'"

"They started on and I said, 'Hold on Billy, if you make another step, I'll shoot you.'"

"He stopped and said, 'You're the most suspicious damn man I ever saw.' He turned back and I pitched him my tobacco. He threw it back and said he didn't want any of my tobacco."

"The boys were gone about an hour to get dinner. I was locked in and Pat had the key in his pocket, and that was a mighty foolish thing to do. He got two of his deputies killed in somewhat the same way." [122]

After the dinner, the party left for Las Vegas.

"As soon as the horses rested a little we were out on the road. Garrett never got hungry or thirsty on the road." [123]

The party traveled all night, reaching Las Vegas in late afternoon, December 26.[124]

Chapter 2 | Jail

"The greatest excitement prevailed yesterday afternoon when the news was noised abroad that Pat Garrett and Frank Stewart had arrived in town bringing with them Billy 'the Kid,' the notorious outlaw and three of his gang. People stood on the muddy street corners and in hotel offices and saloons talking of the great event...."

"Groups of people flocked to the jail and hung around the corners straining their necks to catch a glimpse of... the brave fellows who had brought in the outlaws. But they went quietly from the jail to the corral and from there to the National House where the half-starved, tired men sought to escape the scrutinizing gaze of the scores of hero worshippers." [1]

Many in the boisterous crowd lauding the capture of the four outlaws wanted to immediately *"mete out justice"* to Rudabaugh for the killing of Las Vegas jailor Valdez.[2]

Eleven months earlier, Las Vegas citizenry had done just that, lynching three men they deemed responsible for killing City Constable Joe Carson. Carson was killed when he entered a late-night dance hall and ordered four belligerently drunk Texas cowboys to deposit their arms behind the bar:

"...they refused and immediately firing commenced. Some say the men shot first, others say not. The shooting became general and 30 or 40 shots were exchanged in a moment of time. Carson was shot 4 or 5 times. He fell firing and shot while dying." [3]

One of the cowboys, William Randall, was mortally wounded. A second, James West, was *"shot through the lower bowels and breast."* Two others, Jim Dorsey and Tom "Dutch" Henry, escaped.[4]

Ironically, one of the men in the posse dispatched to apprehend Dorsey and Henry was Rudabaugh, who was a Las Vegas city constable then. (He only got onto the wrong side of the law when he and John Allen decided to break Webb out of jail.) Dorsey and Henry were captured and brought back to the Las Vegas jail.[5]

On February 8, 1880, in the early morning, West, Dorsey, and Henry were lynched:

"...a body of masked and armed men, about 50 in number, marched to the jail, disarmed the guards, and took the three prisoners out to the pump frame in the center of the plaza.... West on account of his wound had to be carried on a stretcher.... a rope was place around [West's] neck and he was swung off into internity (sic), while Dorsey and Henry were placed upon the platform surrounding the well, and perforated with bullets." [6]

"[When the lynchers] put the rope around his neck... [West] exclaimed 'my God I am suffering enough now, can't you let me alone....' He groaned horribly with pain from his wound." [7]

The Las Vegas Plaza windmill where James West was lynched and Tom Dorsey and Tom Henry were *"perforated with bullets,"* February 8, 1880. Courtesy Palace of the Governors Photo Archives (NMHM/DCA), 014386.

It is not known if Rudabaugh was among the lynchers. It is likely, because he and Joe Carson were good friends and fellow constables.

You can see why Billy, Rudabaugh – especially Rudabaugh – Pickett, and Wilson were worried about being lynched in Las Vegas. That fear was the reason they surrendered only after Garrett guaranteed them they would be jailed in Santa Fe, not Las Vegas.

The outlaws' arrival was rousing news. The men were interviewed by both Las Vegas newspapers.

The *Las Vegas Daily Gazette* noted that just prior to their reporter's interview:

"Mike Cosgrove… had just gone in with four large bundles…. One by one the bundles were unpacked disclosing a good suit of clothes for each man. Mr. Cosgrove remarked that he wanted 'to see the boys go away in style.'"

"'Billy, the Kid' and Billy Wilson who were shackled together stood patiently up while a blacksmith took off their shackles and bracelets to allow them an opportunity to make a change of clothing."

The *Daily Gazette* reporter asked Billy:

"'You appear to take it easy?'"

"'Yes! What's the use of looking on the gloomy side of everything. The laugh's on me this time,' he said. Then looking about the placita, he asked 'is the jail at Santa Fe any better than this?'"

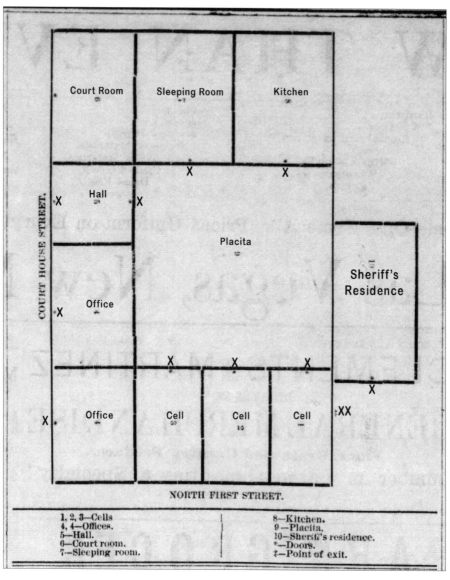

Map showing the layout of the Las Vegas courthouse, which served also as the city jail. "X" marks doors. "XX" marks the point of exit for the jail cells. *Las Vegas Daily Gazette*, December 4, 1881.

Las Vegas train depot, undated photo. Courtesy Center for Southwest Research and Special Collections, UNM.

"This seemed to trouble him considerably, for, as he explained, 'this is a terrible place to put a fellow in.'"

"'There was a big crowd gazing at me wasn't there,' he exclaimed, and then smilingly continued, 'Well, perhaps some of them will think me half man now; everyone seems to think I was some kind of animal.'"

As the cuffs were being cut off, Billy said:

"'I don't suppose you fellows would believe it but this is the first time I ever had bracelets on. But many another better fellow has had them on too.'" [8]

A reporter on the other newspaper, the *Las Vegas Daily Optic*, reported:

"[Billy] was in a talkative mood, but said anything he might say would not be believed. He laughed heartily when told that the papers had built him a reputation second only to Victorio. Kid claims never to have had a large number of men with him."

Rudabaugh, whose nickname was "Dirty Dave," was:

"...dressed about the same as when in Las Vegas [nine months earlier], apparently not having made any raids upon clothing stores.... He inquired anxiously in regard to the feeling in the community, and was told it was very strong against him."

Evidently the *Daily Optic* interview happened before Rudabaugh was gifted his new clothes.

The *Daily Optic* noted that Pickett said he was anxious to *"to under go an examination,"* insisting that his alleged criminal acts were not serious.[9]

Santa Fe

Garrett recognized the menacing threat of the townspeople's spreading anti-Rudabaugh sentiment. He decided to leave Pickett in jail in Las Vegas, as the charges against him for horse stealing were minor. Billy, Rudabaugh, and Wilson he would take to Santa Fe, as promised. He had with him Stewart, East, Emory, and Mason as fellow guards. He asked Michael Cosgrove to join them. For extra help, he wired J. F. Morley in Santa Fe, asking him to rush to Las Vegas. Morley was a U.S. postal inspector.[10]

> *"After breakfast we went to the jail for our prisoners. They turned out the Kid and Wilson to us, who were handcuffed together. We demanded Rudabaugh. They refused to yield him up, saying... they wanted him for murder. I told them my right to the prisoner ranked theirs...."* [11]

Garrett hauled his prisoners by mule wagon to the train depot and loaded them into the smoking car of the Santa Fe train.[12]

While Billy was leaning out of one of the car's windows, a *Daily Gazette* reporter got another chance to question him:

> *"'If it hadn't been for the dead horse in the doorway, I wouldn't be here. I would have ridden out on my bay mare and taken my chances of escaping,' said he. 'But I couldn't ride out over that, for she would have jumped back, and I would have got it in the head. We could have staid in the house but there wouldn't have been anything gained by that for they would have starved us out. I thought it was better to come out and get a good square meal – don't you?'"* [13]

Just after the prisoners were loaded, the train was surrounded by a "posse" of thirty well-armed men led by deputy sheriff Hilario Romero meaning to seize the prisoners by force (and probably lynch Rudabaugh).[14]

Morley gives this account of the events:

> *"...when I arrived at Vegas the mob had the train captured... I at once went on the train where Pat had the Prisoners, Pat told me he was going to cut the Irons off the Boys and let them make a fight for there (sic) lives.... I went up to the residence of A. A. Robinson the Chief Engineer for the Santa Fe RR, and asked him for a train crew to take the train out. Robinson told me I could have all the rolling stock of the Company but would have to man it myself."* [15]

Morley, an ex-train engineer, stoked the steam engine and piloted the train to Santa Fe. By 7:30 that evening, the prisoners were securely locked in the Santa Fe jail.[16]

The jail where the prisoners were incarcerated was the city's "new jail," located on Water Street across from the Herlow Hotel. It had replaced the old jail four months earlier:

> *"The new jail is, of course, in every way far superior to the old. The cells are more secure and larger, and for the perpetrators of serious crimes there is a separate cell built of stone, and so strong that escape from it once its doors have closed behind a prisoner would seem impossible."* [17]

Billy, Rudabaugh, and Wilson were *"shut up in [the windowless] stone cell to which even the light of day is denied admittance...."* [18]

Santa Fe jail, Water Street side. Undated photo. Courtesy Palace of the Governors Photo Archives (NMHM/DCA), 163219.

The next morning, about 11 am, Garrett went to the jail to check on his prisoners:

> *"[He] discovered that they had had not a mouthful to eat since they were put in jail. Upon which one of the posse went down to the keeper of the restaurant who has a contract for feeding United States prisoners and asked him why he had not sent down meals to the three. The man said he had done so, and after a little investigation it was discovered that Jailer Silva or some of his henchmen had eaten the grub themselves. It's pretty rough on prisoners when their jailers eat the meals sent to them."* [19]

Wasting no time, Garrett applied to acting Territorial Governor William Ritch for the reward money. Governor Ritch refused, contending he did not have the authority to make the payment in the absence of the real governor, who was visiting Washington D.C.[20]

The *Santa Fe Daily New Mexican* was displeased when it learned that the reward was not being paid:

> *"The reward of $500 was very small in the first place and should be promptly and cheerfully paid over to the men who have done New Mexico such great service."* [21]

The citizenry were happy to reward Garrett. Billy's capture was called a *"handsome Christmas present"* to the people of New Mexico. The *Las Vegas Daily Optic* opined that

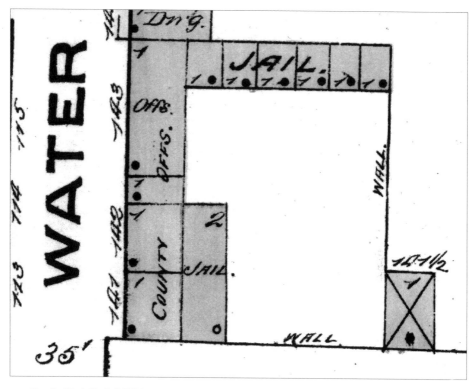

Santa Fe jail. Jail "2" is the windowless stone cell. Detail from the 1883 Santa Fe Sanborn Fire Insurance Map. Courtesy Library of Congress.

Garrett should be retained as *"sheriff of Lincoln Co. for 250 years."* A Dr. Knauer made *"a present to Pat Garrett of $100 in gold."* A Mr. Brunswick of Las Vegas raised a public subscription of $695 for Garrett. One of the donors to the subscription fund was Deputy Sheriff Hilario Romero.[22]

On the last day of the year, Garrett and Stewart returned to Las Vegas. There, Winfield Scott Moore, the owner of the Las Vegas Hot Springs Hotel, made Stewart a present of an *"elegant revolver valued at $60."*

> *"Not to be outdone, Stewart in turn presented Mrs. Moore with 'the Kid's' mare, and she now has the satisfaction of owning one of the best, if not the best animal in the territory."* [23]

Mrs. Moore named the mare *"Kid Stewart Moore."* [24]

On January 13, 1881, Garrett was finally paid the official $500 reward.[25] With the money given to Garrett by citizens, Garrett collected at least $1,500. A share of that money was owed by Garrett to his posse. According to at least one posse member, Calvin Polk, the men had trouble collecting it.[26]

After being paid, East and Emory left for White Oaks, where they had temporarily abandoned their chuck wagons:

"We had a blanket a piece. I [East] got snow blindness as we crossed the Piedranal Plains.... It was below zero.... The snow storm came and froze one of Tom's [Emory's] feet, and froze my face so that my eyelashes came out.... [At White Oaks] we found Charlie Siringo living fat." [27]

Pickett Goes Free

The same day that Billy, Rudabaugh, and Wilson were conveyed by train to Santa Fe, Pickett:

"Was in [town] accompanied by the officers, trying to secure bondsmen. No charge has yet been brought against him, and Major Morrison has concluded to release him without an examination, provided he can give bonds for his appearance at the next term of court in the sum of three hundred dollars." [28]

Pickett claimed that he had not been hanging out with Billy. Instead, he said he was working at Thomas Yerby's ranch as a cowboy. His job was to:

"...ride over certain ranges in order to prevent the cattle from straying away, and it was while on a ride of this kind that he met Kid's party on the fatal day. They rode together to Bowdre's place [he means Stinking Springs] where they were overtaken and captured in a bunch by Garrett's party."

"In regard to the attack upon Garrett at Fort Sumner [when Bowdre was killed], Pickett says that he met the Kid and his gang by chance that day and all rode leisurely into [Fort] Sumner at night, not dreaming of any difficulty, having received a note to the effect that Garrett and his men had abandoned the pursuit and gone home. Pickett claims to have had no connection whatever with the gang which is now broken up and thinks that he should not be held in confinement when the only charge brought against him is that he was in company with them when taken. He feels certain that he can rustle up the required bond now and when his hearing comes, can prove himself innocent of any crime." [29]

Pickett's story that it was just an unlucky coincidence that he was with Billy at Fort Sumner when Bowdre was killed and at Stinking Springs when Billy and the others were captured was not true. But it was true that Picket had no serious charges against him. He was released on bond and never charged with anything connected to being captured with Billy. (See Appendix C for details on his later life.)

Jail Life

On December 28, the morning after his jailing in Santa Fe, Rudabaugh was taken before U.S. Commissioner Samuel Ellison for a preliminary examination. He pleaded guilty to two charges of robbing the U.S. mail. Rudabaugh told the court that:

"...he has nothing to gain by keeping silent longer and resolved to make a clean breast of it. His confession establishes the innocence of the Stokes boys." [30]

The crime he was referring to happened on August 14, 1879, when a stage on the road between Las Vegas and Tecolote was held up and robbed. The robbers took the strongbox, mail sacks, and all the cash in passenger's pockets. Rudabaugh was suspected initially of involvement in the stage robbery, but was released. Three innocent men, including two Stokes brothers, were convicted of the crime. Rudabaugh was a Las Vegas constable at the time and, with his fellow constables, two of whom had joined him in the robbery, engineered the false convictions.[31]

On New Year's Day, Billy wrote Governor Wallace a one-sentence letter:

"I would like to see you for a few moments if you can spare time." [32]

Billy wanted to speak to the governor about the pardon Governor Wallace had promised him (more on this in Chapter 7). Governor Wallace never replied.

On January 8, Boston's *Illustrated Police News* published the story of Billy's hunting and capture. The *Las Vegas Daily Optic* commented that the article contained:

"...a miserably concocted wood-cut of Billy the Kid. If the picture hadn't been labeled, it might have been taken for either Deacon Sanford or Gus Williams, the Dutch comedian." [33]

Three days later, Billy, Rudabaugh, and Wilson were interviewed *"separately and alone"* by Postal Inspector Robert A. Cameron. Cameron reported to his superiors that Billy was *"about 21 or 23 years of age born in New York City, and a graduate from the streets."* He said he suspected Billy of being involved in stage robberies, although Billy denied it.

Of Rudabaugh, Cameron wrote:

"...he has already pled guilty to twice robbing the mails with dangerous weapons. He has without a doubt been engaged in many mail robberies in various parts of the country."

Wilson, Cameron said, was in the *"special business"* of passing counterfeit bills.[34]

On January 17, the Territorial legal machinery began to focus on Billy. On that day, Judge Warren Henry Bristol dispatched an arrest warrant for Billy to Dona Ana County Sheriff James Webster Southwick (was Bristol not reading the newspapers?):

"You are hereby commanded to arrest and take the body of William Bonny alias 'Kid' and him safely keep so that you have his body before the District Court to be begun and held at La Mesilla, New Mexico on the 28th day of March, A. D. 1881 to answer unto an indictment for Murder.

Not surprisingly, Sheriff Southwick replied that he could not locate Billy:

"I hereby certify that diligence (sic) search has been made and that the within named person could not be found in this county." [35]

The Mesilla newspaper *Newman's Thirty-Four* on January 19 published the information that Billy's step-father, William H. Antrim, lived in Silver City.[36]

On January 20, 1881, the *Las Vegas Daily Gazette* published a reporter's interview with causes célèbres Billy and Rudabaugh.

Billy said he had seen the *Police News* article:

"'I got hold of the paper first when it was brought in, but I was ashamed to let the other fellows see it. Wasn't it savage, though?'"

John Joshua Webb sitting in the placita of the Santa Fe jail. His right ankle is ironed. 1881 photo. Courtesy Special Collections and University Archives, NMHU.

The reporter asked:

"'Well, Billy, what do you think of your notoriety?'"

"'I don't see any money in it. Everything that has been done in that country is laid to me,' and he really seemed ashamed of the reputation that he had gained."

"'If you get out, you could get up a show like Buffalo Bill; you have had advertising enough.'"

"'If -----' was his only comment."

Rudabaugh told the reporter:

"'None of them men they've got in jail had anything to do with robbing the stage or train. I'm in for it now, and might as well tell the truth. The Stokes boys are perfectly innocent, and so are all the men who were mistrusted of being mixed up in both affairs. I don't propose to tell who did do either, but they haven't got any of the men but me.'"

"'They've got another innocent man in jail in Vegas.'"

Asked who, Rudabaugh said:

"'Webb; he ain't any more guilty of killing Kelliher than you are. I saw the whole affair and if my word is worth anything, I say that; that man didn't do the killing.'"

"He stoutly adhered to this and said that if he only had a chance to testify he would say so." [37]

The next day the *Las Vegas Daily Optic* opined in a signed editorial:

"Judging from the tone of the remarks found in your contemporary Gazette one would imagine that the editor of that paper thought Kid almost a hero." [38]

The editors of the two Las Vegas newspapers were acrimonious competitors. The *Daily Gazette* editor said of the *Daily Optic* editor:

"Kistler, of the Optic yesterday had a perfect diarrhea of words and a constipation of ideas. This, however, is his normal state." [39]

On January 28, Billy Wilson was brought before Judge Bristol for a preliminary examination. He waived the examination and was committed to trial at the Third District Court in Mesilla in April, 1881. [40]

The following week, Rudabaugh was taken to Las Vegas to testify at John J. Webb's retrial for killing Michael Kelliher. Webb had been sentenced to hang for the killing. He appealed his conviction to the Territorial Supreme Court, claiming innocence. The court grudgingly granted him a new trial. [41]

In the retrial, Rudabaugh, who was in the dance hall when Kelliher was killed, testified that Webb did not do the shooting he was accused of; he merely caught Kelliher's body when he fell, mortally wounded. (Webb did steal Kelliher's wallet with $500 in it, however.) The actual shooter was a man known only as Dutchy. In spite of Rudabaugh's testimony, Webb was convicted again and sentenced to hang. Governor Wallace later commuted Webb's sentence to life in prison. On December 3, 1881, Webb escaped from the Las Vegas jail and died four months later of smallpox.[42]

On February 28, it was discovered that Billy was on the threshold of escaping:

> *"Yesterday afternoon it was discovered that the Kid and his gang had concocted and were stealthily carrying out a plan by which they hoped to gain their freedom and escape the fate that awaits them. And very fortunate it was that the discovery was made just when it was, for a night or two more would have sufficed for the completion of the well laid scheme."* [43]

The "jail delivery" was discovered thanks to a jailhouse snitch who was hired by the sheriff to watch for breakout attempts.

> *"Sheriff Martinez, accompanied by Deputy Marshal Neis, at once proceeded to the jail, and entering the cell, found the men at supper. They examined the room and found that the bed ticking was filled with stones and earth, and removing the mattress discovered a deep hole. Further investigation showed that the men had dug themselves nearly out, and by concealing the loose earth in the bed and covering the hole up with it had almost reached the street without awakening the suspicion of the guard."* [44]

It is clear from this account that the men had been moved from the stone cell of the jail to one of the adobe cells lining the placita wall. The prisoners were permitted regular exercise in the placita – city resident Albert Hyde recounted that he once saw Billy *"hobbling about in the open court of the jail, his ankles heavily ironed."* [45]

Two days after the break attempt, Billy wrote Governor Wallace another letter:

> *"Dear Sir: I wish you would come down to the jail and see me. It will be to your interest to come and see me. I have some matters which date back two years and there are parties who are very anxious to get them, but I will not dispose of them until I see you. That is if you will come immediately."* [46]

The items that *"parties are very anxiouis to get"* that Billy is referring to are the two letters that Wallace wrote to Billy setting up meeting at Justice of the Peace Wilson's home to discuss a pardon offer (see Chapter 7 for details). Wallace deigned to answer.

Two days later, March 4, Billy wrote Governor Wallace again:

> *"I wrote you a little note the day before yesterday but have received no answer. I Expect you have forgotten what you promised me, this Month two Years ago. But I have not, and I think You had might to have come and seen me as I Requested you to. I have done Everything that I promised you I would and you have done nothing that you promised me."*

> *"I think when you think the matter over you will come down and see me, and I can then Explain Everything to you."*

> *"Judge Leonard Passed through here on his way East in January and promised to come and see me on his way back but he did not fulfill his Promise. It looks to me like I am getting left in the Cold. I am not treated right by Sherman. He lets Every Stranger that comes to See me through Curiosity in to see me, but will not let a single one of my friends in, not even an Attorney."*

"I guess they mean to Send me up without giving me any show. But they will have a nice time doing it. I am not entirely without friends."

"I shall Expect to see you Sometime today."

"Patiently Waiting"
"I am Very Truly Yours Respect"
"Wm. H. Bonney" [47]

The governor did not respond. Billy's charge that he was not being granted access to a lawyer must have had some result, though, because ten days later attorney Edgar Caypless filed a writ of replevin against Moore for Billy's bay mare.[48]

Replevin derives from English Common Law. A writ of replevin asserts that one's personal property has been taken unjustly by the state or another person. Replevin is a response to seizure – it can be filed only after the specified property has been taken.

The person filing the writ of replevin must submit a personal bond to the court equal to the value of the disputed property. Once the writ and bond have been filed, the person that took the property is ordered to return it, and it becomes the duty of the court to determine if the property was justly seized.[49]

The writ filed by Caypless asserted that Moore had no legal right to the mare. It asserted that Billy had not given the mare to Stewart; thus Stewart had no right to give the animal to Moore. Further, the writ asserted that Billy was now gifting the mare to Caypless in exchange for legal services. Billy would continue to make this claim throughout his trial, later writing Caypless, *"the mare is about all I can depend upon at present...."* [50]

In anticipation of Billy's upcoming trial, the prosecution issued subpoenas for the witnesses they wanted to testify against him: Isaac Ellis, ex-Sheriff Jacob Mathews, Saturnino Baca, and Bonifacio "Bonnie" Baca:

"You and each of you are hereby commanded to appear before the District Court for the Third Judicial District of said Territory, on the first day of the March 1881 Term thereof, to be held within and for the County of Dona Ana at the Court House of said County, then and there to testify in a certain cause in said Court pending, wherein The Territory is plaintiff and William Bonny is defendant, on the part of the Plaintiff and this do you under penalty of the law" [51]

All four men were required to post bonds of $1,000 to guarantee their appearance at the trial.[52]

Courts of New Mexico

On March 5, in anticipation of the Third District Court Session that would open in Mesilla on March 28, 1881, *Newman's Thirty-Four* published an explanation of the New Mexico Territorial court system:

"The Third Judicial District of New Mexico comprises the counties of Dona Ana, Grant and Lincoln. The court for this district is presided over by an Associate Justice of the Supreme Court of the Territory, who is appointed by the

President of the United States, with the advice and consent of the Senate, for a term of four years."

"This court has original common law and equity jurisdiction of all causes originating under the laws of the Territory and also the jurisdiction of a District and Circuit Court of the United States in cases arising under the laws of the United States."

"Cases arising in any part of the District to which the United States is a party are triable in the county of Dona Ana."

"Terms of court are held, in the county of Dona Ana, commencing on the fourth Monday of March and the first Monday of September of each year and continuing four weeks; in the county of Lincoln, on the first Monday of June and November of each year and continuing for three weeks; in the county of Grant, on the second Monday of July and first Monday of December of each year and continuing for three weeks."

"The District Court is at all times in session and open at any place in the district, where the Judge may be, for the purpose of hearing and determining motions, demurrers and petitions, granting rules and orders and interlocutory decrees, perfecting pleadings and putting causes at issue in all causes in law and equity, and rendering final decrees in equity, as well as for granting all extraordinary writs and issuing every kind and class of process that can be issued by the court at a regular term."

"The officers of the court for the district are Hon. Warren Bristol, Judge, residence, Mesilla, N. M.; Hon. S. B. Newcomb, District Attorney for the Territory, residence, Las Cruces, N. M.; George R. Bowman, Clerk of the Court and Register in Chancery, residence, Mesilla, N. M.; Hon. S. M. Barnes, U.S. Attorney, who prosecutes and defends for the United States in all courts of the Territory, residence, Santa Fe, N.M.; John Sherman, Jr., U.S. Marshal, who executes process in United States cases, residence, Santa Fe, N. M." [53]

Chapter 3 | Mesilla

On Sunday, March 27, 1881, Billy and Billy Wilson were taken from their Santa Fe jail cells to the Coleman & Lujan Blacksmith Shop. There, Mr. Coleman replaced their handcuffs with leg irons. At that time, in New Mexico, few shackles were lockable. Instead, they were forged onto prisoners' limbs by a blacksmith.[1]

The plan was to convey Billy and Wilson to Mesilla for trial that day, but the planned trip was cancelled because of:

> *"...some business obligations of Chief of Police Frank Chavez... who could not get off [that] day. If they had gotten off on that day as was anticipated, they would have found at Rincon a body of perhaps thirty men who were determined and prepared to get away with them even if it were found necessary to dispose of the officials in order to carry out their plans. Judge Thornton was on the train which the crowd thought would bring the Kid, and he was questioned by them as to the day upon which the wanted men would arrive. He was not posted and prudently said that he had heard nothing of their proposed removal...."* [2]

On his return to his cell, Billy hastily scribbled a letter to Governor Wallace and had it hand-delivered to Wallace's office in the Palace of Governors (the Governor's office was a mere two blocks away):

> *"Dear Sir"*
>
> *"for the last time I ask, Will you keep your promise. I start below tomorrow Send answer by bearer"*
>
> *"Yours Respt"*
> *"W. Bonney"* [3]

Billy's distress is evident. The promise to be kept is the pardon offer given to Billy by Governor Wallace in exchange for testifying before the grand jury (see Chapter 7).

The next morning the two prisoners were taken to the A.T. & S.F. train depot and put on the train to Rincon (corner in Spanish). Rincon was as far as the railroad tracks went (the tracks, which were just being laid, would reach Las Cruces five weeks later). Rincon was founded by the railroad and was so young that most residents were living in converted boxcars. Billy and Wilson were escorted by U.S. Marshal Tony Neis and Santa Fe Police Chief Frank Chavez.[4]

Accompanying the prisoners was attorney Ira Edwin Leonard. Leonard had represented Billy in legal matters since April, 1879, when he had written to Governor Wallace on Billy's behalf:

> *"I tell you, Governor, the District Attorney here is no friend of law enforcement. He is bent on going after the Kid. He proposes to destroy his evidence and influence and is bent on pushing him to the wall."* [5]

Rincon train station. Undated photo. Courtesy Palace of the Governors Photo Archives (NMHM/DCA), 066009.

The district attorney Leonard was referring to was William Logan Rynerson. Leonard would also represent Wilson at Mesilla. Rynerson had engineered the transfer of Billy's trial from Lincoln to Mesilla in an effort to guarantee Billy's conviction.

On detraining at Rincon, the five men were confronted by *"six or seven roughs."* One of the "roughs" remarked:

> *"'Let's take them fellows anyhow, 'whereupon Neis replied, 'You don't get them without somebody being killed....'"* [6]

Neis and Chavez herded their shackled prisoners and Leonard to a saloon across the street from the depot, probably Pete Carl's Saloon, and hired a back room, which they barricaded:

> *"The men on the outside then endeavored to organize, while the officers and prisoners awaited anxiously in the room. Neis had a double-barreled gun and six-shooter, and Chavez a rifle. The Kid and Wilson were evidently very uneasy, and Neis not being acquainted with the intentions of the mob suspected that their object was to release the prisoners."* [7]

Some *"disinterested"* men outside the saloon room eventually convinced the "roughs" to disperse.

The next morning the five men boarded the stagecoach to Mesilla, which ran through Las Cruces. On arriving at Las Cruces, they were met by:

> *"...an inquisitive mob gathered around the coach and someone asked which is 'Billy the Kid?' The Kid himself answered by placing his hand on Judge Leonard's shoulder and saying 'this is the man.'"* [8]

After a brief stop to change horses, the stage continued on to Mesilla. There they were met by another crowd. Seeing the *"twenty-odd men"* waiting for him, Billy remarked:

> *"See all those fellows here waiting for me? Not a damn one of them had to attend court, and here they are just to get away with me. They'll take me out of jail and hang me."* [9]

Billy and Wilson were delivered into the custody of Sheriff James Webster Southwick and locked in the Mesilla jail, which the local newspaper described as *"a good jail."* [10]

Mesilla Jail

Mesilla, or La Mesilla as it was then known, was founded March 1, 1850. At that time, it was within territory that the United States had captured from Mexico during the Mexican-American War. When the boundary was being formalized, the border commissioners for the two countries agreed on an initial border point for New Mexico that was about 30 miles north of El Paso, Texas. That decision, thirteen months after Mesilla was founded, moved Mesilla out of the United States and into the State of Chihuahua, Mexico. The Gadsden Purchase three years later moved Mesilla back into the United States. [11]

The lot on which the county courthouse and jail were built was purchased by the county in March, 1865. The money for the structure came half from a Territorial appropriation and half from a tax *"upon all persons in the county of Dona Ana."* [12] The drawing on page 122 shows the layout of the structure, which was built of adobe. When the courthouse room was not in use as the county court, it was used as a primary school. The first office fronting the placita was the sheriff's office. The second was the jailor's office and residence. The two-room, windowless, adobe jail was located inside the placita, as was an outdoor toilet. The floor of the jail was wood. Water was provided to the prisoners in open buckets. A wide door connected the courthouse to the placita. [13]

Although described as a "good jail" by the Santa Fe newspaper, the building was in terrible condition in 1881:

> *"We find [the jail] to be insecure, badly ventilated and entirely unfit for the occupancy of the number of prisoners usually confined there. It is kept as cleanly as its crowded condition will permit; but common humanity would seem to demand that a larger, more comfortable and better ventilated jail should be provided for the unfortunate persons who are required to be deprived of their liberty...."* [14]

> *"[We ask] the people of Dona Ana county, in all fairness, how much longer is this to be borne? How much longer will they tolerate a ruinous, tumble-down adobe building for their jail – a building which is long since fallen into decay, and is so seared with the scars of old-age that it will not safely hold... prisoners – even when extra guards are hired...."* [15]

> *"It must be evident, now, even to the dullest capacity, that the present building is no longer applicable for the purposes of the jail: while the $1200 a year paid for the extra guards to keep prisoners from squeezing between the cracks in its walls, and so making their escape, is not only ineffectual, but is*

so much money thrown away that might be devoted to the erection of the new edifice." [16]

A prisoner, who escaped in 1883, justifying his escape, wrote the following to the local newspaper:

"The place was full of vermin and not fit for a man to live in, and no precaution taken against it by the overseer. Water and soap were unknown in the place." [17]

According to the laws of New Mexico, it was the duty of the District Judge to:

"visit the [jail] at least twice a year, and carefully examine the condition of each cell as to cleanliness and discipline, [and file a lawsuit against the county sheriff] if any of the provisions of law [are being] violated or broken...." [18]

The disgusting condition of the Mesilla jail was due to the failure of District Judge Bristol to meet his legal responsibility to maintain humane jail conditions.

There were numerous breaks from the jail. Here are several that happened in the months following Billy's trial (if he been in the jail longer, he might have escaped too):

"Two more prisoners escaped from the county jail last Wednesday by climbing over the wall." [19]

"Last Friday evening... two more prisoners escaped from in the Mesilla jail.... They managed to become possessed of a small saw, with which they made an opening in the wood floor, and then dug underneath the wall of the jail, and after scaling the outer wall, they found themselves at liberty." [20]

"Another jail delivery occurred at Mesilla on last Thursday night. This time there were four prisoners escaped.... The manner of delivery was to cut through the floor, dig underneath the first wall and then scale the second. It is supposed that they had secreted table knives, brought into their cell with meals, or smuggled in by some of the prisoners' female friends who were permitted to visit the jail indiscriminately and without restraint. Indeed, the latter is the more probable theory, as female footprints were discovered around the morning after the birds had flown."

"[One prisoner] in the same cell refused to leave. Three guards were supposed to be on duty, but it transpires that they were all in bed and sound asleep at the time of the delivery." [21]

"On entering the jail, Mr. Frietze saw the usual sight of a hole in the floor and a great pile of earth and stones near by, showing [the prisoners] had dug themselves out in the same old way. Other prisoners had escaped last fall... thro' the very same hole in the floor, that had simply been patched over... it is not likely they will be caught." [22]

In January, 1882, the Territorial Assembly moved the Dona Ana County Seat from Mesilla to Las Cruces. On June 16, 1883, the prisoners in the Mesilla jail were moved to a new jail in Las Cruces. On October 5, 1885, the county sold the no-longer-needed Mesilla courthouse/jail and lot to the Village of Mesilla for one dollar. [23]

Chapter 4 | The Charges against Billy

Billy faced two murder counts, one for the unlawful death of Lincoln County Sheriff William Brady and one for the unlawful death of Andrew L. "Buckshot" Roberts. Both deaths took place during the first week of April, 1878.

The event that initiated the chain of events that led to Brady's and Robert's killings was the unprovoked, sadistic murder of John Henry Tunstall.

Death of John Henry Tunstall

Tunstall was an Englishman who arrived in Lincoln, New Mexico, on November 6, 1876, with hopes of building a profitable cattle empire. Lincoln at the time was divided into two antagonistic factions, one headed by Lawrence G. Murphy and one headed by Alexander A. McSween. Allied with Murphy were business associates Emil A. Fritz, John H. Riley, and James J. Dolan.[1]

Murphy controlled Lincoln politically and economically. He owned the town's primary mercantile; but the real basis of his power was the exclusive contract he held to sell cattle and supplies to the U.S. Army based at Fort Stanton. The Army needed the cattle to fulfill the Federal Government's treaty obligation to supply food to Native Americans on the Mescalero Apache Reservation. That contract gave Murphy a stranglehold on Lincoln County. It meant that Murphy owned the only forage and livestock market in the county, and he set prices that kept the local ranchers indebted to him.[2]

McSween came to Lincoln as a young lawyer. Initially, he was a Murphy ally. That changed when Fritz died unexpectedly and McSween was hired to collect Fritz's $10,000 life insurance policy benefit from the Merchants Life Assurance Company, which was bankrupt and in receivership. McSween's efforts to obtain the money necessitated a trip to New York, where the company had its office. Here is his account of the difficulties he encountered:

> "I went to New York to ascertain the real condition of the policy on Col. Fritz's life. Whilst there... efforts were made by certain parties to compel me to accept fifty cents on the dollar in full for the policy. When it was found I would not compromise, it was said that the whole claim was lost through my obstinacy. In order to get the policy out of the hands of the party having it, seven to eight hundred dollars had to be paid. Upon payment of this sum the policy was reluctantly surrendered.... I was absent on this business trip two months. I paid all the expenses of the trip out of my own pocket." [3]

Although McSween succeeded in collecting $7,000 of the $10,000 policy, after he charged his commission and expenses against the proceeds, less than one third remained for Fritz's heirs.[4]

That led to a lawsuit that unjustly entangled Tunstall.

It did not take Tunstall long after he arrived in Lincoln with his money (provided by his father) and optimistic plans to begin fighting Murphy's despotic, monopolistic

John Henry Tunstall. Undated photo. Courtesy Palace of the Governors Photo Archives (NMHM/DCA), 066009.

Lawrence Gustave Murphy. Undated photo. Courtesy Center for Southwest Research and Special Collections, UNM.

Emil Adolf Fritz. Undated photo. Courtesy Center for Southwest Research and Special Collections, UNM.

James Joseph Dolan. Undated photo. Courtesy Center for Southwest Research and Special Collections, UNM.

John Henry Riley. Undated photo. Courtesy Center for Southwest Research and Special Collections, UNM.

Alexander Anderson McSween, undated photo. Courtesy Maurice G. Fulton Papers, Special Collections, UA.

control of the county. He acquired a ranch on the Rio Feliz and stocked it with cattle and horses. He followed that insurgent act by opening a general store and bank in Lincoln, across the street from Murphy's. Based solely on scuttlebutt, a rumor spread around Lincoln that McSween was Tunstall's silent financial partner.

When the Fritz suit went to court, the presiding judge, Judge Warren Bristol, ordered the arrest of McSween on fraud charges. Judge Bristol was a long-time ally of Murphy. Judge Bristol would later serve as the presiding judge in Billy's trial in Mesilla.

McSween was visiting Las Vegas when he learned of the order. After a failed attempt to arrest McSween in town, the sheriff of Las Vegas with a posse arrested McSween several miles outside of town.

"[John] Chisum was jerked out head foremost & fell upon his face on the hard road and [was] seized by the throat.... McSween also was jerked out of the ambulanch [sic] and drug off by a lot of the gang & Mrs. McSween was left sitting all alone crying...." (An ambulance was a wagon with leather rather than steel shocks, providing an easier ride.) [5]

McSween was escorted to Lincoln and placed under house arrest. Chisum chose to stay in the Las Vegas jail, not trusting the courts in Lincoln. Judge Bristol announced that he was ill – but nevertheless, he ordered McSween to come to Mesilla for a preliminary examination on the fraud charge, which he ruled would take place in his Mesilla home.[6]

Just before McSween and Tunstall left for Mesilla, Tunstall wrote to the *Mesilla Valley Independent* charging Lincoln County Sheriff William Brady, Riley, and Dolan with tax embezzlement. The letter read, in part:

"Major Brady as the records of the County show, collected over Twenty five hundred dollars, Territorial funds. Of this sum, Alex. A. McSween Esq., of this place, paid him over Fifteen hundred dollars by cheque on the First National Bank of Santa Fe, August 23, 1877."

"Said cheque was presented for payment by John H. Riley, Esq., of the firm of J. J. Dolan & Co., this last amount was paid by the last named gentleman to Underwood and Nash for cattle. This passed away over Fifteen hundred dollars belonging to the Territory of New Mexico."

"Let not Lincoln County suffer for the delinquency of one, two or three men."

"A delinquent tax payer is bad: a delinquent tax collector is worse."

"J. H.T [John Henry Tunstall]" [7]

The letter was published the same day McSween and Tunstall arrived in Mesilla. Dolan shot back in the same newspaper:

"In answer to a communication in reference to taxpayers of Lincoln County published in your issue of the 26th inst. and signed J. H. T., I wish to state that every thing contained therein is false.... Owing to sickness in the family of Sheriff Brady he was unable to be at Santa Fe in time to settle his account with the Territory...."

"If Mr. J. H. T. was recognized as a gentleman, and could be admitted into respectable circles in our community, he might be better posted in public affairs. For my part, I can't see the object of Mr. J. H. T.'s letter, unless it is to have the public believe that A. A. McSween is one of the largest tax-payers in our County, when in fact he is one of the smallest...." [8]

Territory of New Mexico Third Judicial District Judge Warren Henry Bristol.

The McSween hearing in Bristol's residence was irregular and shamelessly biased. No witnesses were sworn, no legal record taken, and Judge Bristol's courtroom statements showed he wholeheartedly supported the prosecution. He ruled that the case should go to the grand jury and McSween should post a bond of $8,000.

The *Cimarron News and Press*, commenting on Judge Bristol, wrote that he made:

"...one of the most partisan charges we ever heard from the bench and which sounds much more like the argument of an attorney seeking to convict McSween of a crime than an address of a judge before whom the facts are likely to come for trial, and who from his high office, is presumed to be impartial and disinterested." [9]

Riley's opinion, expressed in a letter to the *Santa Fe New Mexican*, was:

"McSween who, after a careful investigation before Judge Bristol, (lasting two days.) was bound over for the criminal offence of embezzlement of the money for which attachment was issued.... Every fair-minded and unprejudiced mind, conversant with the facts knows, as I do, that McSween is an unprincipled, scheming villain." [10]

The day McSween and Tunstall left Mesilla, Judge Bristol issued a writ of attachment against Tunstall's property on the basis that McSween was his partner, an assertion

Frederick Tecumseh Waite. Undated photo. Courtesy Maurice G. Fulton Papers,
Special Collections, UA.

that Tunstall had strenuously denied during the hearing. The writ gave the sheriff of Lincoln the authority to:

> "...attach all the right title and interest of Alex A. McSween in and to the goods, chattels, effects and provisions pertinent to the store of Tunstall & Co. in the town of Lincoln, Territory of New Mexico." [11]

Judge Bristol gave the writ to the two men's worst enemy, Dolan, who sped it to Lincoln.

When McSween and Tunstall arrived in Lincoln, they found Sheriff Brady in possession of Tunstall's store. Tunstall, with the reinforcement of Billy, Frederick Waite, and Robert Widenmann, confronted the sheriff. Brady would not back down; rather than pull guns, Tunstall backed down. [12]

Billy, Waite, and Widenmann were hired hands of Tunstall.

Frederick Waite was maybe the best-educated man in Lincoln. As a graduate of Mound City Commercial College, located at St. Louis, Missouri, he had what would be a called a Master's Degree in Business Administration today. After leaving Lincoln, he returned to his family home in Himmonoah, Chickasaw Nation, Oklahoma. He was elected to the Chickasaw House of Representatives and later to the Chickasaw Senate. [13]

Tunstall met and became friends with Widenmann in Santa Fe in August, 1876. At the time of the meeting, neither man had been to Lincoln. Widenmann falsely told Tunstall he had had banking experience in New York and had managed a large cattle ranch in Colorado. Widenmann followed Tunstall to Lincoln a few months later, motivated by financial opportunities he hoped being close to Tunstall would provide. Widenmann had a reputation in Santa Fe as a chiseler. The *Santa Fe Weekly New Mexican* wrote of him:

> "Since this man Wiedermann (sic) made his advent amongst us he has made it his business to earn for himself the character of a first class liar and fraud.... He 'done' many persons in this place by mythical remittances from Europe, which of course, never arrived. To be forewarned is to be forearmed." [14]

During the confrontation at his store, Tunstall forced Brady to release six horses and two mules which were indisputably Tunstall's; these Tunstall sent to his Rio Feliz ranch.

Although Sheriff Brady had already attached property worth three or four times the $8,000 bond mandated by Judge Bristol, Sheriff Brady deputized Jacob B. Mathews to take a posse to Tunstall's ranch and attach his livestock. When the posse reached the ranch, they were confronted by Richard M. Brewer, Tunstall's ranch foreman. Brewer, backed by a number of Tunstall's men, including Billy, refused to permit any stock to be taken. [15]

The next morning, not to be denied, Sheriff Brady put together a much larger posse of *"about twenty four of the best citizens procurable"* – under the leadership of Mathews – and ordered them back to Tunstall's ranch. [16]

Here is Billy's account of what happened at the ranch, given under oath to U.S. Department of Justice Special Investigator Frank Warner Angel:

> "...on the 12th of February A. D. 1878 one J. B. Mathews claiming to be Deputy Sheriff came to the ranch of said J. H. Tunstall in company with

William Brady. Undated photo.
Courtesy Maurice G. Fulton Papers,
Special Collections, UA.

Jacob Basil Mathews. Undated photo.
Courtesy Maurice G. Fulton Papers,
Special Collections, UA.

Robert Adolph Widenmann. Undated
photo. Courtesy Maurice G. Fulton
Papers, Special Collections, UA.

William Logan Rynerson. Undated
photo. Courtesy Archives and Special
Collections, NMSU.

Jessie Evans, Frank Baker, Tom Hill [Tom Chelson] and Rivers [Jack Long], John Hurley, George Hindman, [Buckshot] Roberts and an Indian [Manuel Segovia] and Ponciano [Ponciacho, real name unknown], the latter said to be the murderer of Benito Cruz, for the arrest of murderers of whom the Governor of this Territory offered a reward of $500."

"Before the arrival of said J. B. Mathews, Deputy Sheriff, on his horse, having been informed that said Deputy Sheriff and posse were going to round up all the cattle and drive them off and kill the persons at the ranch, the persons at the ranch cut potholes into the walls of the house and filled sacks with earth, so that they, the persons at the ranch, should they be attacked or their murder attempted, considering the Sheriff's posse was composed of murderers, outlaws and desperate characters some of whom lack any interest at stake in the County, nor being residents of said County." [17]

Sheriff Brady's posse of "best citizens" included four men whom he personally had earlier captured and jailed for robbery and rustling: Jessie Evans, Frank Baker, Tom Hill, and George Davis.[18] The *Mesilla Valley Independent* noted:

"After [their] escape, the cells were found to be liberally supplied with files, knives and augers, as also cotton sacks with rocks weighing from ten to twenty pounds. How is that for vigilance?" [19]

Despite carrying multiple arrest warrants for the escapees, Sheriff Brady made no further effort to arrest them. He purposely included them in his posse because he wanted men with reputations as gunmen whom he knew would cheerfully use force if it came to that. Ponciacho, true name unknown, was wanted for the fatal robbery of Benito Cruz. He had a $250 Territorial bounty on his head for his capture, dead or alive.[20]

Billy's account (dressed in legalese) continues:

"The said Mathews when about 50 yards of the house was called to stop and advance alone and state his business, that said Mathews after arriving at the ranch said that he had come to attach the cattle as property of A. A. McSween, that said Mathews was informed A. A. McSween had no cattle or property there but that if he has, the said Mathews could take it. That said Mathews said, that he thought some of the cattle belonging to R. M. Brewer, whose cattle were also at the ranch of J. H. Tunstall, belonged to A. A. McSween, that said Mathews was told by said Brewer that he, Mathews, could round up the cattle and that he, Brewer, would help him." [21]

Widenmann confronted Jessie Evans, saying he held arrest warrants for him, Baker, and Hill and intended to arrest them (Widenmann was a deputy U.S. marshal). Evans advanced on Widenmann:

"...swinging his gun up and catching it cocked and pointed directly at Widenmann.... Evans told Widenmann, that if he ever came to arrest him he Evans would pick Widenmann as the first man to shoot at, to which Widenmann answered that that was all right, that two could play at that game. That during the talking Frank Baker stood near said Widenmann, swinging his pistol on his finger, catching it full cocked pointing at said Widenmann." [22]

In an attempt to defuse the situation, Brewer asked Mathews into his house to negotiate.

Here is how Sheriff Brady described the events in a later deposition:

> *"I deputized one of my assistants [Mathews] to proceed to the Rio Felix distant some fifty miles from this point, where the company heard [sic] of cattle and horses were held, to attach the same. He took with him four men, and on his arrival he found there one Wiedemann [sic] in charge of some fifteen armed men, and some men against whom the said Wiedemann claims as Deputy U. S. Marshall to have warrants of arrest, these men he invited to partake of his hospitality while the posse were not allowed to approach the house."* [23]

Mathews led his posse back to Lincoln, closely trailed by Billy, Widenmann, and Waite. Billy told Special Investigator Frank Warner Angel:

> *"...that on the road to Lincoln he [Billy] heard said Mathews ask said Widenmann if he Mathews returned to take the cattle, to which said Widenmann answered that no resistance would be offered if the cattle were left at the ranch but if an attempt was made to drive the cattle to the Indian Agency and kill them for keep, as he said Mathews had been heard to say would be done, he said Widenmann, would do all in his power to prevent this."* [24]

The next morning Billy, Widenmann, and Waite returned to Tunstall's ranch.

That same day Dolan and Riley received a letter from Territorial Attorney General William Rynerson explicitly ordering extralegal violence against McSween and Tunstall. The letter read, in part:

> *"Tunstall is in with the swindles with the rogue McSween. They have the money belonging to the Fritz estate and they must be made to give it up. It must be made hot, for them all the hotter the better. Especially is this necessary now that it has been discovered that there is no hell."*

> *"Shake that McSween outfit up till it shouts out and squares up and then shake it out of Lincoln. I will aid to punish the scoundrels all I can. Get the people with you.... You know how to do it. Have good men about to aid Brady and be assured I shall help you all I can for I believe there was never found a more scoundrelly set than that outfit."* [25]

The comment about there being *"no hell,"* so therefore hotness now is even more necessary, is bizarre, but it certainly illustrates Rynerson's attitude.

Three days later, Tunstall arrived at his ranch from Lincoln. Tunstall:

> *"...informed all the persons there, that reliable information had reached him that J. B. Mathews was gathering a large party of outlaws and desperados as a posse and that said posse was coming to the ranch, the Mexicans in the party to gather up the cattle and the balance of the posse to kill the persons at the ranch."*

> *"It was then and there decided that all persons at the ranch except G. Gauss were to leave and Wm. McCloskey was that night sent to the Rio Penasco to inform the posse who were camped there, that they could come over and*

round up the cattle, count them and leave a man there to take care of them and J. H. Tunstall would also leave a man there to help round up and count the cattle and help to take care of them." [26]

This second posse, by several accounts, was over 30 men. Brady later testified under oath that it included only John Hurley, Manuel Segovia, George Hindman, Pantaleón Gallegos, John W. Olinger, Robert W. Beckwith, Ramon Montoya, Thomas Green, Thomas Cochrane, Charles Kruling, George Kitt, Charles Marshall, Sam Perry, and William "Buck" Morton. He did not list posse leader Mathews, nor did he list known members Andrew "Buckshot" Roberts, Ham Mills, Tom Moore, Juan Silva, Felipe Mes, E. H. Wakefield, Pablo Pino, Charles Woltz, Albert Howe, and Ponciacho. Most significantly, he did not list the jail escapees Jessie Evans, Frank Baker, Tom Hill, and George Davis.[27]

Tunstall was persuaded by Billy and others that Mathews' real goal was to kill him. Staying at the ranch only gave Mathews the opportunity he sought. Tunstall decided to abandon the ranch. He was willing to leave his cattle, but not his horses. From childhood on, Tunstall had loved horses (more on this later) – and besides, Sheriff Brady had already agreed the horses were solely his, not jointly owned with McSween.

Tunstall felt he could be safe only at Lincoln. He packed a wagon with supplies and told Waite to drive it to Lincoln using the road. Then, taking Billy, Widenmann, Brewer, and John Middleton with him, Tunstall set off for Lincoln with his string of horses by a safer route, a back trail.

When the posse arrived at Tunstall's ranch and found only Gottfried Gauss, they were furious. Mathews asked Gauss, *"Why did not someone remain to turn over the property?"* Gauss said he was there to do that. Then, according to Gauss:

"[Dolan] came about this time, and he picked out the men to follow after Tunstall's party to bring them back if they caught them before they reached the [Lincoln] Plaza. From their actions I thought that some of the party of Tunstall's would be killed. I heard, I think it was Morton, cry out, 'Hurry up, boys, my knife is sharp and I feel like scalping some one.' They were all excited and seemed as though they were agoing to kill someone." [28]

Pantaleón Gallegos began writing down the names of the men Dolan designated for the chase posse. When Mathews noted that he was including Evans, Baker, Hill, and Davis, he told Gallegos, *"Don't put those boys down at all."* [29]

Mathews deputized Buck Morton to lead the posse.

Because Tunstall and his men were driving horses, it was a simple matter to follow their tracks. Billy recounted what happened next:

"...all the horses which [we] were driving, excepting 3 had been released by Sheriff Brady at Lincoln, that one of these 3 horses belonged to R. M. Brewer, and one other was traded by Brewer to Tunstall for one of the released horses."

"Deposist further says that when he and party had reached to within about 30 miles from the Rio Penasco, he and John Middleton were riding in the rear of the balance of the party and just upon reaching the brow of a hill they saw

a large party of men coming towards them from the rear at full speed and that he and Middleton at once rode forward to inform the balance of the party of the fact."

"Deposist had not more than barely reached Brewer and Widenmann who were some 200 or 300 yards to the left of the trail when the attacking party cleared the brow of the hill and commenced firing at [them]. Deposist, Widenmann and Brewer rode over a hill towards another which was covered with large rocks and trees in order to defend themselves and make a stand. But the attacking party, undoubtedly seeing Tunstall, left off pursuing deposist and the two with him and turned back to the canyon in which the trail was."

"Shortly afterwards we heard two or three separate and distinct shots and the remark then made by Middleton that they the attacking party must have killed Tunstall. Middleton had in the meantime joined deposist, Widenmann and Brewer. Deposist then made the rest of his way to Lincoln in company with Widenmann, Brewer, Waite and Middleton, stopping on the Rio Penasco in order to get men to look for the body of J. H. Tunstall." [30]

Nobody saw the close-up details of the killing of Tunstall except the men who did it, Tom Hill and Buck Morton.[31] Albert Howe, who was in the chase posse, gave the following account under oath:

"Tunstall was some distance off from the road, and when he found he had been deserted by his party, he turned and rode toward Hill and Morton; that when he came in sight of them he seemed very much surprised and hesitated; that Hill called to him to come up and said that he would not be hurt; at the same time both Hill and Morton threw up their guns, resting their stocks on their knees; that after Tunstall came nearer, Morton fired and shot Tunstall through the breast, and then Hill fired and shot Tunstall through the head; someone else fired and wounded or killed Tunstall's horse at the time Tunstall was shot through the head by Hill; that two barrels of Tunstall's revolver were emptied after he was killed; that Tunstall fired no shots, and that Tunstall was killed in cold blood." [32]

To understand why Tunstall did not attempt to defend himself, it is necessary to know the fundamental difference between how English law and U.S. law regarded the act of self-defense. Under English law, you had *"no right to defend yourself"* if there was any option to retreat, no matter how hard or unlikely. You could even be criminally prosecuted if your life was threatened and you did not retreat, as mandated by English law.

Because U.S. law came originally from England, "duty to retreat" was the law in the United States until a series of state and Federal appeal courts in the 1860s and1870s established the legal right of self-defense. Following those rulings, persons facing life-threatening danger had the legal right to use force to defend themselves.[33]

Tunstall was inculcated with English doctrine. In a sense, in the West, he was a fish out of water. He almost never carried a gun, although he did have one with him while retreating to Lincoln. His natural reaction to any threat was to do what he was taught to do since childhood – retreat. That explains why he abandoned his ranch so readily.

It also explains why he did not draw his gun when Hill and Morton approached (you can be certain that Billy would have had his gun out). Tunstall expected that if one of the men threatened violence, he would have an opportunity to retreat. He had no such opportunity; they just shot him.

What was the lawful thing to do for Tunstall was cowardice in the eyes of Hill and Morton.

On their flight to Lincoln, following the killing, Billy and the others stopped at John Newcomb's place and asked him to recover Tunstall's body. The next morning Newcomb and four others found the body:

> "The corpse had evidently been carried by some persons and laid in the position in which we found it; a blanket was found under the corpse and one over it. Tunstall's overcoat was placed under his head, and his hat placed under the head of his dead horse. By the apparent naturalness of the scene we were forced to conclude that the murderers of Mr. Tunstall placed his dead horse in the position indicated, considering the whole affair a burlesque....

> "We found his revolver quite close to the scabbard on the corpse.... We found two chambers empty, but there were no hulls or cartridge shells in the empty chambers; the other four chambers had cartridges in them...."

> "The corpse of Mr. Tunstall was found over 100 yards off the trail on which the horses travelled, in advance of those said to have been driven by Mr. Tunstall, showing clearly, by fresh horse tracks which were seen by us distinctly and plainly, that the horses the posse claimed to have been trying to recover from Mr. Tunstall must have been quite a distance behind Mr. Tunstall, and must have been passed by the posse before they could get Mr. Tunstall." [34]

The killers intended to assert that Tunstall had fired on them, thereby proving they acted in self-defense, but, because the other posse members came upon them so soon after the killing, they only had time to removed two cartridges from the revolver's cylinder.

A number of writers have wondered why Tunstall's horse was shot and posed as it was. The answer is, the murderers knew about Tunstall's deep love of horses, and especially of one horse named "Colonel." The gruesome death-scene posing was a final, depraved act of mockery and contempt.

Tunstall first saw Colonel in a butcher pen at Fort Stanton among cattle that were there to be slaughtered. Appalled, Tunstall asked why the horse was to be killed. He was told the horse was an army cavalry horse that was *"condemned"* because it had gone blind. Tunstall wrote about Colonel to his parents:

> "I gave 27 1/2 dollars for him, & I think I never saw a prettier horse, & I never threw my leg over a finer saddle horse, he walks fast enough to keep my Long Tom horse in a slow job trot, he paces, trots, & goes a single foot gait, that I never saw in England, he can canter on a cabbage leaf & gallop very finely, he is coal black, his mane & tail are as fine as I ever saw, I should think he is nearly thoroughbred, he is not over 7 years old."

"He has never had his eyes doctored, & I think I may cure him, if I could do that, he could not be bought." [35]

"I have taught him to pick up his feet when I tell him we are coming to a bad place in the road, so that he does not strike it, & I can make him understand whether it is an up or down grade we are coming to; he can walk 25 miles in five hours & a half, without any urging, which is all that can be desired of a road horse. He will come when I call, & follow me around just as if he could see." [36]

Although he was not, Tunstall could easily have been riding Colonel when he was killed; Colonel was among the horses he was herding. Like the blind horse he treasured, Tunstall, with his beliefs and character, was unable to see the real nature of the world he so ambitiously set out to conquer. He was blind to the determinative, irrational violence that was embedded in Territorial society.

Tunstall was murdered on February 18, 1878. The coroner's jury met the next day over his body and concluded:

"... the deceased came to his death on the 18th day of February, 1878 by means of divers bullets shot and sent forth out of and from deadly weapons, and upon the head and body of the said John H. Tunstall, which said weapons were held by one or more of the men whose names are herewith written: Jessie Evans, Frank Baker, Thomas Hill, George Hindman, J. J. Dolan, William Norton and others not identified by witnesses that testified before the coroner's jury" [37]

U.S. Army Assistant Surgeon Daniel Appel in his autopsy report stated that Tunstall was shot in the back of the head *"3 inches behind and in a line with the superior border of the right ear"* and in the chest *"2 inches to the right of the medium line, breaking the Clavicle."* He found no powder burns, indicating Tunstall was shot from at least six feet away.[38]

Howe in his testimony stated:

"...we found the skull broken; we found that a rifle or carbine bullet had entered his breast, and a pistol bullet entered the back of his head, coming out in the forehead." [39]

(For a description of Tunstall's murder site and details on how it was relocated and marked 49 years later, see Appendix A.)

Sheriff Brady responded to the news of Tunstall's death at the hands of his posse by sending Territorial Attorney General Rynerson an official report to which he attached a statement by Mathews which claimed:

"...while a portion of the posse were in pursuit of the party, J. H. Tunstall fired on the posse and in the return fire he was shot and killed. It has been falsely aversed (sic) that attached to my Deputy's posse were men against whom U.S. warrants has (sic) been issued." [40]

The day Tunstall was killed, Dr. Taylor F. Ealy, wife Mary, and their two infant children arrived in Lincoln. Their presence in Lincoln was requested of the Santa Fe Presbytery by McSween, who was seeking a Presbyterian minister and teacher for Lincoln. They were lodged in McSween's home.[41]

Mary Ealy gave the following account of what she witnessed after her arrival:

"The following night Tunstall's body was brought to the house of McSween.... Among those who attended the body was Billy the Kid, Dick Brewer, and Fred Waite, men who herded the cattle of Tunstall. They were all good friends of Tunstall and were ready to take the execution of vengeance into their own hands...."

"Tunstall's body was in bad shape, as he had been shot and then beaten until his forehead was battered very badly. Dr. Ealy embalmed the body, which was put in a metal coffin. As Tunstall was an Englishman, it was thought that his friends in England might wish the body sent there. Until such a time the body was to be buried at the east side of what was intended in time to be Tunstall's home."

"The funeral of Mr. Tunstall was held the next morning. As Mrs. McSween was away from home, I was asked to play two or three hymns. Beside the organ on which I played stood Billy the Kid and his cowboy friends, armed to the teeth. Billy's voice was a sweet tenor, and he sang with all his might. The service though was a fearful one, for no one knew when hostilities between the two factions would be resumed, as almost every one connected with the feud was ready to use his gun at a moment's warning." [42]

Mary Ealy affirms what other sources do – Tunstall's face was beaten. Widenmann, in an undated statement, wrote that Tunstall's skull was *"mashed"* with the butt of a gun.[43]

McSween wrote the following to Tunstall's father:

"Thirty of the best men in this County gathered at our house the night his corpse was brought in and remained here until last evening in the hope that parties connected with that murder could be found. They have now dispersed, but have organized themselves into bands and taken to the mountains to hunt the murders...."

"J. J. Dolan & Co. entertained fearful malice toward him and me on account of business. They could not stand to see competition. Without a doubt they planned and executed his death, and it's equally certain that business jealousy was the cause of it." [44]

Tunstall's body was never returned to England. The exact location of his grave is not known.

Knowing that Sheriff Brady would do nothing to investigate Tunstall's murder, or make arrests, Billy and Brewer went to Justice of the Peace John B. Wilson. Wilson issued the following warrants:

"I, John B. Wilson, Justice of the Peace in and for precinct No 1 Lincoln County New Mexico, do hereby certify that on or about the 19th day of February 1878 William Bonney and R. M. Brewer filed in office affidavits charging John J. Dolan, J. Conovar, Frank Baker, Jessie Evans, Tom Hill, George Davis, O. L. Roberts, P. Gilligos, F. Green, J. Awly, A. H. Mills, 'Dutch Charley' proper name

Lincoln resident Miguel Luna standing at the site where Tunstall and later McSween, Harvey Morris, and Chapman were buried. Tunstall was buried in a metal coffin. Luna was a small boy during the Lincoln war and watched Billy escape from the Lincoln jail. Undated photo. Courtesy Maurice G. Fulton Papers, Special Collections, UA.

unknown, R. W. Beckwith, William Morton, George Harmon, J. B. Mathews and others with having murdered and killed one John H. Tunstall at the said County of Lincoln on or about the 18th day of February 1878. I issued warrants on said affidavits for the arrest of the parties above named and directed the same to the Constable of Precinct No One in said County to wit: Antonio Martinez." [45]

Constable Martinez deputized Billy and Brewer to help him serve the warrants.

The three men went to Tunstall's store to arrest any posse men there. They found the store occupied by soldiers from Fort Stanton, who had been summoned by Sheriff Brady. When confronted, Sheriff Brady flatly refused to honor Wilson's warrants.

The killing of Tunstall and the flagrant refusal of legal authorities to hold the known killers – and the organizers of the killers – responsible torched off the Lincoln County War – a two year bloodfest of armed conflict in which as many as 80 men were murdered. On one side were Murphy, Dolan, and the Territorial establishment (widely known as the "Santa Fe Ring"). On the other side were Billy, Widenmann, Brewer, Waite, and as many as 40 others, who began calling themselves "Regulators." (The *New York Times* in a news report called them *"The Wrestlers."*)

Initially, both sides held legal authority. The Regulators had the warrants issued by Justice of the Peace Wilson. Dolan's side had the legal authority of Sheriff Brady and the courts.

On March 8, Territorial Governor Samuel B. Axtell journeyed to Lincoln. The stated purpose of his visit was to ascertain the facts of Tunstall's murder. The next morning, he met with Murphy:

"After hearing the Murphy story, the good governor was satisfied, and had neither time nor patience to hear the people's version of the difficulties. Messrs. Ellis, Shield and Widenmann offered to give him their versions and implored him to visit the people and learn for himself; this his Excellency indignantly refused to do." [46]

On his return to Santa Fe, Governor Axtell issued a proclamation which read in part:

"John B. Wilson's appointment by the County Commissioners as a Justice of the Peace was illegal and void, and all processes issued by him were void, and said Wilson has no authority whatever to act as Justice of the Peace...."

"The appointment of Robt. Widenmann as U.S. Marshall has been revoked...." [47]

Governor Axtell had no legal authority to nullify Wilson's Justice of the Peace office or to revoke Widenmann's U.S. Deputy Marshall appointment. The editor of the *Cimarron News and Press* wrote that Governor Axtell's action had only one purpose – to prevent the arrest of the men responsible for Tunstall's murder:

"On what other hypothesis can this strange action of the Governor's be explained?" [48]

A letter signed by 164 prominent Lincoln County residents published in the *Cimarron News and Press*, said, in part:

"In good faith, [Brewer] went as special constable to arrest the murderers of John H. Tunstall, by virtue of a warrant issued by John B. Wilson, a Justice of the Peace in the town of Lincoln. Before he could make his return thereon, Governor Axtell issued a proclamation to the effect that Wilson was not a legal J. P., although the act of our legislature, by virtue of which said Wilson was appointed justice, was approved by his Excellency. Mr. Wilson had acted as such justice for over a year without having his authority questioned." [49]

Death of Sheriff William Brady

Just after dark, on March 31, 1878, six men sneaked into the town of Lincoln: Billy, Waite, Middleton, Frank McNab, Henry Brown, and Jim French. The last three were hands of Tunstall's before aligning as Regulators.[50] They spent the night in the adobe-walled horse corral attached to Tunstall's store, where they were later joined by Widenmann and Sam Corbet.[51]

The previous day, McSween and about fifteen Regulators had met at John Chisum's South Springs Ranch. McSween told the gathered men that he needed to be in Lincoln to defend himself at the opening session of the district court. He told them that Sheriff Brady was carrying an arrest warrant for him and he was certain that Brady would engineer his "accidental" death once he was in custody. He asked the Regulators to get there in advance to protect him.[52]

McSween also pleaded for military protection from Fort Stanton, which detailed Lt. George Smith to supply an escort. When the escort failed to appear, McSween left for Lincoln without it.[53]

Miguel Luna standing at the spot from where the bullets that killed Brady and Hindman were fired. Undated photo. Courtesy Maurice G. Fulton Papers, Special Collections, UA.

About 9:00 a.m., Sheriff Brady and deputies Mathews, George Hindman, Jack Long, and George Peppin left the Murphy/Dolan store and began walking toward McSween's residence. They were confident McSween was there – and they intended to arrest him. What they did not know was that McSween was delayed by a rainstorm. He was still a few miles outside of Lincoln.[54]

As the five officers neared Tunstall's corral, a sudden flurry of gunshots broke the crisp, morning air, issuing from behind the gate.

Sheriff Brady, who was closest to the corral, was hit by three shots: head, back, left side. He died instantly.

George Hindman was hit by one shot. He stumbled a few steps and fell, mortally wounded. As he was dying, he screamed out, begging for a glass of water (suggesting heavy bleeding).

Jack Long was wounded slightly. He and Mathews and Peppin raced for shelter. Long reached the cover of the town's Torreón, a stone tower built in 1852 as a defense against Native American attacks.[55] Mathews and Peppin gained the safety of a residence.

Nullified Justice of the Peace Wilson, who was gardening outside his house, was hit in the buttocks by a wild bullet.[56]

Two men sprinted from behind the corral wall – Billy and Jim French – and leant over Sheriff Brady's body. Some sources say they were trying to grab the warrant he carried for McSween's arrest. Others, that Billy was trying to recover his Winchester rifle that Brady had confiscated several weeks earlier.

A shot by Mathews wounded French.[57] Dr. Ealy's daughter provided this account of his wounding:

Miguel Luna and an unidentified man standing beside the ruins of the Torreón. Undated photo. Courtesy Maurice G. Fulton Papers, Special Collections, UA.

"*Father stated that someone ran out to pick up either Brady's or Hindman's gun and was shot as he stooped over, not through the bowels as reported, but through the left thigh. Father said that the man came walking through the door and he treated him by drawing a silk handkerchief through the wound and binding it up. Soon the Murphy-Dolan crowd, who had tracked the man by his blood, came to search the house. It seems that Sam Corbett [Corbet] had taken the wounded man in charge and they disappeared. Afterwards, father learned that Sam Corbett had sawed a hole under a bed and laid the man there with a gun in his hand.*" [58]

The Murphy-Dolan supporting *Santa Fe Weekly New Mexican* had a different version:

"*Two of the assassins then attempted to rob the dead and were only prevented from getting off with their arms by being fired at after they picked up the guns of the murdered men, when they dropped them and ran. It is also said that Hindman who did not die for some minutes asked for water, and his murderers threatened to kill any person who should attempt to give him any.*" [59]

French successfully escaped from Lincoln the next day.

The Territorial newspapers had different interpretations of the killings. The *Weekly New Mexican* wrote:

"*McSween being a fugitive from justice had a willing tool in Widerman (sic), a worthless scoundrel and respectable loafer devoid of honor, who left Santa Fe without paying his board bill, and having nothing to lose either morally or financially, in a cowardly manner and in carrying out the instructions of his superior, assassinated one of the United States' best citizens....*" [60]

Torreón after it was restored to its original condition in the early 1930s. Undated postcard.

The *Mesilla Valley Independent* wrote, in an editorial signed by Colonel Albert J. Fountain:

> *"For the past two years, a gang of outlaws consisting of JESSIE EVANS, TOM HILL, FRANK BAKER and ten or twelve others, have systematically plundered the citizens of Lincoln County.... It is alleged that during all this period the outlaws were in the employ of certain persons who had contracts to supply the government with beef cattle and that the cattle stolen from the citizens by the outlaws were turned in to the government on these contracts. All efforts to break up this systematic stealing, and to punish the perpetrators by process of law, failed, for the reason, it is asserted, that the influence of the employers was successfully exerted to protect their outlaw servants from arrest."*

> *"On one occasion they were arrested and the good people of the county began to hope that a better era was dawning; but they were doomed to disappointment; the outlaws walked out of jail, and immediately reentered upon their vile occupation. All these things sorely tested the patience of the suffering citizens, who still, perhaps, would not have resorted to extreme measures had they not been roused to frenzy by an act of unparalleled atrocity."*

> *"A civil writ was placed in the hands of sheriff Brady, directing him to attach the property of A. A. McSween. Brady deputized one Mathews to execute the writ which he proposed to levy upon certain cattle and horses supposed to be the joint property of McSween and Mr. J. H. Tunstall; the latter a prominent*

Graves of William Brady and George Hindman. Undated photo. Courtesy Maurice G. Fulton Papers, Special Collections, UA.

merchant of Lincoln County, who had incurred the enmity of the outlaw gang and their alleged employers. Tunstall's life had been openly threatened by these men and a short time prior to the attempted execution of the writ of attachment. What then must have been his feelings when he beheld these known outlaws, escaped jail birds and refugees from justice, forming a part of the sheriff's posse charged with the execution of a civil writ!" [61]

Colonel Fountain added:

"One of the murderers subsequently stated that Brady was killed by accident; that it was their intention only to kill Hindman, as one of the murderers of Tunstall, and that one of the shots intended for Hindman took effect on Brady." [62]

The *Santa Fe Weekly New Mexican* published the following tribute to Sheriff Brady by Murphy-Dolan ally Riley:

"Poor Brady! After an honorable record of twenty years as a soldier and an officer, a greater portion of which was served in the war of the rebellion, to be so assassinated by a cowardly, sneaking tool of an unprincipled and ambitious man.... Who in New Mexico can say aught against Sheriff Brady? As an officer he was respected and feared by citizens of our county, and as such was in the way of the man McSween. He leaves a wife and nine young children to mourn his untimely death...." [63]

Main building, Blazer's Mill, with family and friends gathered outside. 1878 photo.
This building burned down in the 1880s. Courtesy Maurice G. Fulton Papers,
Special Collections, UA.

Death of Andrew "Buckshot" Roberts

Three days after Sheriff Brady's and Hindman's killings, a band of Regulators galloped into Blazer's Mill (April 4, 1878). The men in the party were: Richard Brewer, Charlie Bowdre, Fred Waite, Jim French, John Middleton, Frank McNab, Henry Brown, Josiah "Doc" Scurlock, Frank Coe, George Coe, Steve Stephens, John Scroggins, Ignacio Gonzales, and Billy.

Blazer's Mill was owned by former dentist Dr. Joseph Hoy Blazer. He and three partners homesteaded the site and built the Mill in 1867. In 1876, Blazer became the sole owner. Water power for the Mill came from the Rio Tularosa. The Mill was located on the *"only practical route through the Sacramento Mountains between the Rio Grande and the Pecos Rivers."* [64]

The Mill was about 40 miles southwest of Lincoln and was a stage stop on the road to El Paso, Texas.

> *"The main building of the mill was an adobe house with three feet thick walls.... It was provided with a look-out box on the roof and port holes in the walls of the second story. These were filled with clay, and could be opened at a moments' notice."* [65]

In 1873, the Federal Government established the Mescalero Apache Reservation. The Mill, now engulfed by the reservation, stayed private land. The government leased an office and quarters for the Reservation Agent in the Mill's main building. The Agent in 1878 was Major Frederick Godfroy.

Dr. Blazer was not a partisan in the Lincoln conflict. His son said of him:

> *"My father maintained a neutral attitude throughout the 'Lincoln County War,' although he had business relations with some of the participants on both sides. In conformity with the customs of the country all transients were welcome to food and horse-feed at all times, so he made no distinction in entertaining partisans of either faction."* [66]

Two days before the Regulators rode in, Buckshot Roberts was at the Mill waiting for a check he expected to come in the U.S. mail (he had sold his ranch a few weeks earlier). He got the nickname "Buckshot" from a load of buckshot he had taken in his right arm. His immobilized right arm left him unable to lift a rifle to his shoulder, so he fired from his hip.[67]

In what should have been fortuitous, the morning of the Regulators' arrival, Dr. Blazer warned Roberts to leave. He told him he had learned that Regulators were in the area and, as a member of the chase posse that murdered Tunstall, he should avoid an encounter.

> *"Roberts had a horse and a mule and that morning he packed the horse with his belongings and rode the mule. The posse was expected to come from the west, which was the direction he wanted to take; instead of going down the road where he would be likely to meet them, he crossed the canyon back of the mill and took the trail down the opposite side."* [68]

Roberts had only gone a short distance when he noticed:

> *"Brewer and his men coming up the road... [Roberts] then turned back and kept in sight of them most of the way until a half mile or so below the mill where the trail runs through a dense cedar thicket.... By the time he came to the edge of the mesa where the cedars end, the posse had their horses in the corral and the men were at dinner in the house so that he saw no sign of them and concluded they had gone on. He had seen the mail buckboard pass up ahead of them and he concluded to see if his letter had come."* [69]

Dr. Blazer's 13-year-old son Almer saw Roberts arrive:

> *"[He] threw his rope around an old stump that stood near the southwest corner of the house and tied his mule.... I remember thinking that he didn't intend to stay long for both his belts were hanging on the saddle horn, and afterward we found that his six shooter was in the scabbard on one of the belts, and his Winchester was in the scabbard on the saddle."*

> *"He had taken a few steps toward the store and we were just in front of the house when some one stepped out and shouted back, 'here is Roberts,' and jumped back into the house."* [70]

Roberts jerked his rifle from its scabbard and ran around the edge of the house. Almer then heard, but did not see, two shots.[71] Bowdre and Roberts had fired at each other. Bowdre's bullet entered Roberts' lower belly. Robert's bullet glanced off Bowdre's cartridge belt and took off George Coe's right *"trigger finger,"* shattering his hand.[72]

Richard M. Brewer, undated photo.
Courtesy Palace of the Governors Photo
Archives (NMHM/DCA), 105400.

Roberts rapidly fired five more shots. One hit Middleton in the chest, wounding him slightly. Three directed at George Coe missed. One sent toward Billy just *"shaved his arm."* Frank Coe said, *"I never saw a man that could handle a Winchester as fast as he [Roberts] could."* [73]

Dr. Blazer's bedroom/office was in the northwest corner of the square building. Although mortally wounded, Roberts managed to get himself into the room. Dr. Blazer's *"officer's pattern"* Springfield rifle was resting on pegs on the wall, along with a supply of shells. Roberts snatched the gun. Then, to defend himself, he dragged a feather mattress off a bed and placed it in doorway so he could lay on it and spot anyone who neared. [74]

"Bruer (sic), who was very much enraged, ordered Dr. Blazer and Major Godfroy to turn Roberts out. This they refused to do. Bruer threatened to burn the house unless the wounded man was turned over to him. Mrs. Godfroy pleaded with Bruer for the life of Roberts (who was a stranger to her), but without avail. Finding that the inmates of the house could not be persuaded or intimidated into turning Roberts out, Bruer proceeded to the Saw mill (about 125 yards from the door of the room in which Roberts had taken shelter) and, getting behind a saw-log, glanced over it at the door. Roberts caught a glimpse of the top of Bruer's head and fired, the ball entering Bruer's eye and killing him instantly." [75]

When the Regulators realized that Brewer was dead and Roberts could defend himself, they rode off.

No one knew how badly Roberts was wounded. Late in the evening Johnny Ryan, who worked for the Reservation Agency, arrived from Tularosa:

"Ryan took his hat in one hand and a large white silk handkerchief in the other to indicate his peaceful mission and walked up the middle road to the foot of the hill near the door from where he called Roberts until he answered. Then he went up to the door and talked to him." [76]

Roberts was made comfortable on a couch in the room. The next morning he died from his wound. The wound was on the right side of the belly with a *"depth of ten inches and of breadth of one half of an inch."*

"Brewer was buried late in the evening of the day he was killed. There were no undertakers, of course, and no ready-made coffins available; but he had a

neat board box covered with black cloth and lined with white [cloth]."

"Roberts died the following day and received the same treatment that Brewer had. Both were buried with every honor respect possible, my sister officiating in the capacity of minister, and they lie side by side in the south west corner of the little cemetery plat on the hill above where they met their fate." [77]

(For a description of the burial site and details on how the graves were relocated and re-marked 54 years later, see Appendix B.)

The letter on Lincoln County events signed by 164 county residents, quoted earlier, paid the following tribute to Brewer:

"We the undersigned residents of Lincoln county, in the Territory of New Mexico, deeply deplore the loss our county sustains by the death of Richard M. Brewer, a young man of irreproachable character, who commanded the respect and admiration of all who knew him. Some of us have been acquainted with him over eight years, and none ever knew his name to be associated with anything of a questionable character. He was a hard working, generous, sober, upright and noble minded young man. Cattle thieves and murderers, and their 'kid-gloved' friends hated him, and promised him a violent death years ago." [78]

James Dolan wrote the following about Brewer in a letter submitted to the *Santa Fe Weekly New Mexican*:

"R. M. Brewer I always considered an honest man and treated him as such until he became contaminated with Mr. McSween, his 'legal adviser.' It didn't take Mr. McSween long to initiate him into the way he should go, as it was only a short time after they became acquainted Mr. Brewer came to me and offered to sell me about twenty head of beef steers, he knowing them to be the property of Mr. Chisum...." [79]

No one seems to have publicly memorialized Buckshot Roberts.

Grand Jury Returns Indictments

On April 7, 1878, the Third District Court opened its session in Lincoln, Judge Bristol presiding. The opening was delayed for one week because of the *"terrible state of anarchy"* in the county. Six days later the court empanelled a grand jury to investigate the county's recent acts of violence. Dr. Blazer was selected jury foreman. [80]

On April 18, the grand jury returned the following indictments:

■ Jessie Evans, Frank Rivers (real name Jack Long), George Davis, and Manuel Segovia for the unlawful killing of John H. Tunstall.

■ James Dolan and Jacob Mathews as accessories for the unlawful killing of John H. Tunstall.

■ William Bonney (alias Kid, alias William Antrim), John Middleton, and Henry Brown for the unlawful killing of Sheriff Brady.

■ Henry Antrim (alias Kid), Charles Bowdre, Doc Scurlock, Henry Brown, John Middleton, Stephen Stevens, John Scroggins, George Coe, Frederick Waite for the unlawful killing of Buckshot Roberts. [81]

The indictment of only Billy, Middleton, and Brown for the killing of Sheriff Brady is surprising. The grand jury based their indictments on witness testimony (unfortunately, no record of those statements exists). The jury might have indicted only the named men because of relevant information learned in their investigation, or they might have simply been unaware of who exactly was behind the corral wall.

Widenmann quickly made it known publicly that he was in the corral only to feed Tunstall's dog – that he was caught entirely by surprise by the shooting and that he had nothing whatsoever to do with it. He became known in the Territorial press as the "dog feeder." Several examples:

"...Wideman [sic] the dog feeder [is] in the guardhouse...." [82]

"Some regret was expressed that there was no warrant issued for McSween and the dog feeder." [83]

"I presume we will have a little peace now for awhile. At least until the 'Dog feeder' returns, who I understand is raising a small army on the Rio Grande." [84]

"This same dog feeder was going to do quite a lot of killing over here once before, but he only got a couple of men killed, some were scared into behaving themselves, at least for a time...." [85]

Issued with the indictments was a report which stated, in part:

"The murder of John H. Tunstall, for brutality and malice, is without a parallel and without a shadow of justification. By this inhuman act our county has lost one of our best and most useful men – one who brought intelligence, industry, and capital to the development of Lincoln county. We equally condemn the most brutal murder of our late sheriff, William Brady, and George Hindman. In each of the cases, where the evidence would warrant it, we have made presentments."

"Had his Excellency, S. B. Axtell, when here, ascertained from the people the causes of our troubles, as he was requested, valuable lives would have been spared our community; especially do we condemn that portion of his proclamation relating to J. B. Wilson as J.P. Mr. Wilson acted in good faith as J.P. [for] over a year. Mr. Brewer, deceased, arrested, as we are informed, some of the alleged murderers of Mr. Tunstall by virtue of warrants issued by Mr. Wilson. The part of the proclamation referred to virtually outlawed Mr. Brewer and posse. In fact, they were hunted to the mountains by our late sheriff with U.S. soldiers. We believe that had the governor done his duty whilst here, these unfortunate occurrences would have been spared us."

"Your honor charged us to investigate the case of Alex. A. McSween, Esq. charged with the embezzlement of ten thousand dollars, belonging to the estate of Emil Fritz, deceased. This we did but were unable to find any evidence that would justify that accusation. We fully exonerate him of the charge and regret that a spirit of persecution has been shown in this matter. [86]

McSween's exoneration would be completely ignored by Lincoln's authorities.

Chapter 5

War in Lincoln

On July 15, 1878, war exploded in Lincoln.

The previous evening, a sleepy Sunday, McSween, Billy, and as many as 60 Regulators, in small groups, slipped silently into Lincoln, undetected by the residents. They had been riding as a band for several weeks, avoiding when they could – and fighting otherwise – a party of gunmen controlled by Dolan.

The Regulators took positions on the north side of the street, in McSween's house and several stores owned by allies. McSween had decided to occupy Lincoln with sufficient firepower to protect him from Dolan while he sought sanctions and redress in the District Court for Dolan's murderous behavior.

Billy, Jim French, Tom O'Folliard, Joe Smith, Thomas Cullins, George Bowers, José Chavez y Chavez, Yginio Salazar, Ignacio Gonzales, Florencio Chaves, Francisco Zamora, and Vincente Romero stationed themselves in McSween's house. They were well armed.[1]

Already resident in McSween's house were McSween's wife Susan, Susan's sister Elizabeth Shield, her children, and Harvey Morris, a visitor who hoped to study law with McSween. David Shield, Elizabeth's husband and McSween's legal partner, was away visiting Santa Fe.

Henry Brown, George Coe, and Sam Smith positioned themselves in what had been Tunstall's store. There already were Dr. Ealy, Mary Ealy, their children, and a school teacher named Susan Gates.

Charlie Bowdre, Doc Scurlock, John Middleton, Steve Stevens, and ten or so other men occupied the Ellis home and store, crowding owner Isaac Ellis, his wife, and their two sons.

Martin Chaves, José Fernando Herrera, and twenty or so other men occupied José Montaño's store. Herrera was the father of Manuela Herrera, Charlie Bowdre's future wife. His daughter Antonia Miguela Herrera was married already to Doc Scurlock.

> *"On Monday morning just as Dr. Ealy was opening the shutters and preparing for school one of the Shield's boys came in and said, 'There will be no school today as both parties are in town.' He told us the Murphy-Dolan party were divided; part at a tower just east of where we lived, and the other at the Murphy place. The McSween party were at his house and at the houses of Montana [sic] and Ellis at the far east of the town."* [2]

Dolan, who was living at the Wortley Hotel in Lincoln, was caught by surprise. He had few of his men with him. He frantically ordered Sheriff George W. Peppin to round up armed supporters.

McSween's U-shaped house was made of thick adobe walls, which provided excellent protection from gun shots (see drawing page 78). To further fortify the shelter, the men inside blocked the windows and doors with adobe bricks and drilled gun ports in

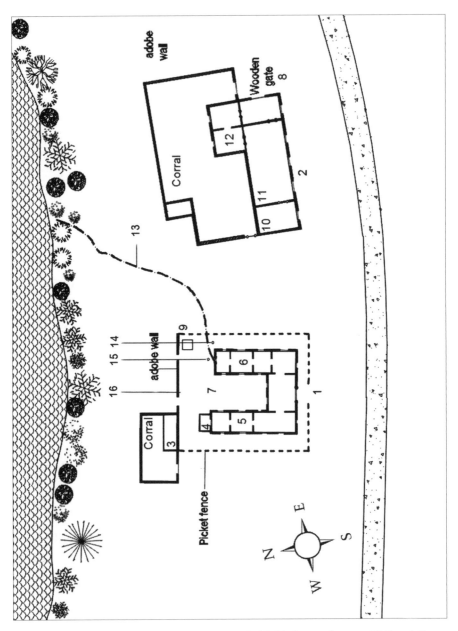

Lincoln, New Mexico, July 19, 1878, detail. (1) McSween house, (2) Tunstall store/residence, (3) Stable, (4) Kitchen shed, (5) McSween's wing, (6) Shield's wing, (7) Courtyard, (8) Corral gate (9) Outdoor toilet, (10) McSween law office, (11) Tunstall's store, (12) Tunstall's residence, (13) Route Billy, Thomas O'Folliard, Jim French, and José Chavez y Chavez took to escape, (14) Harvey Morris killed here, (15) McSween killed here, (16) Francisco Zamora and Vincente Romero killed here.

the walls. A high parapet lined the roof of the house, providing an ideal defensive bastion from which rifles could be aimed. In a strange twist of fate, Sheriff Peppin had built the house for McSween only a year earlier.[3]

By late afternoon, Sheriff Peppin was back in Lincoln with a party almost as large as McSween's. Dolan's heavily-armed fighters now included Jessie Evans, Robert and Wallace Olinger; Robert Beckwith; John, Tom, and Jim Jones; Milo Pierce; William Johnson; John Kinney; Charlie Hart; John Chambers; Sam Collins; Charlie "Lallacooler" Crawford; Andrew Boyle; John and Jim Hurley; Tom Cochrane; José Chavez y Baca, Pantaleón Gallegos, and 20 others.[4]

Dolan's men took positions in the Torreón, the Wortley Hotel, and Hamilton Mills' and Juan Chaves' houses.

Shooting between the two sides was sporadic, until Dolan's reinforcements arrived. Then the firing exploded. During a lull in the fighting, Sheriff Peppin delegated Deputy Jack Long to approach the McSween house and serve arrest warrants on McSween, Billy, Scurlock, Bowdre, Brown, and Frank and George Coe. He was refused by gunfire.[5]

In an attempt to force out the Dolan men who were firing from the Torreón and an adjacent adobe, McSween had a messenger hand-deliver an eviction notice to Saturnino Baca, who owned the Torreón but was renting the adobe from McSween:

"I want you to vacate the property now occupied by you at once. Unless you leave the house within three days, proceedings will be instituted against you without further notice."

"You have consented to improper use of the property by murderers for the purpose of taking my life, and I can no longer consent to your occupancy thereof." [6]

(That is truly a lawyer's perspective: issuing an eviction notice in the midst of fighting for one's life during a ferocious gun battle.)

When evening darkness fell, firing turned sporadic again. Mary Ealy reported:

"There was scarcely a minute that day that a shot did not ring out – sometimes a whole volley. That evening or more some time in the night, a Mr. Green [Justice of the Peace John Wilson] who lived close to us came to the window and called the Doctor in a whisper, saying, 'There is a man over here dying,' and asked him to go see him. They started off and immediately those in the tower began to shoot. Green called them 'Don't shoot; I am taking the doctor to see a dying man.' The shooting stopped. The house where the man lived was just beside the tower, and the man told Dr. Ealy the cursing and swearing was distressing. The man was very low and died before morning." [7]

The next day, the second day of the war, firing continued all day and into the night. Mary Ealy wrote:

"During our stay in Lincoln we got all our drinking water from the neighbors, but all the other water for cooking, etc., from the river at the foot of a little hill back of the corral. By this time the children and all of us were suffering for water; so Wednesday morning Miss Gates said, 'I am going to the river for

Mary and Taylor Ealy. 1874 tintype. Courtesy Center for Southwest Research and Special Collections, UNM.

water; if we don't get water we will die anyway.' So we started and were not molested. We carried several buckets of water, which lasted while we were kept in the house." [8]

Dolan's men were making no progress, leaving Sheriff Peppin seething. After he could tolerate it no longer, he sent a note to Colonel Nathan Dudley, the commander of Fort Stanton:

"I have the honor to respectfully state that mostly all the men for whom I have united states [sic] warrants are in town, and are being protected by A. A. McSween and a large party of his followers.... They are resisting, and it is impossible for me to serve the warrants. If it is in your power to loan me one of your Howitzers, I am of the opinion the parties for whom I have said warrants would surrender...." [9]

Colonel Dudley recorded his response to the sheriff's request in a report to his superiors:

"I after careful deliberation and a long consultation with my Officers came to the conclusion to refuse the request, deeply regretting that I was compelled to do so." [10]

The third day of the battle, shooting between the two sides alternated between periods of heavy fire and counter fire, and periods of eerie quiet. It worsened at sundown, however. Mary Ealy wrote:

"Wednesday night was worse yet. Fighting, cursing, screaming – everything to frighten people from the East – went on incessantly. We barricaded our windows with our trunks and laid our beds on the floor. That night Ben Ellis, a friend whom we had made, was shot. Two men from his father's place waded up the river until they came opposite to our house; then they crawled up to the corral and managed to reach our door although many shots were fired at them from the tower. Dr. Ealy went with them and tried to reach Ellis', but he was not able to wade the river and could not get there." [11]

Early Thursday morning, the fourth day of the war, Dr. Ealy decided – no matter what the risk – he would provide medical care to Ben Ellis. Mary Ealy recounted:

"[Dr. Ealy] took [our] baby in his arms and led our little Pearl, and we all walked down the street to Ellis'. He felt sure even such desperadoes would not hurt women and children. The wound was a bad one, and the man had lost much blood. As Dr. Ealy was dressing the wound, we learned that Ben Ellis had been shot while in the corral feeding his horses." [12]

Recognizing that his men were making no progress – and that time was not on his side – Dolan decided, as Sheriff Peppin had earlier, that the only way to win was to bring in the army. He rode to Fort Stanton and met with Colonel Dudley.

Colonel Dudley greeted Dolan heartily. He had been aching for an excuse to intervene in the war.

Nathan Augustus Monroe Dudley. 1863 photo. Courtesy Library of Congress.

Alexander Rudder, a laborer at Fort Stanton, was in a room next to where Dolan and Colonel Dudley met. Rudder was there *"rubbing the dust off the windows."* He overheard Colonel Dudley say:

"...he would go down as soon as he could, the cannon was broke some way or other and Mr. Nelson, blacksmith, worked on it all night." [13]

Samuel Beard also heard the conversation:

"...I was out in front of [Dudley's] quarters. I heard him, Colonel Dudley, tell Mr. Dolan as he was getting on his horse to leave, to go down and stand them off and he would be there by 12 o'clock." [14]

When Dolan was asked later under oath if he was at Fort Stanton on the day in question, he replied, no, he was in Lincoln all day. He added:

"I think I was at the butcher shop, slaughter pen, I had dinner there with Mr. McVeagh." [15]

The next day, the fifth day of the war, at 10 a.m., Colonel Dudley marched into Lincoln with his entire command: officers, cavalry, infantry:

"On the morning of the 19th inst. I took every officer of the post including the post surgeon... [and] proceeded to Lincoln taking with me the Gatling Gun and 2,000 rounds of ammunition, also the Howitzer with ample supply of ammunition for any emergency that might arise, with three days rations."

"I personally headed the column..." [16]

Colonel Dudley pitched camp in the center of town opposite the Montaño store.

When the McSween men in the Montaño store peered out, they saw a howitzer cannon being unhitched from two horses. The gun was *"unlimbered"* and pointed directly at their shelter. Three soldiers began *"cleaning it and putting up their homespike."* One of the soldiers was *"fixing his lanyard and fuse"* in preparation for firing the howitzer. The Gatling gun was assembled and set up alongside the howitzer.[17]

When one of the men in Montaño's store questioned Colonel Dudley about the guns, he replied:

"...that if a shot was fired from that house into my command wounding or killing any of my officers or men, I should open fire with my Howitzer on it at once...." [18]

Martin Chaves, the leader of the Montaño contingent, said:

"I saw a cannon pointing toward [us]. I went out of the house with the men that were there, when I was entering the house of Ellis I saw the same piece turned and directed toward the Ellis house. I went out from there and went down the river...." [19]

Sam Corbet reported:

"I saw the cannon placed toward the Montaño house. After the men left Montaño and went to the Ellis house, the cannon was then turned toward that

Alex H. McSween,
David P. Shield,

"B"

Said Office
of
McSween and Shield
Lincoln County Bank Building
Lincoln New Mexico. 7/19 1878
Gen. Dudley U.S.A.— Would
you have the kindness to let me
know why soldiers surround my
house. Before blowing up my
property I would like to know
the reason. The Constable is here
and has warrants for the
arrest of Sheriff Peppin and
Posse for murder and larceny.
Respectfully
(Signed) A. H. McSween.

a true copy
M. F. Goodwin
2" Lieut 9" Cavalry
Post Adjutant

A certified copy of the note sent by McSween to Colonel Dudley asking why he
intended to blow up McSween's house. Introduced as Exhibit B, Dudley Court of
Inquiry. Courtesy NARA.

house. After they left the Ellis house, the cannon moved off about 150 yards from his camp towards the river." [20]

With these simple maneuvers, Colonel Dudley scared off McSween's protectors in the Montaño and Ellis stores. McSween was left with only those men sheltering with him within his residence.

Dolan's men took advantage of the turn in fortune delivered by the arrival of the army to rush the McSween house:

"I saw about 13 or 14 men run down the road from the Wortley Hotel to the McSween building and take positions around the house against the adobe walls, some four or five others of the same party took possession of Stanley's house across the street from the McSween building. This was about 3/4 of an hour from the passage of the troops."

"Some of them attempted to pry under shields (sic) with kitchen knives as far as I could see, and were shouting demands to surrender." [21]

Colonel Dudley would laud this action in a report:

"Men who have the reckless courage to attack a building in bright mid-day, its walls forming a perfect protection against any modern musketry to its inmates, pierced as this castle of McSween's was, with scores of loop holes for rifles in every side and angle, to say nothing of the flat roof protected by a perfect wall of defense, and for hours hugging the walls, exposed to the fire of not only from the loop holes, but from the roof of adjacent buildings... charging this position across a space perfectly exposed to the fire of McSween's men for a distance of nearly three hundred yards, are not of a character to be easily induced to abandon a course they believe is only half completed." [22]

Deputy Marion Turner, one of the men who stormed McSween's house, said he shouted through a slit in a window that he had a warrant for McSween and for those inside to surrender. He said Jim French yelled back:

"Our warrants are in our guns you c**k s**cking sons of bitches." [23]

At the Stanley house, Dolan's men posted a black flag, a kind of flag used during the Civil War to signal to opponents they would be afforded no mercy. Susan McSween described the flag:

"It was a black Cashmere shawl, about a yard and a half long, hung from the top of the door, in front of the house." [24]

Seeing his position weakening, McSween sent a note to Colonel Dudley by the hand of his little niece, Minnie Shield:

"Would you have the kindness to let me know why soldiers surround my house. Before blowing up my property I would like to know the reason. The Constable [Antonio Martinez] is here and has warrants for the arrest of Sheriff Peppin and <u>posse</u> *for murder and larceny."* [25]

Susan Ellen McSween. Undated photo. Courtesy Center for Southwest Research and Special Collections, UNM.

Colonel Dudley recorded his nasty response in a report to his superiors:

"I received through a little girl about 7 years of age a communication signed A. A. McSween, probably the last letter he ever wrote; to which I returned the following reply in lead pencil, through my Adjutant Lieutenant Goodwin, by the same messenger – viz – I am directed by the Commanding Officer to inform you that my soldiers have surrounded your house and that he desires to hold no correspondence with you; if you desire to blow up your house, the Commanding Officer does not object providing it does not injure any U.S. soldiers." [26]

After receiving this reply, McSween held a war conference. Susan McSween told the group:

"I believe that I could go down to his camp and talk with him [Dudley] myself. Perhaps I could get some satisfaction from him or could perhaps have some influence with him by talking with him." [27]

She crossed to Dudley's camp, partly on her hands and knees to avoid being shot. He met her outside his tent.

"I then asked him why he camped there in the middle of the town just on that day.... I then said it looked strange to me to see his men, or soldiers I should say, guarding Peppin back and forth through town and sending soldiers around our house, and sending us word as he had sent us, if he had nothing to do with it." [28]

The two argued about the warrant for McSween's arrest. Susan said there was no warrant for McSween, and thus no basis for army involvement. Colonel Dudley said there was indeed a warrant for McSween. Although he did not tell her, he had just forced Justice of the Peace Wilson to write such a warrant, which Wilson did only after being bodily threatened by several of Dudley's officers.[29]

Susan said that McSween had *"always regarded the military with the greatest esteem."*

"Colonel Dudley then said in a spurley way, I am pleased to hear this, and he made fun of my remark, and said Mr. McSween was a mean man, that he had no principles.... He then made sport of me being Mrs. McSween as though it was degrading to be called Mrs. McSween."

"He then got very angry with me, used abusive language towards me and those with my husband. He said I was not a woman of good character." [30]

Colonel Dudley was alluding to a calumny circulating in Lincoln that Susan had had an affair with Francisco Gomez. Sheriff Peppin, in an affidavit signed four months later, claimed that he had personally witnessed Susan *"in actual lascivious contact"* with Gomez, Saturnino Baca's son-in-law.[31]

Susan asked Dudley why he threatened to blow up her house. Colonel Dudley replied that it was McSween, not he, who intended to blow up her house. Susan said he had misunderstood her husband's letter, to let her have it, and she would explain it to him.

"He then brought out the letter. I reached out my hand for the letter, he pushed it away and said, [he] did not want [me] to have the letter, [I would] keep

it. I told him, no Sir, I will not do that, I merely wanted to show him he could be so mistaken in what McSween had written. He then handed the letter to me and said to a soldier, or a guard, or a Sargt., 'I'll thank you to shoot this lady if she takes this letter.'" [32]

Colonel Dudley was pretending that McSween's sentence, *"Before blowing up my property I would like to know the reason..."* meant *"Before I blow up my property...,"* an intentionally dense interpretation that Dudley knew was bogus.

After more arguing:

"...he [Dudley] ordered me out of the camp, ordered the guard to put me out of the camp. He walked away. I then called him back. ...I see through your whole intention now." [33]

Elizabeth (Hummer) Shield, Susan McSween's sister. Courtesy Maurice G. Fulton Papers, Special Collections, UA.

While Colonel Dudley was denigrating Susan, Dolan and Sheriff Peppin were putting in motion the plan they knew would end the war. It started at Isaac Ellis' house:

"Peppin with nine men came to my house, fired off their guns a number of times and shot in the house. One of the men [Beckwith] asked me for coal oil. I told him I had none in cans. He told me to get something and draw some so that they could carry it. I got them a bucket and drawed [sic] some oil for them. They took it and went off with it, went up the road, did not see them further until they got to Colonel Dudley's camp. Then he went out and was standing with them...." [34]

Before Susan could get back to her home, she noticed *"three soldiers standing near the house"* and *"some Murphy men standing close up to the wall of the house."* She saw one of the men *"pour coal oil on the floor of my sister's house."* She saw *"Jack Long throw something that popped, something like a torpedo."* [35]

Deputy Jack Long, questioned under oath, explained what they were doing.

*"**QUESTION**: Do you know anything about setting fire to the McSween house that day?"*

*"**LONG**: Yes sir, I know about setting the house afire. I poured coal oil on the floor and gave a man some matches out of my pocket to start the coal oil fire."*

*"**QUESTION**: About what time did you pour the coal oil on the floor of the McSween house?"*

*"**LONG**: About half past one in the afternoon."*

"QUESTION: In what part of the house was the coal oil poured?"

"LONG: In the northeast kitchen, they did have two kitchens."

"QUESTION: State whether or not this attempt to set the house on fire was successful."

"LONG: It was not."

"QUESTION: After you poured the coal oil on the floor of the kitchen, where did you go?

"LONG: I was shot at and I ran outside the fence and got into a privy sink, it was dug into the bank, privy sink was open facing the river. Buck Powell was with me." [Thomas Benton "Buck" Powell was one of Peppin's deputies.]

"QUESTION: How long did you remain there?"

"LONG: I was there until after dark. Ascequa [sic] was running within 15 feet but I could not get to it, neither me or Buck." [36]

Long had tried to start the fire at the wing of the house occupied by Elizabeth Shield and her five children.

George Coe, in his autobiography, wrote about Long cowering in the stinking toilet hole:

"All day when we had nothing better to do, we made that [the outhouse] our target and shot it full of holes. The result was that he was forced to crawl down into the pit rather than meet certain death. He afterwards remarked that it was the most gruesome experience of his life, but beat dying...." [37]

After the disappointing failure of the first attempt to fire the house, Peppin organized a second. Andrew Boyle testified:

"QUESTION: Do you know when the McSween house was set on fire at the place where the fire was successfully started?"

"BOYLE: It was about one o'clock in the afternoon."

"QUESTION: Where you present at the time?"

"BOYLE: I was."

"QUESTION: On which side of what part of the house was this?"

"BOYLE: It was at the back door of the kitchen on the northwest corner of the house."

"QUESTION: Describe, if you know, the way the fire took effect and its course of progress upon the house."

"BOYLE: I set it on fire with a sack of shavings and chips and used what timber there was on top of the stable to make it burn. It burned very slowly all the afternoon from one room to another turning a circle around the house." [38]

Boyle has started his fire at the McSween wing of the building.

Asked under oath, Boyle confirmed the firing was ordered by Sheriff Peppin:

Juan Batista Patron's house, where the Ealys, Miss Gates, Susan McSween, and Elizabeth Shield and her five children took shelter. Undated photo. Courtesy Maurice G. Fulton Papers, Special Collections, UA.

> *"**QUESTION**: When did Sheriff Peppin order you if you could not get the McSween party out without burning it, to burn it?"*
> *"**BOYLE**: In the morning when I started to go down there."* [39]

Seeing the McSween house in flames, Dr. and Mary Ealy in the Tunstall store about *"30 steps"* away became frightened that their refuge would be burned next. They had been told that Colonel Dudley would accept no communication from them, so Mary wrote two notes and sent them to Dr. Appel by the hand of school teacher Susan Gates. Miss Gates asked Dr. Appel to pass the second note to Colonel Dudley. The note to Dr. Appel read:

> *"Please use your influence with Colonel Dudley to protect us. We will remember you for it. We are afraid the store will be set on fire."* [40]

The note to Colonel Dudley read:

> *"Please give us a guard of Soldiers from this building. We have no place to go. We ask you for protection."* [41]

Colonel Dudley refused to order any of his men to help the Ealys, but Dr. Appel and several others volunteered to do so. They commandeered a wagon to haul the Ealy possessions to safety. Dr. Ealy, Mary, their children, and Miss Gates were escorted to the Juan Patron house which was only few feet from Dudley's camp. [42]

While Dr. Appel was loading the Ealys' possessions, Susan McSween approached him, saying she and her sister wanted to leave the burning McSween house and asking would he protect them also. Appel agreed and Susan and Elizabeth Shield and her five terrified children were conducted without incident to the Patron house. Susan abandoned her husband with great reluctance, having vowed earlier to see it through with him no matter how it ended.[43]

Boyle started the fire about one o'clock. It burned all afternoon, consuming one room after another, forcing the men inside to crowd into a smaller and smaller space. *"About the late afternoon,"* when the fire reached the cross-connecting portion of the house, a gunpowder keg exploded.[44]

By evening, the entire house was burning, except for one room, ironically, the room where Long had tried to start the first fire. In spite of the spreading darkness, the fire, in Billy's words, *"made it almost light as day for a short distance all around."* [45]

> *"The house was in a great blaze lighting up the hills on both sides of the town."* [46]

Colonel Dudley asked his officers to estimate how many rounds had been fired since the fire was started:

> *"The estimate made by my officers was that over two thousand shots were exchanged during the evening."* [47]

The men in the house faced a stark choice, stay and burn to death or run for it.

In an attempt to save McSween's life, Billy, Thomas O'Folliard, Jim French, José Chavez y Chavez, and Harvey Morris volunteered to make a break for Tunstall's store, exiting the house to the east. That was the most exposed route and would draw the most fire. Simultaneously, McSween, Yginio Salazar, Thomas Cullins, George Bowers, Ignacio Gonzales, Francisco Zamora, Vincente Romero, and Florencio Chaves would dash straight back, aiming for the cover of the river.

Billy and his group dashed into a wall of fire. Morris, who was in the lead, was killed before he got six feet, *"inside the gate inside the McSween yard."* [48]

It was impossible to reach the Tunstall store, as Billy later explained under oath:

> *"**QUESTION**: In what direction did you go upon your escape from the McSween house?"*
> *"**BILLY**: Ran towards the Tunstall store, was fired at, and there turned towards the river."* [49]

Both Billy and José Chavez y Chavez later testified that the fire that killed Morris came from three soldiers shooting from the cover of the Tunstall store.

> *"**QUESTION**: How many soldiers fired at you?"*
> *"**BILLY**: Three."*

> *"**QUESTION**: How many shots did those soldiers fire, that you say shot from the Tunstall building?"*
> *"**BILLY**: I could not swear to that on account of firing on all sides, I could not hear. I seen them fire one volley."*

> *"**QUESTION**: What did they fire at?"*
> *"**BILLY**: Myself and José Chavez."* [50]

Yginio Salazar. Undated photo. Courtesy Maurice G. Fulton Papers, Special Collections, UA.

The McSween party fared worse. Boyle described what he saw:

"...McSween and two Mexicans got as far as the back house. [They] ran back in the corner [of the fence] and stayed five minutes. Then they tried to run out the gate a second time, we shot at them and they ran back again, then stayed there under cover for about 10 minutes more, McSween called out, 'I shall surrender.'"

"Robert Beckwith replied, 'I am a deputy sheriff and I have got a warrant for you.' He went then to the back door to serve the warrant. McSween then cried, 'I shall never surrender.' Then the fire became promiscuous and that was the time the big killing was made."

"When McSween said he would not surrender every one of them commenced to shoot. Robert Beckwith fell first, McSween next, on top of Beckwith, the two Mexicans fell next to them. Two more Mexicans went into the chicken house, and two more fell between the door and the back house." [51]

Colonel Dudley reported to his superiors:

"I regret to report as follows: A. A. McSween, José Chavez (sic), Vincente Romero, Harvey Morris were killed. Thomas Cullins and another man name unknown were wounded or killed and reported as buried in the burned house of McSween... it is reported that one man was killed on the 18th inst, and buried in the cellar of McSween's house.... Jim French and Kid Antrim are reported missing and it is generally supposed they are in the ruins of the building, as during the burning of the building, a large number of cartridges were heard exploding." [52]

The toll according to the coroner's jury was five:

> *"A. A. McSween with 5 shots in his body, Harvey Morris with 1 shot in his body, Bincente [Vincente] Romero with 3 shots in his body and leg, Francisco Samora [Zamora] with eight shots in his body, and Robert Beckwith with two shots, one in the head and one in the wrist."* [53]

No attempt was made to determine if there were any bodies in the burned-out rubble. [54]

Yginio Salazar, fleeing with McSween's group, was shot in two places and knocked unconscious. He was assumed to be dead by the victors, so was further ignored. Yginio was 15 years old. He later recounted:

> *"After the house was set on fire, we resisted until dusk. When the last room was burning, then we started out of the house one at a time, and there were thirteen who left the house.... I sat down at the wall only fifteen yards from the posse when I was shot and fainted away; and about 8 or 9 o'clock that night I started away."* [55]

Yginio crawled 1,000 yards to his sister-in-law's house, leaving a trail of blood and reaching the house about midnight. Dr. Appel was called and he treated Yginio's wounds.[56]

Beckwith's body was removed the same night he was killed, taken to Fort Stanton, and buried there. He was given a formal funeral with one of the Fort's officers reading the funeral oration.[57] Romero and Zamora were buried in private plots by their families. Susan refused to let Colonel Dudley have anything to do with the burial of her husband. He was *"buried near where Tunstall had been buried,"* as was Harvey Morris.[58]

Colonel Dudley wrote:

> *"McSween's body, unwashed was wrapped up in a blanket, placed in a box and buried without ceremony."* [59]

The next morning, after a night of revelry and hard drinking, Dolan's men and some of Dudley's soldiers broke into Tunstall's store (property of Tunstall's heirs), taking what they wanted. The looting continued for three days. Sam Corbet, who was in charge of the store, testified:

> *"**QUESTION**: Who was in the store when you went in there, and what were the persons doing?"*
> *"**CORBET**: There was so many in there, I could not tell who they was. Peppin and Andy Boyle, and a good many of his posse were in there. I asked Peppin if he could not stop his men from taking goods out of there. He told me he was not responsible for anything done. That he had taken something himself that he would pay for it."* [60]

Colonel Dudley refused to use his men to prevent the robbing. He was even seen in the store himself.[61]

By late afternoon, Colonel Dudley had packed up his tents, hitched up his howitzer and Gatling gun, and marched back to Fort Stanton. Victory was sweet.

George Coe pointing at the site of the burned-down McSween home. 1940 photo.
Courtesy Archives and Special Collections, NMSU.

Chapter 6 | Governor Wallace's Amnesty Proclamation

Removing Governor Samuel B. Axtell

On September 4, 1878, U.S. President Rutherford B. Hayes removed Axtell as New Mexico Territorial Governor and replaced him with Lewis "Lew" Wallace:

> "I transmit herewith an order from the President for the suspension of Mr. Samuel B. Axtell from his office as Governor of the Territory of New Mexico, together with a designation for yourself to perform the duties of said suspended officer, subject to all provisions of law applicable thereto."

> "You will deliver said order of suspension to Governor Axtell upon your arrival at the capitol of New Mexico, and when you enter upon the duties of your office you will at once repost the fact to this Department." [1]

As signaled by the tone of the letter by Secretary of the Interior Carl Shurz, President Hayes was most dissatisfied with Axtell's job performance.

The Territorial establishment was vociferously unhappy with Axtell's removal. The *Las Vegas Daily Gazette* wrote:

> "We infer from the action of the president directly after the return of Mr. Frank Warner Angell [sic] to the capital that the quarrel between him and Gov. Axtell had more to do with the latter's removal than any misdemeanors in office. Mr. Angell is a satrap of Carl Shurz sent out on the European plan, with a wave of the hand like a Bismarck, and instructed that if any one presumes to differ with you, refer them to me. Angell got mad, went off huffy, reported Axtell, and Shurz at once recommended removal." [2]

The *Santa Fe New Mexican* wrote:

> "There probably never was less partisan politics or demagoguism in a territorial administration than that of Governor S. B. Axtell.... the most respectable and intelligent portion of this people have come to and still do regard Gov. Axtell as the purest and best executive ever appointed over them. Hence, we, with them, and the people generally, learn with profound regret of his suspension or removal." [3]

Frank Angel was a special investigator dispatched by the Secretary of the Interior to investigate the atrocities ripping Lincoln County apart. He arrived in the county five weeks after Tunstall's savage murder and began taking depositions in the form of interrogatories from participants and witnesses. His report to the Secretary, submitted October 7, 1878, included 39 sworn statements. (The account of Tunstall's murder by Billy on page 57 is from Billy's statement to Angel.)

His report made 12 formal charges against Axtell. Here are the most serious ones:

■ The Governor has taken strictly partisan actions....
■ He refused to listen to complaints by the people....
■ He was paid $2,000 to influence his actions....

Lewis "Lew" Wallace. Undated photo. Courtesy Center for Southwest Research and Special Collections, UNM.

- He arbitrarily removed Territorial officials thereby outlawing citizens and usurping the functions of the judiciary....
- He knowingly appointed bad men to office....
- He was a tool of designing men....
- He conspired to murder innocent and law abiding citizens because they opposed his wishes.... [4]

Wallace arrived in Santa Fe by buckboard late in the evening of September 30 after an exhausting trip from Trinidad, Colorado – *"sick in every bone, dead in every muscle."*

Early the next day he called on Governor Axtell at the Palace of Governors to deliver Secretary Shurz's letter and assume the governor's office:

> *"I found him [Axtell] in what is called the Executive Office – a large, low, dark chamber, one of many in the palace. The carpet was old and dirty. There was a large table in the center, a settee covered with stained and greasy calico, a few chairs – these constituted the furniture.... On the north wall there was a great map almost as yellow as the walls themselves. The ceiling was of dirty muslin tacked to the rafters.... In every corner hung dusty cabinets, every crack and catch was a mass of sooty dust."*
>
> *"As you may imagine, the interview was not a pleasant one...."* [5]

Despite his dismissal for his dreadful performance as governor, Axtell was appointed the Chief Justice of the New Mexico Territorial Supreme Court four years later by President Chester A. Arthur.[6]

Amnesty

Lew Wallace was a Mexican-American and Civil War veteran. In the Civil War he attained the rank of major general. Beginning May 12, 1865, Wallace served as a judge on the military commission that convicted eight persons of murdering, conspiring to murder, and/or aiding the murder of President Abraham Lincoln. The commission sentenced three men and one woman to hang: Lewis Powell, George Atzerodt, David Herold, and Mary Surratt. Three others were sentenced to life at hard labor: Samuel Arnold, Dr. Samuel Mudd, and Michael O'Laughlen. One man, Edman Spangler, was sentenced to six years in prison.[7]

Beginning August 23, 1865, Wallace was the presiding judge on the trial of Heinrich H. Wirz for his actions as commander of the infamous Confederate military prison at Andersonville. Wirz was convicted of murder, personal cruelty, and injuring the health of the Union prisoners in his custody. He was hanged November 10, 1865. [8]

Five years before his appointment as New Mexico governor, Wallace published *"The Fair God,"* a novel based on the Spanish conquest of Mexico. The title is an allegorical interpretation of Quetzalcoatl, the Aztec god of wind, air, and learning. During his time in New Mexico, Wallace would also write *"Ben-Hur."*

From the moment of his appointment, Wallace had a plan to restore order to Lincoln County.

On his second day in office, he received what he had asked from President Hayes:

Proclamation by the Governor.

For the information of the people of the United States, and of the citizens of New Mexico in especial, the undersigned announces that the disorders lately prevalent in Lincoln County in said Territory, have been happily brought to an end. Persons having business and property interests therein, and who are themselves peaceably disposed, may go to and from that County without hinderance or molestation. Individuals resident there, but who have been driven away, or who, from choice, sought safety elsewhere, are invited to return, under assurance that ample measures have been taken, and are now and will be continued in force. to make them secure in person and property. And that the people of Lincoln County may be helped more speedily to the management of their civil affairs, as contemplated by law, and to induce them to lay aside forever the divisions and feuds which, by national notoriety, have been so prejudicial to their locality and the whole Territory. the undersigned, by virtue of authority in him vested, further proclaims a general pardon for misdemeanors and offenses committed in the said County of Lincoln against the laws of the said Territory in connection with the aforesaid disorders, between the first day of February, 1878, and the date of this proclamation.

And it is expressly understood that the foregoing pardon is upon the conditions and limitations following:

It shall not apply to officers of the United States Army stationed in the said County during the said disorders, and to persons who, at the time of the commission of the offense or misdemeanor of which they may be accused. were, with good intent, resident citizens of the said Territory, and who shall have hereafter kept the peace, and conducted themselves in all respects as becomes good citizens.

Neither shall it be pleaded by any person in bar of conviction under indictment now found and returned for any such crimes or misdemeanors, nor operate the release of any party undergoing pains and penalties consequent upon sentence heretofore had for any crime or misdemeanor.

In witness whereof I have hereunto set may hand and caused the seal of the Territory of New Mexico to be affixed.

{ SEAL. } Done at the city of Santa Fé, this 13th day of November, A D. 1878.
LEWIS WALLACE,

By the Governor,
W. G. RITCH,
Secretary.

Para la informacion del pueblo de los Estados Unidos, y de los ciudadanos del Territorio de Nuevo Mojico en lo especial, el abajo firmado anuncia que los desórdenes que hace poco tiempo predominaban en el Condado de Lincoln, en dicho Territorio, han llegado felizmente á su fin. Personas que tengan negocios y propiedad é intereses en él mismo, y que están pacificamente dispuestas pueden entrar y salir de ese condado sin obstaculo ni vejacion. Individuos residentes alli, pero que han sido impelidos á salir, ó que por escojimiento han buscado seguridad en otras partes, son invitadas de regresar, bajo la seguridad que se han tomado medidas amplias y están ahora y serán continuadas en fuerza, para asegurarles en su propiedad.

Y para que el pueblo del condado de Lincoln sea mas prontamente ayudado en el manejo de sus asuntos locales como contemplado por la ley, y para inducirles de dejar á un lado y para siempre las divisiones y disensiones, que por notoriedad nacional han sido tan perjudiciales á su localidad y á todo el Territorio, el abajo firmado, por virtud de autoridad en él investida, además proclama un perdon general por malos procederes y ofensas cometidas en el dicho condado de Lincoln contra las leyes del dicho territorio, en coneccion con los arriba dichos desordenes, entre el dia primero de Febrero mil ochocientos setenta y ocho y la fecha de esta proclamacion.

Y es expresamente entendido que el perdon arriba dicho es sobre las condiciones y limitaciones siguientes: No se aplicará excepto á oficiales del Ejercito de los Estados Unidos apostados en dicho condado durante los dichos desórdenes, y á personas que, al tiempo de cometer la ofensa ó mal proceder de la cual puedan ser acusados, eran con buena intencion ciudadanos residentes de dicho territorio, y quienes en lo de adelante guarden la paz y se conduscan en todos respectos como conviene á ciudadanos buenos. Ni tampoco se alegará por ninguna persona en foro de conviccion bajo querella ahora hallada y retornada por cualesquier tales crimenes ó malos procederes, ni obrará la exoneracion de ninguna parte sufriendo castigos y penas consecuentes sobre sentencia dada antes por ningun crimen ó mal proceder.

En testimonio de lo cual he puesto á esta mi mano, y he causado que sea fijado el sello del Territorio de Nuevo Mejico.

{ SELLO } Hecha en la ciudad de Santa Fé, este dia 13 de Noviembre, A. D., 1878,
LEWIS WALLACE,

Por el Gobernador:
W. G. RITCH, Secretario.

Pardon issued by Territorial Governor Lewis "Lew" Wallace, November 13, 1878.
Courtesy Lew Wallace Collection, Indiana State Historical Society.

"In accordance with your verbal request I submitted to the President and Cabinet the question as to the extent of your authority as Governor of New Mexico to grant amnesty or pardon to persons charged with offenses. The result of the discussion was the conclusion that you have full power to grant pardons and reprieves and to reduce fines and forfeitures for all offenses against the laws of the Territory. Also to grant respites for offenses against the United States until the decision of the President can be known thereon. See Section 1841, Revised Statues."

"I have the honor to be, Sir,"
"Very respectfully your Obedient Servant,"
"Geo. W. McCrary"
"Sec'y of War" [9]

After taking 40 days to inform himself on conditions in Lincoln County, Wallace, on November 13, 1878, issued an amnesty proclamation. It read, in part:

"And that the people of Lincoln county may be helped more speedily to the management of their civil affairs, as contemplated by law, and to induce them to lay aside forever the division and feuds which, by national notoriety, have been so prejudicial to their locality and the whole Territory, the undersigned, by virtue of authority in him vested, further proclaims a general pardon for misdemeanors and offenses committed in the said county of Lincoln against the laws of the said Territory, in connection with the aforesaid disorders, between the first day of February, eighteen hundred and seventy eight and the date of this proclamation."

"And it is expressly understood that the foregoing pardon is upon the conditions and limitations following: It shall not apply except to officers of the United States army stationed in the said county during the said disorders, and to persons who, at the time of the commission of the offense or misdemeanor of which they may be accused, were with good intent, resident citizens of the said Territory, and who shall have hereafter kept the peace and conducted themselves in all respects as becoming good citizens. Neither shall it be pleaded by any person in bar of conviction under indictment now found and returned for any such crimes or misdemeanors, nor operate the release of any party undergoing pains and penalties consequent upon sentence heretofore had for any crime or misdemeanor." [10]

The amnesty was for crimes committed between February 1, 1878, and November 13, 1878.

The Territorial establishment did not respond favorably. The *Mesilla News* wrote:

"We have been a close observant of the course of Gov. Wallace since his advent in this territory and have been anxious to find something in his official career for approval. It seems we are doomed to disappointment...."

"What has the governor done in the premises; simply sat down in Santa Fe and perhaps consulted with men of unenviable reputation and limited information, or what is worse prejudiced or biased in regard to Lincoln co.

affairs. He has not consulted with impartial and well informed citizens in regard to affairs there; he has not visited the country; as far as we can learn the Gov. has acted entirely on his own judgment or at least without having consulted any of the district court in regard to matters in Lincoln co. The proclamation of gov. W. pardoning with a scratch of the pen all the guilty crew that have run riot in Lincoln co. the past year is an outrage; in the first place the murderers of sheriff Brady and his deputy, of Roberts, of Bernstein and the unoffending Mexicans Chaves and others should not have been pardoned at all." [11]

The *Mesilla News* was wrong in the detail that most outraged the newspaper's editor, a detail that would determine Billy's fate. The amnesty did not apply to persons already indicted.

Governor Wallace's Pardon Betrayal

Peace Conference and Death of Chapman

On February 17, 1879, Billy wrote a letter to Jessie Evans proposing the Dolan men and the Regulators make peace. Billy's letter is lost, unfortunately. Evans showed the letter to Dolan and, revealing the extent to which the Fort Stanton commander was a loyal ally of the Dolan faction, to Colonel Dudley. Colonel Dudley wrote about the letter:

> *"Yesterday morning I was shown a letter from Bonney, alias 'Kid', the party indicted for the murder of the late Sheriff Brady, addressed to one of the Dolan faction, wanting to know whether they proposed peace or fight etc. 'Kid' was in the [Lincoln] Plaza walking the streets openly, all through the day, accompanied by two other parties, one a Mexican for whom the Sheriff has a warrant, and Joe Bowers, who is charged with stealing the band of horses from Fritz's ranch."*

> *"I learn that the Dolan men sent word to 'Kid' and others of the McSween faction that they would come to the Plaza in the evening, and meet him and his friends, and have a talk. As I am persuaded, a truce was agreed upon. The Dolan party went to the Plaza, met 'Kid' and his friends, and outside of hard expressions, no breach of the peace occurred."*

> *"The Sheriff returned to the Plaza in the evening, and found 'Kid' and his party in town, but was unable to obtain the assistance of more than one man to help Deputies [capture] these outlaws. 'Kid' told the Sheriff if the warrant for him was for murder, that he would not be taken alive. The Sheriff rode out of town, and came to the Post for military assistance...."* [1]

The peace parley took place February 18, 1879, on the one-year anniversary of Tunstall's murder.

Accompanying Billy were Thomas O'Folliard, Doc Scurlock, George Bowers, and José Salazar. Dolan had Jacob Mathews, Billy Campbell, and Edgar Waltz. The irony of Mathews being present, the man who selected the members of the chase-posse that killed Tunstall, would have escaped none of them.

The two sides met in the street near the Wortley Hotel:

> *"'The Kid' put out his hand to Evans who said I will not shake hands with you for you have murdered my friends and your friends and I ought to kill you; 'The Kid' said the understanding was they were to meet as friends and he did not want any trouble."*

> *"After talking on about the same strain for about 10 minutes, Dolan by persuasion got the guns and pistols from both of them, afterwards they continued to talk in an angry way for about 15 minutes more, they shook hands and made friends which caused all to make friends, and the two locked arms and all passed to Copeland's saloon where all took 6 to 8 drinks...."* [2]

Whortley Hotel, known in later years as the Lincoln Hotel. 1930s postcard.

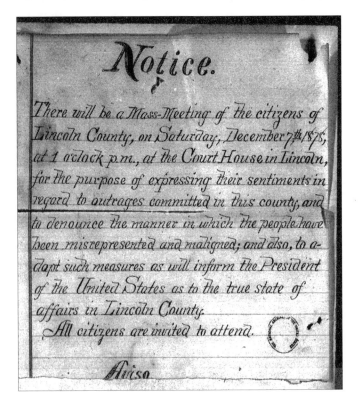

The notice posted by Huston Chapman announcing the meeting to protest the killings of Tunstall and McSween, December 7, 1878. Courtesy NARA.

Coincident with the peace meeting, Huston Chapman was riding into Lincoln from Santa Fe. Chapman was a young lawyer who Susan McSween had hired to handle her husband's estate and to pursue criminal charges against Colonel Dudley for the murder of her husband. As a thirteen-old youth, Chapman lost his left arm in a self-inflicted gun accident.[3]

Chapman's purpose in visiting Santa Fe was to get copies of the reports that Colonel Dudley had submitted to his superiors on Lincoln affairs and use them as the basis for obtaining an arrest warrant for Colonel Dudley. He was refused those reports.[4]

Colonel Dudley was hugely annoyed at Chapman's energetic and persistent efforts on Susan's behalf. Chapman wrote Governor Wallace and other U.S. officials demanding justice and supplying incriminating details about McSween's murder.

In December, 1878, shortly after he was hired by Susan, in an action that particularly enraged Colonel Dudley, Chapman organized a county-wide meeting of Lincoln citizens:

> *"...for the purpose of expressing their sentiments in regard to outrages committed in this county... and to adopt such measures as will inform the President of the United States as to the true state of affairs in Lincoln County."* [5]

Shortly after this community meeting, Chapman:

> *"...was by order of the post commandant excluded from the privileges of the post and denounced as one of the outlaws of Lincoln county."* [6]

After the two groups of peace-makers left John Copeland's saloon, they went to Allen J. Ballard's store for supper. On leaving Ballard's, the "friends" ran into Chapman and Juan Patron. Waltz described what happened next, under oath:

> *"Campbell stepped up on the ax of [the] buggy, shook hands with them and I supposed he was telling them that all had made friends, then all went to Mrs. McSween's, met and shook hands with Chapman, spent a pleasant half hour there then went to Montana's [Montaño's] where all drank more, then went to Juan Patron's while there some talk of old matters come up and Campbell in his drunkenness tried to shoot Patron but was prevented by Ballard, Dolan and others, from there went to Capt. [Saturnino] Baca's, drank more and had a pleasant time, then started to Copeland's saloon."* [7] (In the Whortley Hotel.)

Chapman left the group when it was at Susan McSween's *"to get some bread to make a poultice for his face. He was suffering with a severe attack of neuralgia."* He was in the street walking to his law office just as the peace-makers left Copeland's saloon. It was about 10 in the evening. Waltz's testimony continued:

> *"Campbell stopped Chapman and said I would like to see you dance, he replied my face is frozen and I don't care to dance for a drunken crowd; then Campbell said well you better dance anyhow. Chapman replied I'll be damn if I'll dance for you or for anybody else, and it will take a lot more than you to make me."*

> *"...in about 15 seconds Campbell who kept his pistol pointed close to Chapman's breast fired, as Chapman fell he said 'Oh! my God I'm killed' and threw his arms up and fell backwards."*

Miguel Luna and Gorgonio Wilson, son of Justice of the Peace Wilson, standing at the reputed spot where Chapman was murdered by Campbell and Dolan. Courtesy Maurice G. Fulton Papers, Special Collections, UA.

"We all started to walk up the street to the saloon, when about 30 feet from the body Campbell said I promised my God and Gen. Dudley that I would kill him and Scase, and I will now go up to the post and kill Scase and skin out of the country. When we got to the saloon, I [Waltz] had not taken a drink all evening, Campbell asked me to take a drink, and as he looked at me with the same smile as when he killed Chapman I concluded that I better take a drink." [8]

An anonymous letter writer, who identified himself only as Max, gave this account:

"When they met, one of the Dolan party asked 'who are you and where are you going?' Chapman answered and told them he was attending to his business. He was told to talk differently or they would make him. He answered, raising a bandage from his face, 'You cannot scare me, boys. I know you and it's no use. You have tried that before.' Then said Campbell 'I'll settle you,' and fired his pistol, the ball going in at the breast and coming out at the back. As he fell Dolan shot him with his Winchester. They then set fire to his body. It is thought they soaked his clothes with whiskey to make them burn." [9]

Chapman's body was left in the street where it fell. It was found there several hours later by Sergeant Dawson:

"...the body was very badly burned and most of the clothing off the upper portion of the body was burned. We then proceeded to the Justice of the Peace (Wilson) and informed him of the fact that the body was lying in the road, he said he was aware of it, but was unable to get any person to assist him in removing it." [10]

The coroner's jury ruled *"that Chapman received two wounds, either of which would have proved fatal."* Both were in the chest.[11]

Chapman had two bullet holes in him – as you would expect – since Campbell fired once and Dolan fired once. But Dolan, in a signed letter to the *Mesilla News*, wrote:

> *"...I met him [Chapman] on the evening of the occurrence after dark on his arrival entering the house of Mrs. McSween, where a party of citizens were assembled, Mrs. McSween giving a Musical entertainment. Salutations passed between us, he expressing himself as being pleased with the proceeding of the afternoon. I in like manner, after which we parted, he retiring to his room. This was the last time I saw Mr. Chapman."* [12]

When Dolan was forced to testify under oath, he said:

> *"He saw nothing nor did he know anything about the shooting of Chapman. He did not see Chapman shot, and did not know that he was killed until after his arrival at the hotel. He acknowledged that he fired a shot, but stated that he fired it 'to attract the attention of the party' – to call the boys off. Heard Evans talking but did not know who he was talking to. In short, [he] knew nothing about the killing of Chapman, although he was not ten feet away."* [13]

Additional testimony under oath established that after Chapman's killing:

> *"Dolan mounted a horse and went to Fort Stanton. The next morning Evans and Campbell also went to the post and with Dolan had a long conference with General Dudley. We are not advised as to what this interview was about. If Campbell's story of the promise to General Dudley is true, the visit to the post the next day was probably to report the result of his labors so far, and to hunt up and murder Scase. They did hunt through the post for Scase and he only escaped by disguising himself in a soldier's uniform."* (Charley Scase worked for Susan. Two years later Campbell would be lynched at St. John, Arizona, for killing two men for money.) [14]

The killing of Chapman persuaded Governor Wallace that civil order could be restored to Lincoln only if he took command of the county. He would delegate to himself the powers of martial law without actually declaring martial law. He travelled to Fort Stanton and then to Lincoln. At Fort Stanton, he ordered Colonel Dudley to place a detachment of soldiers at his disposal for his personal protection.[15]

Then, bypassing Colonel Dudley, he wrote to Colonel Edward Hatch, commander of all military forces in New Mexico, and ordered him to dispatch soldiers and arrest Dolan, Campbell, Evans, and Mathews for the murder of Chapman. The four men were found and brought to Fort Stanton. Campbell, Evans, and Mathews were placed in cells. Dolan was confined to the fort library for two days, then released on self-parole.[16]

Governor Wallace wrote to Juan Patron, who had organized a private militia, called the Rangers, to use his men to arrest Billy and Scurlock. That effort led to nothing.[17]

Two days after asking Colonel Hatch to arrest the Dolan men, Governor Wallace wrote to Colonel Hatch requesting that he dismiss Colonel Dudley from command of Fort Stanton:

"...it is charged that Lt. Col. Dudley is responsible for the killing of McSween and the men who were shot with that person; that he was an influential participant in that affair, and yet is an active partisan. I have information also connecting him with the more recent murder of H. J. Chapman; to the effect that he knew the man would be killed, and announced it the day of the night of the killing, and that one of the murderers stated publically that he had promised Colonel Dudley to do the deed." [18]

The next day, Colonel Hatch issued a special field order relieving Colonel Dudley of his command. Captain Henry Carroll was given the command. [19]

Two days later, Governor Wallace ordered Dolan be re-arrested and Campbell, Evans, and Mathews be transferred to Fort Union, which had more secure jail cells. [20]

Pardon Negotiations

Several days after the order to arrest Dolan, Billy wrote a letter to Governor Wallace that a friend hand-delivered (spelling and grammar uncorrected):

"Dear Sir I have heard that You will give one thousand $ dollars for my body which as I can understand it means alive as a witness. I know it is as a witness against those that Murdered Mr. Chapman. if it was so as that I could appear at Court I could give the desired information. but I have indictments against me for things that happened in the late Lincoln County War and am afraid to give up because my Enemies would Kill me the day Mr. Chapman was murdered I was in Lincoln, at the request of good Citizens to meet Mr. J.J. Dolan to meet as Friends, so as to be able to lay aside our arms and go to Work. I was present when Mr. Chapman was murderded and know who did it and if it were not for those indictments I would have made it clear before now if it is in your power to Annully those indictments I hope you will do so so as to give a chance to explain. please send me an annser telling me what you can do You can send annser by bearer"

"I have no wish to fight any more indeed I have not raised an arm since Your proclamation. as to my Character I refer to any of the Citizens, for the majority of them are my Friends and have been helping me all they could. I am called Kid Antrim but Antrim is my stepfathers name."

"Waiting for an annser I remain Your Obedeint Servant"
"W. H. Bonney." [21]

Governor Wallace responded:

"Lincoln, March 15, 1879"
"W. H. Bonney."

"Come to the house of Old Squire Wilson (not the lawyer) at nine (9) o'clock next Monday night alone. I don't mean his office, but his residence. Follow along the floor of the mountain south of town, come in at that side, and knock on the east door. I have the authority to exempt you from prosecution, if you will testify to what you say you knew."

"The object of the meeting at Squire Wilson's is to arrange the matter in a way to make your life safe. To do that the utmost secrecy is to be used. So come alone. Don't tell anybody – not a living soul – where you are coming or the object. If you could trust Jesse [Jessie] Evans, you can trust me."

"Lew Wallace" [22]

The reference to Evans was to the failed peace conference.

Twenty-one years later, Wallace gave an account of their meeting to the *Indianapolis News*. Not surprisingly, for a best-selling novelist, it is heavily fictionalized and dramatized. It is also full of errors, with Wallace saying the meeting was in Santa Fe at midnight:

"There he stands in the doorway of the little adobe house, his form outlined by moonlight at his back, his face illuminated by the glow of the little lamp.... I invited him in. The door flew open, and there stood the most feared man in New Mexico. The room was covered by a winchester rifle, held in one hand. In the other was a colt's revolver."

"It was a musical growl that said: "I was to meet the Governor here at midnight. It is midnight. Is he here?" [23]

In the account, Wallace falsely claimed that he initiated the meeting by asking a third party to write to Billy.

Two years later, Wallace published in the *New York Times* a much longer, more theatrical account of the meeting, with made-up dialog:

"When 'Billy the Kid' stepped to the chair opposite me, I lost no time in stating my proposition."

"'Testify,' I said, 'before the Grand Jury and the trial court and convict the murderer of Chapman and I will let you go scott-free with a pardon in your pocket for all your misdeeds.'"

"Billy heard me in silence; he thought several minutes without reply."

"'Governor,' said he, 'if I were to do what you ask they would kill me.'" [24]

In exchange for Governor Wallace's pardon promise, Billy agreed to permit himself to be arrested by Patron's Rangers – who he could trust to not kill him – and to testify before the grand jury about Chapman's murder at the upcoming District Court session.

The day after the secret meeting, Evans and Campbell escaped from Fort Stanton. They were aided in their escape by the soldier assigned to guard them, a man known as "Texas Jack." They may have escaped as they were being readied to be sent to Fort Union. [25]

Evans and Campbell's escape put Billy's life in danger. The two had been striving to kill him before the peace conference. Now he was going to voluntarily confine himself and give evidence against them – he would be an easy target and they would have a self-preservation reason to kill him.

Uncertain if their pardon agreement still held, Billy wrote to Wallace through ex-Justice of the Peace Wilson:

> *"Friend Wilson"*
>
> *"Please tell You know who that I do not know what to do, now as those Prisoners have escaped. to send word by bearer, a note through You it may be that he has made different arrangements if not and he still wants it the same to Send 'William Hudgins' as Deputy. to the Junction tomorrow at three Oclock with some men you know to be right. Send a note telling me what to do"*
>
> *"W. H. Bonney"*
>
> *"P.S. Do not send Soldiers"* [26]

Governor Wallace confirmed the agreement in a return note (the strikethroughs are Wallace's):

> *"The escape makes no difference in arrangements. ~~I will comply with my part, if you will with yours.~~"*
>
> *"To remove all suspicions of ~~arrangement~~ understanding, I think it better to put the arresting party in charge of Sheriff Kimball, who will be instructed to see that no violence is used."*
>
> *"This will go to you tonight. ~~If you still insist upon Hudgins, let me know:~~ If I don't get ~~receive~~ other word from you the party (all citizens) will be at the junction by three o'clock tomorrow."* [27]

Billy then sent detailed instructions as to how he would surrender:

> *"General Lew Wallace"*
>
> *"I will keep the appointment I made but be sure and have men come that you can depend on I am not afraid to die like a man fighting but I would not like to be killed like a dog unarmed. tell Kimbal [Kimbrell] to let his men be placed around the house and for him to come in alone: and he can arrest us. all I am afraid of is that in the Fort we might be poisoned or killed through a Window at night. but You can arrange that all right. Tell the Commanding Officer to Watch Lt Goodwin he would not hesitate to do anything there will be danger on the road of somebody way laying us to kill us on the road to the Fort."*
>
> *"You will never catch those fellows on the Road Watch Fritzes, Captain Bacas ranch and the Brewery they will either go to Seven Rivers or to Jacarilla Mountains they will stay around close until the scouting parties come in give a Spy a pair of glasses and let him get on the mountain back of Fritzes and watch and if they are there ther will be provision carried to them. it is not my place to advise you, but I am anxious to have them caught. and perhaps know how men hid from soldiers better than you. please excuse me for having so much to say and still remain"*
>
> *"Yours Truly"*
> *"W. H. Bonney"*

"P. S. I have changed my mind Send Kimbal to Gutierez just below San Patricio one mile. because Sanger and Ballard are or were great friends of Camels [Campbell] Ballard told me yesterday to leave for you were doing everything to catch me. it was a blind to get me to leave. Tell Kimbal not to come before 3 oclock for I may not be there before." [28]

Sheriff Kimbrell was not a Dolan man; Billy could trust him. 'Us" refers to Billy and Tom O'Folliard. Lt. Goodwin was a known, strong supporter of Dolan. In the reference to the two ranches, Fritz's refers to Emil Fritz's ranch, inherited by his brother Charles Fritz after Emil's death. Captain Baca is Saturnino Baca, who became an enemy of McSween after McSween tried to evict him during the war in Lincoln. Saturnino Baca will testify against Billy in his trial.

Billy's letter reveals a lot about himself. It shows a man aware of the risks to his life and intent on preserving it, not for cowardly reasons, but because he believed dying, if it happened, should be honorable – the "code of the West." His detailed instructions reveal a confident and cautious man, not a man with a "devil may care" attitude, as attributed to him in most movies and books. The poor grammar reflects his lack of formal education.

As promised, Billy and O'Folliard surrendered to Sheriff Kimbrell and Patron's Rangers at the agreed time and place. The date was March 21, 1879.

Billy was placed in the Lincoln jail for one night and then moved to a building behind Patron's house. It was not a totally unpleasant confinement: friends, good food, and, as Governor Wallace noted in a letter, music some evenings. Patron would later bill the county a dollar a day for boarding Billy and stabling his horse.[29]

Two days after his confinement, Billy was interrogated by Governor Wallace. The Governor's notes show that Billy detailed numerous unrecognized killings by a group calling themselves the "Rustlers" who were affiliated with the Murphy-Dolan faction. Their livelihood was livestock stealing. He described the trails used by the Rustlers to move stolen cattle to markets. He named the hideouts used by the Rustlers: Shedd's Ranch (later the W. W. Cox San Augustine ranch), Mormon City on the Rio Mimbres, San Nicolas Spring west of Tularosa, the settlement of Seven Rivers, and the Heiskell Jones Ranch at Rocky Arroyo.[30]

Here is an example of the kind of detail Billy provided Governor Wallace:

"The trail used going from Seven Rivers to Shedd's was round the S.W. part of the Guadalupe Mts by a tank on the right hand of trail: from Shedd's the drive would be over to Las Cruces. Jesse [Jessie] Evans, Frank Baker (killed), Jim McDaniels (at Cruces ranging between Cruces and El Paso) Reed [Reade] at Shedd's bought cattle – also sold cattle to E. C. Priest butcher in Cruces." [31]

District Court Opens

The District Court session opened April 14, 1879, Judge Warren Bristol presiding. Billy testified before the grand jury exactly as he had promised Governor Wallace. The transcripts of his and the other witness testimonies, if they ever existed, are lost.

Governor Wallace reported of the grand jury:

"...the grand jury empanelled... was, with one or two exceptions, composed of men accounted of the McSween or anti-Dolan party, making it undeniable that nearly all citizens eligible for such position are of that persuasion. They found nearly 200 indictments [over 100 for murder], almost altogether accusatory of Dolan people. Nearly 200 indictments in a county of a voting population of 150 total. You cannot fail to see what would have come of trial thereunder – how long they would have lasted – the expense to a county already bankrupt...." [32]

The grand jury, led by Isaac Ellis, indicted Colonel Dudley, Sheriff Peppin, and John Kinney for burning down McSween's house. It indicted *"Dolan and Campbell for the Chapman murder, in which the Kid [was] the principal witness."* Jessie Evans was indicted as an accessory in Chapman's killing. Marion Turner and John Jones were indicted for shooting McSween, *"in and upon the head, breast, and belly."* O'Folliard was indicted for stealing horses from Fritz's ranch. [33]

Also indicted and charged with murder were Sheriff Peppin posse members Jack Long, Jacob Mathews, Buck Powell, and 25 other men,. They pled Governor Wallace's amnesty and walked out of courtroom free men. [34]

Dolan, who did not qualify for a pardon, got Judge Bristol to grant him a change of venue to Socorro. [35]

The grand jury did not indict Billy, or any McSween defender, for any action during the five-day Lincoln war. District Attorney Rynerson well understood what that meant. A jury of peers in Lincoln would not convict Billy for Brady's or Roberts' killings, because they also had experienced the circumstances that provoked the shootings, the relentless hounding and sadistic murder of Tunstall.

Governor Wallace asked Rynerson to quash Billy's murder indictments; he refused:

"The District Attorney would not consent to the release of Kid for turning state's evidence." [36]

The *Mesilla News* noted:

"That Col. Rynerson district attorney refused to consent to it [Governor Wallace asking for the quashing], that sharp words passed between them; that Col. R. is reticent and will not say anything about it." [37]

Rynerson was not content with just refusing Governor Wallace's appeal. As a Murphy-Dolan partisan, he wanted Billy convicted as the best-known, still living supporter of the Tunstall-McSween side, and he wanted the conviction guaranteed. To that end, he renewed the Brady and Roberts indictments against Billy and asked Judge Bristol to move the cases to Mesilla, where no one had first-hand knowledge of the events that motivated Billy's actions:

"W. L. Rynerson District Attorney... says that justice cannot be done [in] the Territory on the trial of the said defendant William Bonny alias Kid alias William Antrim in the said County of Lincoln for the reason that jurors in attendance and all those liable to be summoned for the trial of said defendant, by reason of partisanship in the late and existing troubles and lawlessness in said County

have so prejudiced the said jurors that they cannot fairly and impartially try the said defendant; and for the further reason that said jurors and the witnesses in said cause are so intimidated by lawless men in said Lincoln County by fear of violence and lawlessness against their persons and property on the part of lawless men that they said Jurors and witnesses cannot fearlessly and justly perform their respective duties at said trial in said Lincoln County." [38]

The risible hypocrisy of this motion is that it was the Dolan side that practiced violent physical intimidation to dominate Lincoln County.

Judge Bristol granted the change of venue for Billy's cases.

Susan McSween with the aid of her lawyer Ira Leonard (who had replaced Chapman) filed a civil suit against Colonel Dudley for the destruction of her home, asking $25,000 in damages.[39]

Colonel Dudley, just before being indicted by the grand jury, complained to the Adjutant of the Army in Washington D. C. that the jury was composed of *"all Mexicans but one."*

"Of course if indicted I do not propose to take the chances of being tried by any such class of men." [40]

Colonel Dudley's slander was a lie. The grand jury was composed of seven Anglos and eight Hispanics.

After his indictment and Susan's filing of the civil suit against him, Dudley wrote the Attorney General of the United States claiming he had already spent $5,000 in legal fees defending himself and begging that the Federal government pay his legal costs. The request was denied.[41]

Dudley Court of Inquiry

Following his demand that Colonel Dudley be dismissed, Governor Wallace requested that Dudley be tried for his actions during the Lincoln war. Rather than order a trial, Brigadier General John Pope, commander of the Department of the Missouri, the jurisdiction of which included New Mexico, ordered a Court of Inquiry. The purpose of the Court was to determine whether Colonel Dudley should be court-martialed.[42]

After some preliminaries, the Court opened May 7, 1879. The judges were Colonel Galusha Pennypacker, presiding, Major N. W. Osborne, and Captain H. R. Brinkerhoff. The prosecutor, representing the Army, was Captain Henry H. Humphreys. Assisting Captain Humphreys was Susan's attorney, Ira Leonard. Defending Colonel Dudley was Santa Fe lawyer Henry L. Waldo. The location was Fort Stanton.

The seven charges leveled against Colonel Dudley were (summarized):

■ Leading his command of 60 men, howitzer, and Gatling gun to Lincoln for the purpose of *"giving aid to an armed band of outlaws,"* aiding in the burning of a building containing women and children, and aiding in the death of Alexander A. McSween.

■ Forcing Justice of the Peace Wilson by a threat of *"ironing and imprisonment"* to write a warrant for McSween's arrest.

Fort Stanton. 1898 photo. Courtesy Archives and Special Collections, NMSU.

- Plundering himself and allowing his soldiers to plunder *"upwards of six thousand dollars worth of goods"* from Tunstall's store.

- Procuring *"base and wicked men to make false and slanderous charges against the character"* of Mrs. Susan McSween.

- Forcing David Easton, to retain his contract to sell corn to Fort Stanton, to swear in an affidavit to slanderous charges against Mrs. Susan McSween.

- Writing a letter to the *Santa Fe New Mexican* for publication *"which was calculated and intended to foment the disturbances then rife in"* Lincoln. Said letter also made false and malicious charges against the character of Mrs. Susan McSween.

- Dispatching a squad of men commanded by Lieutenant James H. French that illegally forced entry into the homes of John Copeland, Alexander A. McSween, and a man known only as Maximo. That Lieutenant French, in an intoxicated state, abused the occupants of the homes in *"a shameful manner."* [43]

Given the events that Colonel Dudley had participated in or had influenced, this seems a weak – even trivial – batch of charges. The charges suggest weak lawyering on the part of the prosecution. The one charge that would have seriously worried the defense, "conspiracy to aid" the Dolan side, is missing. Maybe the prosecution thought they had covered that in the first charge, but by not explicitly charging conspiracy, they removed the element of planning to aid the Dolan faction from Dudley's actions – and there was obvious evidence of such planning. Planning a crime with others, even if there is no commission, is convictable (an inchoate offense).

The prosecution tried to introduce evidence of conspiracy during the trial, but the defense objected, and the judges ruled all such evidence and argument inadmissible because no "conspiracy charge" was among the charges being tried. Here is the ruling:

> *"The Court has no allegation of conspiracy before it. The authorities quoted in support of the question refer to admission of evidence in conspiring. Therefore it is decided that the answer to the question shall be disregarded as evidence and further that no evidence will be entertained looking to the estab-lishment of offenses other than those charged."* [44]

The Court called over 85 witnesses, almost everybody who had had a role in the Lincoln war who were still alive or who were not on the run.[45]

Testifying for the McSween side were: Governor Lew Wallace, Susan McSween, Billy, Dr. Taylor F. Ealy, José Chavez y Chavez, Samuel Corbet, Isaac Ellis, David Easton, Joe Dixon, John O'Brian, and ex-Justice of the Peace John B. Wilson.

Testifying for the Dolan side were: James Dolan, Sheriff George Peppin, Andrew Boyle, José Chavez y Baca, John Hurley, John Long, ex-Sheriff Jacob B. Mathews, Saturnino Baca, Robert Olinger, Thomas "Buck" Powell, Marion Turner, Captain George A. Purington, and 2nd Lt. M. F. Goodwin.

Colonel Dudley testified in his own defense. He was the last witness to testify. During his examination by Waldo, he pled ignorance of almost every event that happened in Lincoln on July 19. The few times he did not plead ignorance, he denied that the event occurred.

Bizarrely, the prosecution lawyer asked him only four questions! Here are the questions and answers:

> *"**PROSECUTOR**: What induced you to think it was your solemn duty to go to Lincoln on the 19th day of July last, upon what authority did you base that action, and was your sole and only object that of a humanitarian?"*
>
> *"**DUDLEY**: My knowledge of the situation of affairs in Lincoln, my sense of duty as an Officer of the Army. It was decidedly as I understand that word."*
>
> *"**PROSECUTOR**: If you were there in the capacity of a humanitarian why did you not carry out that purpose and prevent the bloodshed and destruc-tion of property that was going on there instead of promoting the distur-bances by allowing a warrant to be issued against McSween and others?"*
>
> *"**OBJECTED TO BY DEFENSE COUNSEL**. Question objected to because it assumes that Gen. Dudley was engaged in fomenting disturbances and assumes that he allowed a warrant to be issued against McSween."*
>
> *"Prosecutor stated he had no reply to make."*
>
> *"Objection sustained."*
>
> *"**PROSECUTOR**: If you were there in the capacity of a humanitarian why did you not carry out that object and prevent the bloodshed and destruction of property that took place on that occasion?"*
>
> *"Objected to by Court"*

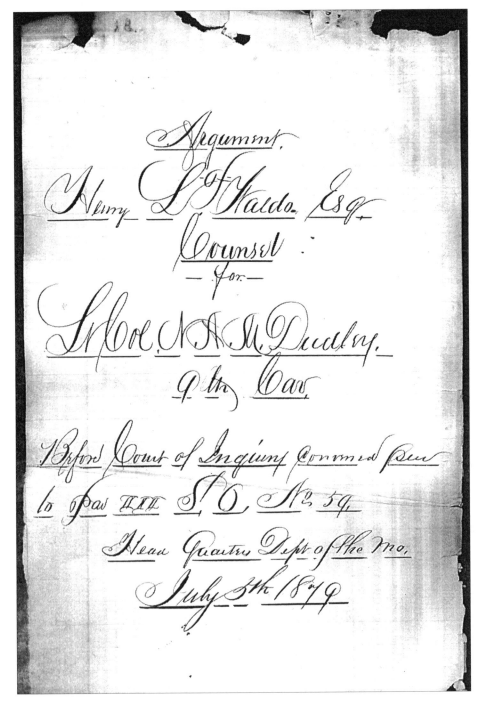

Cover sheet for Attorney Henry Linn Waldo's 75-page closing argument at the
Dudley Court of Inquiry. Courtesy NARA.

*"**PROSECUTOR**: When and where did you have the conversation with J. B. Wilson in the camp that you spoke to him and reference was made to a Board of Officers?"*

*"**DUDLEY**: In Lincoln, just shortly after the troops got into camp. That's all the conversation."*

"Prosecution stated he had finished with the witness." [46]

It is impossible to imagine such a performance by any other prosecutor. No attempt to make him detail his actions, no attempt to confront him with contradictory testimony, no attempt to probe for partisanship, no attempt to explore whether his duty as an officer included the duty to let a house sheltering women and children to be started on fire (for an alleged civil offense that a grand jury had exonerated him of!).

The net effect of the testimony was that for every McSween witness that offered evidence in support of a charge against Colonel Dudley, there was a Dolan witness to contradict that evidence. That left it to the judges to choose the witnesses (or side) they wanted to believe.

In an ironic table-turn, in his summation to the judges, Defense Attorney Waldo agreed that, yes, there was a conspiracy at play in the case – but it was a conspiracy against Colonel Dudley promulgated by Governor Lew Wallace, Susan's attorney Ira Leonard, and Susan McSween.

Waldo had demeaning words for all of Susan McSween's witnesses. Wilson was *"a stupid and ignorant old man."* Joe Dixon was *"a dull slow kind of fellow."* John O'Brian's testimony was *"the result of a cramming process."* Sam Corbet *"literally knows nothing about the incidents of July 19."* Dr. Ealy's testimony shows *"to what violent extremes of bitterness and malice the prompting of injured vanity may carry a man."* Alexander Rudder had *"a known weakness of mind."*

Susan McSween's testimony was *"so muddled, confused, self-contradictory and inconsistent as to deprive it of any weight or force whatsoever."* About Billy's testimony, Waldo asserted, *"under a rule of law of imperative force, outside of its inherent improbability, the Court will be constrained to reject it."* (Huh?) [47]

The Court ruling, as attorney Leonard suspected before it was issued, was exoneration. He wrote to Governor Wallace:

"There is nothing to be looked for or hoped from this tribunal, it is a farce on judicial investigation and ought to be called and designated 'The Mutual Admiration Inquiry.'" [48]

Before giving its opinion, the Court issued a finding of facts, all of which explicitly contradicted the charges against Colonel Dudley. The most notable finding was that on July 19, 1878:

"Colonel Dudley did not extend any aid or assistance to either party and that both he and the officers and men of his command did all that could properly have been done to protect the lives and the property of peaceable and law abiding citizens." (Note the careful parsing of words – protection is owed only to those Dudley himself deemed law-abiding.) [49]

The Court took only a few hours to consider and render its opinion. Here is the full text:

> *"In view of the evidence adduced the court is of the opinion that Lieut Colonel N A M Dudley 9th Calvary has not been guilty of any violation of law or of orders that the act of proceeding with his command to the town of Lincoln on the 19th of July 1878 was prompted by the most human and worthy motives and by good military judgment under exceptional circumstances."*

> *"The court is of the opinion that none of the allegations made against Lieut Colonel Dudley by His Excellency the Governor of New Mexico or by Ira E Leonard have been sustained and that proceedings before a Court Martial are therefore unnecessary."* [50]

Attorney Leonard characterized the trial as *"an expensive and stupendous farce."* The only protection Dudley gave women and children was of the *"kind that a wolf would naturally give to the lamb."* [51] The author agrees with both of these characterizations.

On receiving the record of the Court, Brigadier-General Pope wrote:

> *"Having carefully considered the evidence in the foregoing case, the Department Commander disapproved the opinion expressed by the court of inquiry."* [52]

The Judge Advocate of the Department of the Missouri, after an extensive review of the case, concluded:

> *"That Lieut. Dudley did not go with his command on the 19th of July 1879 to the town of Lincoln for the protection of women and children, but for the purpose of aiding and assisting the Dolan-Riley party, and to further their schemes, and objects, against the McSween party."* [53]

The Court session ended July 6, 1879, having lasted over 60 days. The costs to the army exceeded $25,000. [54]

Billy testified May 28. He was escorted to and from the Court under armed guard. During his testimony there was one particularly interesting exchange:

> *"**PROSECUTOR**: In addition to the names you have given, are you also known as the 'Kid?'"*
> *"**BILLY**: I have already answered that question. Yes sir, I am, but not 'Billy Kid' that I know of."* [55]

On June 17, Billy walked out of Patron's indifferent confinement and left Lincoln. He was joined by O'Folliard.

After his acquittal, Colonel Dudley was transferred to command of Fort Union. He responded by complaining that Fort Stanton was his *"rightful"* command and being moved to Fort Union was nothing less than *"disgrace and exile."* [56] He was later transferred to command of Fort Cummings, then to commands in Kansas and Colorado. He served a term as commander of the Department of Oklahoma. He retired from the army in 1889. [57]

Colonel Dudley was addressed as colonel and sometimes general by contemporaries because he had received brevet promotions to both colonel and brigadier general during the Civil War. A brevet promotion was usually awarded as a reward for gallantry or meritorious conduct in battle, but could be given for non-combat reasons. His actual army rank while in command of Fort Stanton was Lieutenant Colonel. In 1904, in recognition of his service during the Civil War, he made Brigadier General.

Susan McSween's Civil Suit

Events were hurtling Colonel Dudley's way: full exoneration for the killings in Lincoln, a new fort command, and broad public support by the Territorial newspapers. One problem only remained: Susan McSween's $25,000 civil suit against him for burning down her house.

Judge Bristol solved that problem for Colonel Dudley. He transferred the case to the court in Mesilla: trial in Lincoln – conviction; trial in Mesilla – virtually no chance of conviction.

The case was scheduled for the week of November 17, 1879. On November 4, Colonel Dudley wrote the Army Adjutant General

"I have the honor to request that transportation be furnished me from Fort Union New Mexico to Mesilla... I am under bonds to appear before [the court] at Mesilla N. M. to answer to an indictment found against me by the grand jury of Lincoln County... The Honorable Attorney General of the United States... has directed the United States District Attorney (Barnes) for the Territory of New Mexico to defend me in this suit." [58]

Denial of his request, Colonel Dudley complained, would:

"...necessitate my paying out of my private means the exorbitant fare by Stage, which I believe is about twenty cents per mile." [59]

Colonel Dudley did not get his transport paid, but he did get the free services of Territorial Attorney General Sidney M. Barnes, one of New Mexico's finest lawyers.

On November 17, the day her suit was called, Susan was not in the courtroom. Leonard, who was representing her, had promised to travel to Lincoln and escort her to Mesilla. For reasons never explained, he did not show. When she realized she would not be present, she wrote Judge Bristol asking for a continuance. Judge Bristol refused and ordered her $1,000 bond forfeited. He further ordered arrest warrants *"for Mrs. McSween and the other witnesses for the prosecution to appear at once."* [60]

By November 26, Susan was in Mesilla with one witness, Sebrian Bates. Why not more witnesses? Probably because she had to pay their expenses. The trial began the next morning. With Leonard still missing, Susan was represented by Rynerson.[61] What a perverted twist! There was no more vociferous supporter of the Dolan-Murphy side than Rynerson. During the April court session in Lincoln, he did all he could to defeat every indictment brought against the Dolan side. He engineered the transfer of Billy's case to Mesilla. Now he was representing Susan against Colonel Dudley?

Bates was an ex-soldier. He worked for Susan as a servant. He had testified in the Court of Inquiry and had been appallingly insulted and abused by Waldo. Examples:

"I say now and here, it is an infamous outrage that in the investigation of the conduct of a gentleman and an Officer the testimony of a degraded and brutal person like this should be offered for the purpose of sustaining a single accusations against him."

"[His testimony] reeking of the foulest distillation of perjury vapored forth at every breath of the slimy, crawling reptile thing that gave it utterance." [62]

Bates repeated his Court of Inquiry testimony at Mesilla, that he had been forced by soldiers to carry some of the wood that was used to start the McSween house on fire. He testified that he heard Dudley ask Sheriff Peppin:

"... have you got those fellows burned out yet, Peppin? ...you were a hell of a while getting those fellows out of there. Peppin said they ain't got but one more room to stand in and then we'll have them burnt out." [63]

The trial lasted two days and parts of two nights. The *Mesilla News* noted:

"There had been throughout the trial more interest manifested than had been seen in any case tried here for years, and when the jury after being out about half an hour, came in, the court room was crowded." [64]

The verdict, after only two minutes of deliberation, was not guilty. The ruling was greeted by *"a spontaneous outburst of applause."*

Billy's Pardon

Here is how Governor Wallace described his pardon deal with Billy in the *Indianapolis News*:

"The note contained a promise that if Billy would appear as a witness, he should receive a pardon for all his past offenses."

"According to the terms of the compact he was to be a free man and receive a pardon covering all his offenses as soon as the murderers of Chapman were convicted." [65]

Here is how he described it in his *New York Times* account:

"'Testify,' I said, 'before the Grand Jury and the trial court and convict the murderer of Chapman and I will let you go scott-free with a pardon in your pocket for all your misdeeds.'" [66]

Both of these descriptions required that Billy testify before the grand jury <u>and</u> that Dolan be convicted before Wallace granted a pardon.

I do not believe the "conviction" stipulation was part of the deal. There is no indication of such in Governor Wallace's first offer of a deal in his first letter to Billy:

"I have the authority to exempt you from prosecution, if you will testify to what you say you knew." [67] (Letter quoted in full on page 106.)

Billy's letters to Wallace always indicted that he believed he had fully met the terms of the agreement. The "conviction" provision appears to have been made up and added by Governor Wallace to his newspaper stories – written 21 years later – to justify his dishonorable failure to fulfill his agreement.

When Billy walked out of Patron's house, saddled his horse, and rode out of Lincoln, his feelings were probably exhilaration – he was free.

Billy had much to reflect on: the sadistic murder of Tunstall, Governor Axtell's illegal nullifying of the arrest warrants for the men who murdered Tunstall, weeks of running gun battles with Dolan's men, and the five-day war that erupted following McSween's return to Lincoln.

He saw, on the last day of the Lincoln war, Colonel Dudley bring his troops and artillery into Lincoln to help Dolan's men. He saw Colonel Dudley frighten away all of McSween's supporters except those few barricaded with McSween in his home. He saw Colonel Dudley encourage the firing of McSween's home. He saw the fire consume room after room of the house until the only choices for those trapped inside were burn to death or try to escape through the scorching gunfire of Dolan's men.

He saw McSween, Harvey Morris, Vincente Romero, and Francisco Zamora killed in their valiant escape attempt.

He saw Governor Wallace issue a blanket amnesty, which covered as many as 200 men, for crimes ranging from simple misdemeanors to cold-blooded murder, including Tunstall's murder, but which explicitly exempted him.

He sought and obtained a secret meeting with Governor Wallace in which the Governor promised him a pardon in exchange for his testimony against the murderers of Chapman. He met fully his end of that agreement.

When Billy rode out of Lincoln, Colonel Dudley's Court of Inquiry was half over. He and most of Lincoln County expected Dudley to be ordered to a court martial trial.

Billy probably expected Governor Wallace to issue his pardon following Dudley's Court of Inquiry.

As the months passed following Dudley's exoneration, Billy must have begun to question Governor Wallace's pledge. But surely, he must have thought, a decorated Civil War general, speaking in his official capacity as the Governor of the Territory of New Mexico, would not renege on his word?

After his capture at Stinking Springs, Billy wrote Governor Wallace asking for his pardon:

> *"I wrote you a little note the day before yesterday but have received no answer. I Expect you have forgotten what you promised me, this Month two Years ago. But I have not, and I think You had might to have come and seen me as I Requested you to. I have done Everything that I promised you I would and you have done nothing that you promised me."* [68] (Letter quoted in full on page 44.)

Twenty-three days later, Billy asked again:

> *"for the last time I ask, Will you keep your promise...."* [69] (Quoted in full on page 47.)

Governor Wallace did not reply – he was determined not to honor his promise.

Dolan Escapes Punishment

In October, 1879, session of the District Court, convening in Socorro, Judge Bristol granted the request of Dolan's lawyers that the two murder charges against him be dismissed. He had been facing one count as accessory to the unlawful killing of Tunstall and one count for the unlawful killing of Chapman.[70]

Dolan was so confident he would escape any penalty for his actions that several months earlier (July 13, 1879) he had married Caroline Fritz, daughter of Charles Fritz.[71]

Dolan's best man at the wedding was Jack Long. Long had an outlaw past and numerous aliases, including Frank Rivers and Barry Longmont. Long was in the sub-posse that killed Tunstall and was indicted for Tunstall's murder. He was walking down the street beside Sheriff Brady when Brady was shot. He set the first fire at McSween's house. He was one of the two men who were forced to take shelter in the toilet hole during the final hours of the Lincoln war. Long pled Wallace's amnesty for his murderous actions and collected a pardon.

Allan J. Ballard, the owner of the establishment where Chapman's murderers had supped the night they killed him, gave the bride away. Present at the wedding, the *Mesilla News* noted, were:

> "...personal friends of the bride and bride groom, who throughout all the vicissitudes of fortune, prosperity, slander and calumny still were ever true and devoted friends." [72]

So ended the Lincoln County War: not with a bang of consequences for the self-evident perpetrators, but with the War's master schemer stealthily absolved of his actions by a colluding judge.

Chapter 8 | Trial in Mesilla

Billy and Billy Wilson were delivered into the custody of Dona Ana Sheriff and Deputy U. S. Marshal James W. Southwick on March 29, 1881.

Southwick had been elected sheriff just five months earlier. Before winning the sheriff's office, Southwick was the Mesilla postmaster. During the Civil War, Southwick had fought for the Union:

> *"After the war, Major Southwick spent some years in the west and in Mexico. When the Union Pacific railroad was built from Leavenworth, Kans., to Ogden, Utah, he received the contract for furnishing the ties. He also bore the distinction of driving the golden spike which united Northern and Southern Pacific railroads into the Union Pacific."* [1]

The two Billys were placed in the Mesilla jail with fourteen other prisoners. Guarding the prisoners were head jailor Anacleto Maese and assistant jailors José Maese and Francisco Bustillos. [2]

John Webster Southwick, March 24, 1922, *Illinois State Journal.*

Courtroom

The Dona Ana County courthouse was located at the southeast corner of the Mesilla plaza. The courtroom occupied the front quarter of the lot. The courtroom portion of the courthouse still stands today (see drawing on the next page).

The layout of the courtroom reflected its secondary function as the village school:

> *"At the back end of the room is a small platform on which are a table and chair for the judge. On either side of the platform is a small table with two chairs. In one corner of the back wall is a large bookcase with the glass missing from one door. At the other corner is a stove in front of the fireplace. There is no other furniture in the room except sixteen or eighteen wooden benches without backs."* [3]

> *"In front of the desk was a small clearance where the lawyers came to make their pleas."* [4]

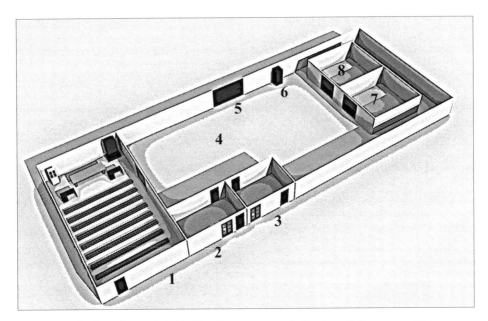

Mesilla Courthouse lot. (1) Courthouse room. In the back left corner was a bookcase, in the back right corner a stove. The judge sat at a table. The attorneys had desks in front of the judge. The seats were benches. The jury sat in the first two rows of benches. (2) Office of the sheriff. (3) Office and residence of the head jailor. (4) Placita. (5) Gate providing access to the placita and jail. (6) Toilet. (7) Jail cell 1. (8) Jail cell 2.

Mesilla courthouse, circa 1883. Courtesy Palace of the Governors Photo Archives (NMHM/DCA), 057238.

The adobe walls of the wooden-floored courtroom were whitewashed. Two large doors opened into an attached placita, which served as an exercise yard and enclosed the two-celled jail. A gate at the back of the placita provided secure access to the compound. Katherine Stoes, who was a young student in the courtroom school the year Billy was tried, gave this description:

"When court was in session, the judge lent dignity to the rickety platform and desk.... Wide doors led into an inner court and into the jail where iron-grilled bars opened and closed on Mexican and Gringo alike. Across the court yard could be seen ragged prisoners gazing sadly outside, or sitting idly within."

"Centipedes, mice, and bats, homing in the ceiling, fell from the latillas. But no one bothered too much. A few screams from the girls and the big boys with teen-age bravado squashed them; and lessons went on."[5]

The jurors sat in the first two rows of benches. For their deliberations, the jurors were secluded in Joshua S. Sledd's Casino Hotel, located on the block south of the plaza. Witnesses were also isolated there prior to their testimony. The court paid Sledd two dollars a day to use his hotel. Sledd's hotel was one of the three hotels in Mesilla at the time. The other two were the Corn Exchange Hotel (now the La Posta Restaurant) and the Texas Pacific Hotel.[6]

Court Convenes

The Third District Court, like all Territorial District Courts, had jurisdiction over both Federal and Territorial cases. Regulations of the court required it to address Federal business before Territorial business. Each morning the court would open in Federal session. After the Federal business was finished, that session would adjourn and a Territorial session would open. The District Judge presided over both sessions. The lawyers of the Territory would sometimes serve as prosecutor in Federal cases and as defense lawyer in Territorial cases, and visa versa. The court met six days a week, resting on Sundays.

The Court opened Monday, March 28, 1881. Present on opening were:

- Warren Bristol, Associate Justice of the Supreme Court of the Territory of New Mexico and Presiding Judge of the Third Judicial District
- Sidney M. Barnes, U. S. Attorney for New Mexico by Simon B. Newcomb, his representative
- Ira E. Leonard, attorney
- John D. Bail, attorney
- William Logan Rynerson, attorney
- Colonel Albert J. Fountain, attorney
- John Sherman, Jr., Territorial Marshal, by his Deputy, James W. Southwick
- George R. Bowman, court clerk
- Bailiffs for the term: Anastacio Garcia, Vincente Lopez, Martin Trujillo, and Jesus Arvizu
- Eugene Van Patten, interpreter (translator)
- Joshua S. Sledd, levier[7]

José Maese, one of the two assistant jailors who guarded Billy during his Mesilla trial. Undated photo. Courtsey Joe Lopez.

Mesilla courthouse (second building on right). Plaza and San Albino church visible on left. Photo circa 1894. Courtesy Archives and Special Collections, NMSU.

The back of the Mesilla courthouse lot, showing the ruins of the placita and jail, which fell down in the 1890s. Photo circa 1894. Courtesy Joseph Lopez.

A. J. Lopez bought the Mesilla courthouse in 1905 and opened it as the Elephant Butte Saloon, naming it after the Elephant Butte Dam. The apparent brick wall is painted on. Undated photo. Left to right: Juan Lopez, Frank Lopez, Gustavo Audetat, and Blas Pino. Courtesy Archives and Special Collections, NMSU.

Mesilla courthouse, circa 1918. The Elephant Butte Saloon closed in 1915. Courtesy Joseph Lopez.

Mesilla courthouse, circa 1918. On right, Robert G. Gamboa. Second man
unidentified. Courtesy Bob Gamboa.

Mesilla courthouse today. 2017 photo.

Ira Edwin Leonard. Undated photo.
Courtesy Beth Wilson.

The duty of the levier was to accept monies paid to the court for fees, fines, bonds, etc. He also disbursed monies owed prosecution witnesses for travel expenses and the stipends due jurors for their jury service.

Visitors at the Court included Dr. Blazer, John Delaney, Samuel Terrell, Samuel Corbet, and Patrick Coghlan. James Dolan, José Montaño, and David Easton were present as witnesses against Billy Wilson. Jacob B. Mathews, Saturnino Baca, Bonifacio J. Baca, and Isaac Ellis were present as witnesses against Billy.[8]

Day 1, March 28. was a Federal session. The court adjourned at 10 a.m. By the end of Day 2, the grand jurors for Federal cases were selected.[9]

Day 3, March 30: The Court began hearing Federal cases. The first case was U.S. versus Victorio (Apache name Bi-du-ya), Nana (Kastziden), and Mangus (son of Mangas Coloradas) for stealing horses, mules, and pistols. At acting District Attorney Newcomb's request, the case was stricken from the docket with leave to reinstate. The three Native American Chiefs were in not custody, hence no trial.

Next the court took up U.S. versus Henry Antrim, alias 'Kid," for the murder of Buckshot Roberts. The case was being pursued as a Federal case because the site of the killing, Blazer's Mill, was located on the Mescalero Reservation. Jurisdiction over reservations was limited to the Federal Government.

"Defendant Henry Antrim, alias "Kid," appearing in his own proper person and it appearing to the Court that he has no attorney and no means to employ one, the Court now appoints Ira E. Leonard, Esq, an Attorney of this Court, to defend said Defendant" [10]

Leonard, on behalf of Billy, asked the court for time to prepare Billy's defense. The court granted the motion.

Day 4, March 31: Billy appeared before Judge Bristol for pleading. Billy pled not guilty to Roberts' murder.

Territorial Attorney General Sidney M. Barnes arrived in Mesilla from Santa Fe.

Day 5, April 1: Frank C. Clark appeared before Judge Bristol and pled not guilty in his case, Territory versus F. C. Clark, for the murder of Robert R. Mann. Clark was one of five men being tried for murder in the session (more on Clark's case later). Sidney Barnes and John Bail were appointed as his attorneys. Newcomb represented the Territory.

Day 6, April 2: The Federal session consisted of swearing in new U.S. citizens. The Territorial session dealt with civil litigation. Deputy U.S. Marshal Robert Olinger arrived in Mesilla with two mules, allegedly stolen by Billy from the N. M. & T. Co. railroad.[11]

Newman's Semi-Weekly published an editorial warning that there was a high danger of Billy escaping, writing:

> *"Lincoln which has suffered so long from his crimes, cannot afford to see him escape; and yet every hour that he is confined in the Mesilla jail is a threat to the peace of that community. There are a hundred good citizens of Lincoln who would not sleep soundly in their beds did they know that he were at large."* [12]

The court was not in session Sunday, April 3.

Simon Bolivar Newcomb. Undated photo. Courtesy Center for Southwest Research and Special Collections, UNM.

Day 7, April 4: Billy Wilson pled not guilty to three Federal counts of passing counterfeit notes.

In the Territorial session, Martin Abeita appeared before Judge Bristol to plead his case, Territory versus Martin Abeita, murder. The case was stricken from the docket at the request of acting District Attorney Newcomb.

Selection of the jury for Clark's trial began. It took two days. The two sides fought furiously over jurors, exhausting the jury pool and going through 64 talesmen before a panel of 12 jurors were agreed upon. One of the talesmen was Dolan, who was rejected by the defense on the ground that he was could not act impartially. (Talesmen are people detained in the street or wherever they can be found by the court bailiff and ordered into court as potential jurors.)

Day 8, April 5: Anastacio Garcia was excused as bailiff and David Wood appointed in his place. Wood was also appointed deputy sheriff.

Fighting over the jurors for Clark's trial took most of the Territorial session.

Day 9, April 6: In the Federal session, Billy's trial for killing Roberts opened. At the suggestion of attorney Albert J. Fountain, Billy's attorney Leonard moved that Billy's not-guilty plea be withdrawn and the case dismissed because the Federal Government lacked jurisdiction. Leonard argued that although Blazer's Mill, the site of Robert's killing, was on a reservation, Blazer's Mill itself was on private land. Thus, the site was under Territorial jurisdiction.[13]

Acting Attorney General Newcomb filed a demurrer, arguing that while it was true that the Federal Government did not have jurisdiction, that fact was irrelevant to the case.

"Whereupon the Court took said matters under advisement, and after being fully advised upon the matters arising upon said demurrer to said plea over-ruled said demurrer and sustains said Defendant's plea to the jurisdiction of this Court. It is therefore considered by the Court here that said indictment be and the same hereby is quashed and that said Defendant Henry Antrim alias 'Kid' as to said indictment go hence without delay."

Of course, Billy was not free to walk out of the court. After granting the dismissal, Judge Bristol remanded Billy to the custody of Sheriff Southwick to be held for his trial for killing Brady.

Although only Billy was being tried for Buckshot Roberts' killing – because he was the only one present – eight other men were under indictment for the crime: Charles Bowdre (deceased), Doc Scurlock, Henry Brown, John Middleton, Stephen Stevens, John Scroggins, George Coe and Frederick Waite. The causes against those men were quashed by Judge Bristol for the same reason he quashed Billy's case, lack of jurisdiction.

In the Territorial session, jury selection was taken up again for Clark's trial. By the end of the session, twelve jurors had been agreed upon.

Days 10, April 7: In the Federal session, Billy Wilson's counterfeiting trial opened. The first act of his defense attorney was to ask for a change of venue to Santa Fe. The motion was opposed by acting Attorney General Newcomb. Judge Bristol agreed to send the case to Santa Fe.

Frank Clark's murder trial opened. He was found guilty of murdering Mann in the first degree and sentenced to death. See "Territory versus Clark, Murder of Robert R. Mann" for details.

Day 11, April 8: In the Territorial session, Pedro Rivera, charged with the murder of Jesus Chacon, appeared before Judge Bristol and pled destitution. The court assigned Rynerson and Barnes as his lawyers.

Billy appeared before Judge Bristol to answer for his Brady murder case and pled destitution. Newcomb represented the Territory. The court assigned Colonel Albert J. Fountain and Bail as his lawyers. The selection of jurors for his case took the remainder of the court session.

Day 12, April 9: The day was spent on Billy's Brady murder trial. Billy was found guilty of murder in the first degree and sentenced to death by the jury. See "Territory versus Billy, Murder of Sheriff Brady" for details.

The court was not in session Sunday, April 10.

Day 13, April 11: In the Territorial session, Santos Barela, charged with the murder of José Jojola, appeared before Judge Bristol and pled destitution. Newcomb represented the Territory. The court assigned Bail and Rynerson as his lawyers. The same day, Santos Barela was charged with the rape of Mrs. Jojola by the grand jury. That case was added to the session docket.

Daniel Frietze, charged with murder, appeared before Judge Bristol with his lawyer Newcomb. Newcomb requested a continuance to the next term of the court for Frietze's trial. Judge Bristol so ordered.

Day 14, April 12: In the Territorial session, Santos Barela, charged with rape, appeared before Judge Bristol and pled destitution. Barnes was assigned as his lawyer.

Pedro Rivera's murder trial began with the selection of his jury. The session ended with the jury panel partially selected. Jury selection was continued to the next day. Rivera's attorneys were Rynerson and Barnes.

Day 15, April 13: In the Territorial session, jury selection for Pedro Rivera's trial was completed. Rivera's trial was held and he was found guilty of murder in the fifth degree and sentenced to one year's imprisonment.

Frank Clark was called into court to hear his formal sentence. Judge Bristol sentenced him to hang on May 13.

Billy was called into court to hear his formal sentence. Judge Bristol sentenced him to hang on May 13.

Day 16, April 14: In the Territorial session, the only woman being tried, Mariana Heungues, charged with adultery, had her case dismissed by the court after the grand jury refused to indict her for that charge.

Days 17-20: Nothing of relevance to Billy or the Lincoln County War.

Day 21, April 20: The jury for Santos Barela's murder trail was selected. His trial opened and he was convicted of first degree murder and sentenced to death. See "Territory versus Barela, Murder of José Jojola" for details.

Day 22, April 21: Territory versus Cristobal Barela, murder, was ordered continued to the next term of the court.

Day 23, April 22: No relevant business.

Day 24, April 23: Santos Barela was called into court to hear his formal sentence. Judge Bristol sentenced him to hang on May 20.

Among the cases handled by the court and not detailed here were cases for rape, assault with intent to commit murder, extortion, burglary, larceny, robbery, chancery (fraud), forgery, trespass, selling liquor without a license, carrying a weapon, drawing a weapon, permitting gaming, and violation of the Sunday law.

Following Barela's sentencing and some final business, the District Court adjourned sine die.[14]

Territorial Law

New Mexico Territorial law at the time recognized five degrees of murder, *"according to the facts and circumstances of each case."* [15]

Murder in the first degree was defined as a killing perpetrated from a premeditated design to effect the death of the person killed. The punishment was death by hanging on the 30th day after the person's conviction.

Murder in the second degree was defined as a killing by a person engaged in the commission of any felony. The punishment was imprisonment in the county jail or Territorial prison for not more than fourteen years nor less than seven years.

Murder in the third, fourth, or fifth degree was defined as a killing by the act, procurement, or omission of another, when such killing shall not be murder according to the definitions of first or second degree. The punishment was determined by the jury.[16]

A defendant had the right in all cases of final judgment to appeal to the Territorial Supreme Court, if applied for during the term at which such judgment was rendered.[17]

The right of appeal had this disheartening limitation:

"No such appeal shall stay the execution of such judgment unless the circuit court shall be of opinion that there is probable cause for such appeal, or so much doubt as to render it expedient to take the judgment of the superior court thereof, and shall make an order expressly directing that such appeal shall operate as stay of proceedings." [18]

This constraint on the right of appeal gave the judge who sentenced a defendant the sole power to decide whether that defendant's appeal was submitted to the Territorial Supreme Court. It also defined as a default that no appeal by a defendant stayed the execution of a judgment ordered by a court (even a hanging).

New Mexico at the time had three judicial districts, each with its own presiding judge. The Third District had jurisdiction over Dona Ana, Grant, and Lincoln Counties. The three District Judges made up the Territorial Supreme Court. Thus, the judge who convicted a defendant also sat on the court that handled any appeal by that defendant.

In appeals, the judge who presided over a case was permitted to argue the case before the other justices, but constrained from voting on the appeal unless he was voting to reverse his lower court ruling.

"But the judge who tried the case in the court below may give his reasons for any opinion which he may have given, and quote authorities to sustain such decision." [19]

The New Mexico Supreme Court met twice a year. As a result, there would often be no Supreme Court session during the 30-day time period between a defendants' death sentencing and the person's hanging. In such a case, the sentencing judge had the power to stay an execution until an appeal could be heard. He had no legal obligation to do so. If the sentencing judge did not stay the execution, the defendant could petition the Territorial Governor for such a stay.

Regarding the question of ironing, the Territorial Supreme Court had ruled:

"A prisoner when brought to the bar of the court for trial, is entitled to have his irons removed before the trial commences, unless the court be of the opinion that their retention upon the limbs of the prisoner is a reasonable precaution to prevent an escape or to insure the safety of the by-standers and the orderly conduct of the prisoner."

"The calling and examination of jurors is a part of the proceedings of a trial, and it is irregular to compel the prisoner at this stage of the trial to appear

at the bar in irons for no better reason than that it would be inconvenient to remove them, or that their removal would cause a delay of a few hours in the trial." [20]

In a murder case a few months after Billy's trial, Territory versus Edward M. Kelly, the presiding judge did not order Kelly's irons removed during his trial because:

"The sheriff having the prisoner in charge, informed the court, 'That the irons were riveted on, and in order to remove them, the prisoner would have to be taken to a blacksmith's shop; that no such shop was open at that hour, and he did not believe he could find a blacksmith; and that even in the day time it would take quite a while.'" [21]

Kelly appealed his first degree murder conviction based on that issue. The Territorial Supreme Court, in an opinion written by Judge Bristol, ruled:

"In my opinion, an action of the court without evident necessity that imposes physical burdens, pains and restraints upon a prisoner during the process of his trial, inevitably tends to confuse and embarrass his mental faculties, and thereby materially abridge and prejudicially affect his constitutional rights of defense." [22]

In spite of Judge Bristol's opinion, Kelly, known as "Choctaw" Kelley, was not granted a new trial. Kelly's lawyer was Edgar Caypless, who waged an indefatigable campaign to convince the Territorial public that Kelly's sentence was unjustly harsh (Kelly had killed John Reardon in a drunken barroom fight). On the day before he was to hang a telegram:

"Largely signed by the members of the bar here [Las Vegas] was sent to-day to President Arthur for a respite until the case can be presented to him." [23]

U.S. President Arthur responded by commuting Kelly's sentence to life imprisonment. On September 10, 1893, Kelly was released from prison and granted a full pardon by then Territorial Governor Thornton.[24]

Trial Transcript?

Almost every author who has written about the Billy and the Lincoln County War has questioned why there is no transcript of Billy's trial. Most have speculated that either no transcript was made or else the transcript was lost or stolen.

The truth is, there was a transcript taken by the court clerk. But the rule of the court was that if a case was not appealed, then the court did not pay the clerk to make a formal transcript for the case file. That was an unnecessary expense for an unappealed case:

"When an appeal shall be taken which operates as a stay of proceedings, it shall be the duty of the clerk of the district court to make out a transcript of the record in the case, and certify and return the same to the office of the clerk of the supreme court without delay." [25]

This practice continued throughout the Territory until at least as late as May, 1909, when Jesse Wayne Brazel was tried for killing Pat Garrett (see *"Killing Pat Garrett, the Wild West's Most Famous Lawman – Murder or Self-Defense?"* for details on Brazel's trial).

Colonel Albert J. Fountain. Undated photo. Courtesy Archives and Special Collections, NMSU.

Territory versus Billy, Murder of Sheriff Brady

Shortly after Billy was jailed in Mesilla, he was given a new suit (black according to Stoes) and shoes by the Las Cruces Sisters of the Loretta Academy. They probably provided Billy Wilson new clothes as well. Neither man had changed his clothes since they were gifted *"good suits"* three months earlier by Michael Cosgrove at the Las Vegas jail. It was common practice, as well, for the Sisters to take food to the prisoners in the Mesilla jail. Conditions in the jail were inhumane, as described in Chapter 3.[26]

Stoes remembered that the prisoners *"slept in their clothes on the dirt floor weeks on end, and smelled."* [27]

The first act in Billy's trail, after his pleading, was the selection of the jury. The two sides went through the jury pool and 36 talesmen before 12 mutually acceptable jurors were found. Almost all of the potential jurors were Hispanic. An analysis of Colonel Fountain's jury strategy shows that he rejected the only four Anglos in the jury pool: Henry C. Haring, John Wood, Peter Ott, and James West. Colonel Fountain obviously felt that his client had a better chance with an all-Hispanic jury. The prosecution made only six objections; they found all four Anglos acceptable.

The 12 jurors chosen were:

Crescencio Bustillos	Merced Lucero	Pedro Onopa
Felipe Lopez	Pedro Serna	Jesus Silva
Refugio Bernal	Pedro Martinez	Hilario Moreno
Jesus Telles	Luis Sedillos	Benito Montoya

Census data reveals the following information about the jurors: they ranged in age from 27 to 56. All were married except Pedro Martinez who was widowed. Six were farmers and two were freighters. Five could not read or write. Crescencio Bustillos was the brother of jail guard Francisco Bustillos. Felipe Lopez was the great uncle of Joseph E. Lopez, to whom I dedicate this book.[28]

Territorial law required that jurors be between 21 and 60 years of age. They must have resided in the county for at least six months prior to jury selection and be citizens of the United States. They must be heads of families. They were paid two dollars a day for their service.[29]

When court convened on April 9, 1881, the prosecution had four witnesses present to testify against Billy: Jacob B. Mathews, Saturnino Baca, Bonifacio Baca, and Isaac Ellis. With no transcript, it is necessary to reconstruct their testimony.[30]

Mathews was one of the four deputies walking down the street with Sheriff Brady when Brady was killed. Mathews would have testified about suddenly coming under fire, Brady's shooting, sprinting to shelter, and returning the fire of the ambushers. He would have identified the source of the firing – Tunstall's corral. He would have recounted how he saw Billy and Jim French run out from behind the corral wall and seemingly attempt to recover something from Brady's body.

Saturnino Baca was teaching school in the Torreón when Brady was killed. Bonifacio Baca, Saturnino's oldest son, was in the street when the killing occurred. Both probably testified to seeing Brady killed and seeing Billy and French run to the body. Both were

Saturnino Baca, age 91. 1921 photo. Courtesy Maurice G. Fulton Papers, Special Collections, UA.

opponents of the McSween faction during the Lincoln War. Saturnino testified in Colonel Dudley's defense during the Dudley Court of Inquiry.

Ellis must also have testified to seeing Brady's killing.

The critical question is: did any of these witnesses see who did the shooting that killed Sheriff Brady? There were eight men behind the 10 feet high corral wall: Billy, Waite, Middleton, McNab, Brown, French, Widenmann, and Corbet. Yet, strikingly, only Billy, Middleton, and Brown were indicted by the grand jury. Did the jury have an evidentiary basis for selecting only those three for indictments, or did they just not know who all were behind the wall? (Remember, Widenmann assuaged his potential culpability by claiming he was there only to feed Tunstall's dog.)

Billy had no witnesses for his defense.

Most authors have asserted that Billy was shackled during his trial. Given the Supreme Court ruling on ironing authored by Judge Bristol (quoted earlier), it would seem unlikely. There is no doubt that Billy and the other prisoners were ironed while in jail. The Mesilla blacksmith charged the county $54 for handcuffs and shackles during the court session. Sheriff Southwick charged the county $899 to feed the prisoners during the session.

Testifying in One's Own Defense

Many researchers have wondered if Billy testified in his own defense. He did not.

The history of testifying in one's own defense is surprising. Being able to tell your side of events when accused of a crime would seem to be a fundamental right. Yet, it is a relatively recent legal right of a defendant.

Under English common law, a defendant had no right to testify in their own defense, because that person was assumed to be an unreliable witness. This was true for both civil and criminal cases.

> *"It was considered certain that the defendant's fear of punishment, whether he was guilty or innocent, would cause him to perjure himself, and to avoid this, he was not allowed to testify."* [31]

Because English common law formed the basis for United States law, defendants in the U.S. also had no right to testify in their own defense. That began to change in the 1860s when U.S. legal scholars started to advocate for such a right. The first state to permit testifying in one's own defense in civil cases was Maine in 1864. Maine was followed by Massachusetts in 1866 and Connecticut in 1867.[32]

Legal reformers argued that defendants should be able to testify in their own defense in criminal cases also. New York, in 1869, became the first state to permit the practice in criminal cases.

In February, 1880, the New Mexico Territorial Legislature passed a law that permitted a defendant to testify in their own defense:

> *"In the trial of all indictments, informations, complaints and other proceedings against persons charged with the commission of crimes, offenses and misdemeanors in the courts of this territory, the person so charged shall,*

at his own request, but not otherwise, be a competent witness; and his failure to make such request shall not create any presumption against him." [33]

New Mexico was relatively late making this reform. The last state to make this a right in a criminal case was Alaska in 1899.[34]

Thus, Billy had the right to tell his side of the shooting to the jury. Why did he not?

Perhaps Colonel Fountain was so unfamiliar with the new idea of a defendant testifying that he did not consider the option. The author has been unable to find any case prior to Billy's in which Colonel Fountain put a defendant on the stand to testify in his own defense. The first case in which Colonel Fountain apparently did so was Territory versus Sehero Gomez, for murdering his wife. The trial took place September 2, 1882, in Mesilla. Testifying was a winning strategy for Gomez – he was only convicted of fifth degree murder. A fifth degree conviction was amazing since Gomez testified he had knifed his wife to death four days after he caught her in flagrante delicto, and after he had told her father he intended to kill her.[35]

Another explanation is that Billy simply refused to tell the jury that he did not shoot Brady – he had done it, Brady deserved it, and he was not going to lie about it. This explanation seems unlikely. As recounted in Chapter 4, Colonel Fountain, the editor of the *Mesilla Valley Independent* at the time of Brady's killing, interviewed one of the men behind the corral wall (likely it was Billy). Colonel Fountain reported:

> *"One of the murderers subsequently stated that Brady was killed by accident; that it was their intention only to kill Hindman, as one of the murderers of Tunstall, and that one of the shots intended for Hindman took effect on Brady."* [36]

Colonel Fountain had grounds with that statement to argue that the killing of Brady was not intentional. He could have called defense witnesses to bolster the argument. Sam Corbet was in Mesilla during Billy's trial. He was behind the corral wall when Brady was shot. <u>Why was he not called as a witness?</u> (Also surprising, since he was behind the corral wall, why was he not charged with Brady's killing?)

Instead, Colonel Fountain called no defense witnesses. Billy's defense consisted only of what Colonel Fountain could tell the jury on his behalf. It appears that Colonel Fountain provided Billy with something less than the most vigorous defense.

War of Jury Instructions

Usually in murder cases, if a defendant was convicted, it was left to the jury to decide the degree of murder, as in the case of Sehero Gomez discussed above. In the cases of Billy, Clark, and Barela, the jury was given no choice. The only charge they were permitted to consider by Judge Bristol was first degree murder.

The Territorial law required that to convict a defendant of first degree murder, the jury must be certain beyond a reasonable doubt that the defendant did it, and they must be equally certain that the act was intentional.

Colonel Fountain prepared the following instructions to be given to the jury before they began deliberation:

> *"1st Instruction asked:"*

"Under the evidence the jury must either find the defendant guilty of Murder in the 1st degree or acquit him."

"2nd Instruction asked:"

"The Jury will not be justified in finding the defendant guilty of Murder in the 1st degree unless they are satisfied, from the evidence, to the exclusion of all reasonable doubt, that the defendant actually fired the shot that caused the death of the deceased Brady, and that such shot was fired by the defendant with a premeditated design to effect the death of the deceased, or that the defendant was present and actually assisted in firing the fatal shot or shots that caused the death of the deceased, and that he was present and in a position to render such assistance and actually rendered such assistance from a premeditated design to effect the death of the deceased."

"3rd Instruction asked:"

"If the Jury are satisfied from the evidence to the exclusion of all reasonable doubt that the defendant was present at the time of the firing of the shot or shots that caused the death of the deceased Brady, yet, before they will be justified in finding the defendant guilty, they must be further satisfied from the evidence and the evidence alone, to the exclusion of all reasonable doubt, that the defendant either fired the shots that killed the deceased, or some one of them, or that he assisted in firing said shot or shots, and that he fired said shot or shots, or assisted in firing the same, or assisted the parties who fired the same either by his advice, encouragement or procurement or command, from a premeditated design to effect the death of Brady. If the Jury entertains any reasonable doubt upon any of these points they must find a verdict of acquittal." [37]

These instructions would not be out of place in a trial today. They well address both legal requirements for convicting a defendant of first degree murder.

Judge Bristol rejected Colonel Fountain's instructions and substituted his own:

"Gentlemen of the Jury:"

"The defendant in this case William Bonny (sic) alias Kid alias William Antrim is charged in and by the indictment against him which has been laid before you with having committed in connection with certain other persons the crime of murder in the County of Lincoln in the 3d Judicial District of the Territory of New Mexico in the month of April of the year 1878 by then and there unlawfully killing one William Brady by inflicting upon his body certain fatal gun shot wounds from a premeditated design to effect his death."

"The case is here for trial by a change of venue from the said County of Lincoln."

"The facts alleged in the indictment if true constitute Murder in the 1st and highest degree and whether these allegations are true or not are for you to determine from the evidence which you have heard and which is now submitted to you for your careful consideration."

"The Trial of Billy the Kid," Joseph E. Lopez.

"In the matter of determining what your verdict shall be it will be improper for you to consider anything except the evidence before you."

"You as Jurors are the exclusive judges of the weight of the evidence. You are the exclusive judges of the credibility of the witnesses. It is for you to determine whether the testimony of any witness whom you have heard is to be believed or not. You are also the exclusive judges whether the evidence is sufficiently clear and strong to satisfy your minds that the defendant is guilty."

"There is no evidence tending to show that the killing of Brady was either justifiable or excusable in law. As a matter of law therefore such killing was unlawful and whoever committed the deed or was present and advised or aided or abetted and consented to such killing committed the crime of murder in some one of the degrees of murder."

"There is no evidence before you showing that the killing of Brady is murder in any other degree than the first."

"Your verdict therefore should be either that the defendant is guilty of murder in the 1st degree or that he is not guilty at all under this indictment."

"Murder in the 1st degree consists in the killing of one human being by another without authority of law and from a premeditated design to effect the death of the person killed."

"Every killing of one human being by another that is not justifiable or excusable would be necessarily a killing without authority of law."

"As I have already instructed you to constitute murder in the 1st degree it is necessary that the killing should have been perpetrated from a premeditated design to effect the death of the person killed."

"As to this premeditated design I charge you that to render a design to kill premeditated it is not necessary that such design to kill should exist in the mind for any considerable length of time before the killing."

"If the design to kill is completely formed in the mind but for a moment before inflicting the fatal wounds it would be premeditated and in law the effect would be the same as though the design to kill had existed for a long time."

"In this case in order to justify you in finding this defendant guilty of murder in the 1st degree under the peculiar circumstances as presented by the indictment and the evidence you should be satisfied and believe from the evidence to the exclusion of every reasonable doubt of the truth of several propositions."

"1st That the defendant either inflicted one or more of the fatal wounds causing Brady's death or that he was present at the time and place of the killing and encouraged – incited – aided in – abetted – advised or commanded such killing."

"2d That such killing was without justification or excuse."

"*3d That such killing of Brady was caused by inflicting upon his body a fatal gun shot wound.*"

"*And 4th that such fatal wound was either inflicted by the defendant from a premeditated design to effect Brady's death or that he was present at the time and place of the killing of Brady and from a premeditated design to effect his death he then and there encouraged – incited – aided in – abetted – advised or commanded such killing.*"

"*If he was so present – encouraging – inciting – aiding in – abbetting (sic) – advising or commanding the killing of Brady he is as much as guilty as though he fired the fatal shot.*"

"*I have charged you that to justify you in finding the defendant guilty of murder in the 1st degree you should be satisfied from the evidence to the exclusion of every reasonable doubt that the defendant is actually guilty.*"

"*As to what would be or would not be a reasonable doubt of guilty I charge you that belief in the guilt of the defendant to the exclusion of every reasonable doubt does not require you to so believe absolutely and to a mathematical certainty – That is to justify a verdict of guilty it is not necessary for you to be as certain that the defendant is guilty as you are that two and two are four or that two and three are five.*"

"*Merely a vague conjecture or bare possibility that the defendant may be innocent is not sufficient to raise a reasonable doubt of his guilt.*"

"*If all the evidence before you which you believe to be true convinces and directs your understanding and satisfies your reason and judgment while acting upon it conscientiously under your oath as jurors and if this evidence leaves in your minds an abiding conviction to a moral certainty that the defendant is guilty of the crime charged against him: then this would be proof of guilt to the exclusion of every reasonable doubt and would justify you in finding the defendant guilty.*"

"*You will apply the evidence to this case according to the instructions I have given you and determine whether the defendant is guilty of murder in the 1st degree or not guilty.*"

"*Murder in the 1st degree is the greatest crime known to our laws. The Legislature of this Territory has enacted a law prescribing that the punishment for murder in the 1st degree shall be death.*"

"*This then is the law: No other punishment than death can be imposed – for murder in the 1st degree.*"

"*If you believe and are satisfied therefore from the evidence before you to the exclusion of every reasonable doubt that the defendant is guilty of murder in the 1st degree then it will be your duty to find a verdict that the defendant is guilty of murder in that degree naming murder in the 1st degree in your verdict and also saying in your verdict that the defendant shall suffer the punishment of death.*"

"If from the evidence you do not believe to the exclusion of every reasonable doubt that the defendant is guilty of murder in the 1st degree or if you entertain a reasonable doubt as to the guilt of the defendant, then in that case your verdict should be not guilty." [38]

It is important to see this document in its entirety because it is the reason Billy was convicted of first degree murder. On the issue of premeditation, Judge Bristol asserted that the *"design to kill"* need exist for only a *"moment"* to qualify as premeditation. Intention is tricky. If the men behind Tunstall's corral wall were intending to shoot Hindman and not Sheriff Brady, does that mean they "intended" to kill Brady? Judge Bristol defines intention (premeditation) as the *"design to kill."* But he doesn't really mean that a defendant must have thought, "I am going to kill Brady." That can never be proved. Thoughts are hidden. What Judge Bristol means is "decision to act." In Billy's case, it means the decision to fire a weapon in Brady's direction, whatever the consequences.

Judge Bristol's definition of intention would qualify almost every crime as premeditated. Decision to act is so universal that the jury probably did not give the question of intention serious consideration.

With the question of intentionality removed from the jurors' minds, Judge Bristol then defined culpability so broadly that Billy's mere known presence at the scene was evidence sufficient to convict him of the crime. Billy was guilty – even if he did not shoot Brady himself – if he encouraged, incited, aided, abetted, advised, or commanded Brady's shooting. None of these actions could be proven without the testimony of a participant in the conversations preceding the shooting. They are irrelevant. Their purpose in the instructions was to confuse the jury – a jury that Judge Bristol knew was unsophisticated.

Colonel Fountain in his instructions required the jury to be certain that Billy *"either fired the shots that killed the deceased, or some one of them or that the defendant was present and actually assisted in firing the fatal shot or shots that caused the death of the deceased."* Judge Bristol was well aware that the jury did not know if Billy fired the killing shots, or assisted in firing them, given the evidence presented. That is why he substituted his own instructions.

If the jury had been able to consider all five degrees of murder, they may well have decided that Billy's crime fit the definition of murder in the third, fourth, or fifth degree.

Judge Bristol's three-page, complex instructions were read to the jury in English, and then given to them in written form in English to take with them to the Casino Hotel for their deliberations. Few of the jurors spoke English. The editor of *Newman's Semi-Weekly* addressed this problem in regards to Clark's trial:

"...we desire to call the attention of the court and bar to the manner in which trials are conducted in this county through the medium of interpreters. It is unfortunate that we cannot get juries composed of men who understand the English language; but, inasmuch as this is impossible, it is certainly necessary in order that justice may be intelligently and impartially administered, that the evidence of witnesses, the arguments of lawyers and the rulings, instructions and charges of the court be correctly and intelligently presented to the minds of the jurors."

"We on Thursday watched for several hours the progress of the trial of Clark for murder. Here was a man being tried for the highest crime known to the law; his life hung in the balance and he was certainly entitled to all the protection and all the guaranties which the court and the laws of his country could throw around him. He was entitled to an impartial trial; and in this term 'impartial' is embraced the right of his attorneys to advance and explain any theory of the case which they might consider would relieve him of the terrible suspicion resting upon him. If their theory is not thoroughly and lucidly explained and the abstract principles and ideas advanced by them are not interpreted to the jurors in a manner to be perfectly understood by them, then it appears to us that Clark has just ground of complaint that a fair trial has been denied him. We maintain that this was not done; and any Spanish scholar who watched the proceedings will bear us out."

"We believe Clark to be guilty of the crime of which he has been convicted, but nevertheless, we cannot but view that part of his trial which we saw as a mockery upon justice." [39]

There is no reason to believe that these devastating obstacles to a fair trial did not exist in Billy's trial also – *"a mockery upon justice."*

Billy's Death Sentence

Billy was convicted of murdering Brady on April 9, 1881. *Newman's Semi-Weekly* reported:

"The case of Kid was submitted to the jury on Wednesday, and after an absence of about three hours the jury brought in a verdict of 'guilty,' which consigns the prisoner to the gallows.... Kid will be taken to Lincoln for execution and the gallows will probably be erected over the spot where Brady fell." [40]

On April 13, Billy was brought into court to hear his death sentence read:

"It is therefore considered by the Court here that the said defendant, William Bonny (sic), alias Kid, alias William Antrim, be taken to the County of Lincoln, in the Third Judicial District of the Territory of New Mexico, by the Sheriff of the County of Dona Ana in said Judicial District and Territory and there by him delivered into the custody of the Sheriff of the said County of Lincoln, and that he, the said William Bonny, alias Kid, alias William Antrim, be confined in prison in said County of Lincoln by the Sheriff of such County until on Friday, the 13th day of May, in the Year of our Lord One Thousand Eight Hundred and Eighty-One."

"That on the day aforesaid, between the hours of nine of the clock in the forenoon and three of the clock in the afternoon, he, the said William Bonny, alias Kid, alias William Antrim, be taken from such prison to some suitable and convenient place of execution within said County of Lincoln, by the Sheriff of said County, and that then and there on that day and between the aforesaid hours thereof by the Sheriff of said County of Lincoln, he, the said William Bonny, alias Kid, alias William Antrim, be hanged by the neck until his body be dead." [41]

The sentence is to be performed on Billy's body. The unspoken assumption is that Billy has a soul which would not be killed.

Billy was ordered to Lincoln to hang, rather than hanged in Mesilla, because Lincoln was where the crime was committed, as required by Territorial law.

Louisa Bristol, Judge Bristol's wife, in an interview given after her husband's death, said:

> *"In the trial of Billy the Kid, the judge afterwards related that knowing Billy's desperate nature and what he might do if the bailiffs with their weapons came within 'snatching' distance of him, he, the judge, never lost sight of the criminal during the entire trial.... The judge in passing sentence always did it as briefly as possible."* [42]

Judge Bristol's habit of not lecturing a defendant before sentencing spared Billy an exhortation such as this one given by Judge Benedict in sentencing José Maria Martin to death by hanging:

> *"As a usual thing it is a painful duty, José Maria Martin, for the judge of a court of justice to pronounce upon a human being the sentence of death."*

> *"Happily, however, your case is relieved of all such unpleasant features; the court takes positive delight in sentencing you to death. You are a young man, José Maria Martin, apparently of good physical condition and robust health. Ordinarily you might have looked forward to many years of life, and the court has no doubt that you have, and have expected to die at a good old age; but you are about to be cut off in consequence of your act."*

> *"José Maria Martin, it is now the spring time, in a little while the grass will be springing up green in these beautiful valleys, and on these broad mesas and mountain sides flowers will be blooming, birds will be singing their sweet carols, and nature will be putting on her most attractive and gorgeous robes, and life will be pleasant and men will want to stay; but none of this for you, José Maria Martin, the flowers will not bloom for you, José Maria Martin; the birds will not carol for you, José Maria Martin; you will not gladden the masses of men; you will be occupying a hole about six by two beneath the earth and the green grass and the beautiful flowers will be growing above your lowly head."* [43]

The Murphy-Dolan cheerleading *Daily New Mexican* was euphoric at the prospect of Billy's demise:

> *"Billy the Kid who was convicted of murder in the first degree at the La Mesilla court, is said to be weakening. His spirit has been broken and he finds that he is not likely to escape so easily this time as heretofore. When the Kid's execution comes off it will probably attract more people than any similar event that ever occurred in the Territory. Certainly this consideration ought to flatter and console the young gentleman."* [44]

> *"They made short work of trying and convicting the Kid. Now if they will be as prompt with the hanging the territory will soon be rid of one of its worst characters."* [45]

Interview with Billy

Following his sentencing, Billy was interviewed by Ira M. Bond, editor of the *Mesilla News*:

> *"Shortly after sentence was passed upon the Kid, a reporter of the Mesilla News interviewed him with the following effect. Said the Kid, after a considerable delay:"*

> *"'Well, I had intended at one time to not say a word in my own behalf, because persons would say, 'Oh, he lied'; Newman gave me a rough deal; he created prejudice against me, and is trying to incite a mob to lynch me. He sent me a paper which shows it; I think it a dirty, mean advantage to take of me considering my situation and knowing I could not defend myself by word or act. But I suppose he thought he would give me a kick down hill. Newman came to see me the other day; I refused to talk to him or tell him anything; but I believe the News is always willing to give its readers both sides of a question.'"*

> *"'If mob law is going to rule, better dismiss judge, sheriff, etc., and let all take chances alike. I expect to be lynched in going to Lincoln. Advise persons never to engage in killing.'"*

> *"Editor – 'Think you will be taken through safe? Do you expect a pardon from the Governor?'"*

> *"'Considering the active part Wallace took on our side and the friendly relations that existed between him and me, I think he ought to pardon me. Don't know that he will do it. When I was arrested for that murder, he let me out and gave me the freedom of the town and let me go about with my arms. When I got ready to go I left. Think it hard that I should be the only one to suffer the extreme penalties of the law.'"*

> *"Here the sheriff led us away and said we had talked long enough."* [46]

Billy's comment – *"after a considerable delay"* – that he had decided to not speak out in his defense because he thought he would not be believed, suggests that he had a defense to the charge of killing Brady – such as he did not shoot him. This statement reinforces the conclusion that Colonel Fountain made a serious error in not putting Billy on the stand to tell his side of events.

Billy's comments on the unfair press he had received shows a modern recognition of the extent to which the press influences – and taints – events. Billy's jury may well have decided he was guilty based on what the press was touting, rather than on courtroom evidence. Billy's grievance against Simeon H. Newman, owner and editor of *Newman's Thirty-Four*, derived from published comments by Newman such as:

> *"His [Billy's] conviction is beyond a reasonable doubt, and his execution by due process of law would have a most beneficial effect on the lawless element of the Territory."* [47]

Billy's sardonic comment on *"mob law"* is amazing. It is a subtle, sarcastic commentary on this line in a Newman editorial:

"Mob law must be avoided. Kid himself has been the most terrible exponent of that law in Southern New Mexico and his punishment should be meted out in due form and with all the solemnity attaching to the dignity of the laws he has outraged." [48]

Probably most *Mesilla News* readers missed Billy's ironic jab. It was the Murphy-Dolan "mob" that initiated mob law in Lincoln. It was the Murphy-Dolan mob that kicked off the Lincoln County War by killing Tunstall. Knowing this, and knowing the Murphy-Dolan mob was completely successful in achieving their aims, Billy pretends to suggest that if the mob is to rule, then dismiss the law – exactly what the Murphy-Dolan mob did. He pretends to counsel against killing – such as the killing of Tunstall and McSween. The irony of his statement is that he – and only he – was derided by Newman for precisely what the Murphy-Dolan mob did.

The question regarding a potential pardon shows that the deal Wallace made with Billy was widely known. Unlike in his letters to Governor Wallace, Billy does not assert that Wallace had not honored his end of the deal, as he did in his March 4 letter:

"I have done Everything that I promised you I would and you have done nothing that you promised me." (The full text of the letter is on page 44.) [49]

Not publically accusing Governor Wallace of breaking his word was a diplomatic move. Billy still hoped for a pardon.

Billy points out – truthfully – that of all the killings committed during the Lincoln County War – maybe as many as 80 – he is the only one paying any legal penalty.

What a loss to history that Sheriff Southwick did not permit the *Mesilla News* editor to ask more questions!

Attempt to Appeal

Two days after being sentenced, on April 15, Billy wrote to attorney Edgar Caypless:

"I would have written before this but could get no paper. My United States case was thrown out of court and I was rushed to trial on my Territorial charge. Was convicted of murder in the first degree and am to be hanged on the 13th of May. Mr. A. J. Fountain was appointed to defend me and has done the best he could for me. He is willing to carry the case further if I can raise the money to bear his expenses."

"The mare is about all I can depend upon at present, so I hope you will settle the case right away and give him the money you get for her. If you do not settle the matter with Scott Moore, and have to go to court about [it], either give him the mare or sell her at auction and give him the money. Please do as he wishes you to do in the matter. I know you will do the best you can for me in this. I shall be taken to Lincoln to-morrow. Please write and direct care of Garrett, sheriff. Excuse bad writing. I have my handcuffs on." [50]

Territorial law required the court to pay for a defendant's defense lawyer if the defendant was penniless. But there was no requirement for the court to pay for an appeal.

The bay mare that Billy had been riding when he was captured at Stinking Springs was Billy's only asset. His ownership was in question because of claims that he had given the mare away. While in the Las Vegas jail he had asked Caypless to get the mare back from Moore, who was given the mare by Frank Stewart.

That action was dismissed by the court, so Caypless filed a second writ of replevin on April 19, asking return of the horse and $500 in damages. The horse was described in the writ as:

> "...one bay mare about fifteen hands high, with white star on forehead, branded -7 on left shoulder, which said mare is generally known and described as 'Billy the Kid's mare' and which was formerly owned by William Bonney alias 'Billy the Kid,' which said property is unlawfully withheld from him" [51]

That action was dismissed by the court also, so Caypless filed a writ of assumpsit. Assumpsit asserts that the party being sued has enriched themselves unjustly. In the case of the mare, Moore got the mare for nothing.[52]

On July 26, 1881, the court awarded Caypless a judgment of $50.95. By that date, the money could do Billy no good.[53]

Grounds for Appeal

Billy had several grounds for the appeal he never received.

In Territory versus Richard Romine, Romine was charged with murdering Patrick Rafferty with a hammer. (Rafferty was one of the 600 cavalryman in the military action known to history as "Charge of the Light Brigade" during the Crimean War.) Romine appealed his first degree murder conviction on two grounds relative to Billy's case: (1) the jury was all-Hispanic and spoke no English and (2) the instructions to the jury were given to the jury only in English. The Territorial Supreme Court denied the appeal.[54]

In Territory versus Damian Romero, Romero was charged with murdering William L. Brocksmit. Romero was 16 at the time of the killing. His victim was 17. Romero appealed based on two grounds: (1) one of the jurors in his trial was not a U.S. citizen and (2) the instructions to the jury did not permit the jury to consider any degree of murder except first degree, or any evidence that did not directly relate to the first degree murder charge. The Territorial Supreme Court denied the appeal on the citizen issue because the *"question was not raised until after the verdict."* On the issue of the jury instructions, the court, after reviewing the evidence in the case, ruled:

> "We cannot see how, under the circumstances disclosed by this evidence, and all the other evidence in the case, the court could have been required, or even justified, in leaving the case to the jury on any other degree of crime than that of murder in the first degree." [55]

Given these rulings, and with no witness (even Billy) to testify that Billy did not fire the shot or shots that killed Brady, an appeal by Billy would have been denied (even assuming no bias – probably a false assumption).

Conducting Billy to Lincoln

On April 15, two days after Billy's sentencing, Sheriff Southwick appointed Robert Olinger a special deputy:

"...charged with the special task of taking William Bonny (sic) alias the Kid alias Henry Antrim from the county seat of Dona Ana Co. and delivering him to the Sheriff of Lincoln County with full power and authority to summons posse or to do any and all things necessary for the safe delivery of said prisoner." [56]

The next day, in the evening, Billy began his trip to Lincoln:

"On Saturday night about ten o'clock deputy U. S. marshal Robt. Olinger with deputy sheriff David Wood and a posse of five men (Tom Williams, Billy Mathews, John Kinney, D. M. Reade and W. A. Lockhart) started for Lincoln with Henry Antrim alias the Kid. The fact that they intended to leave at that time had been purposely concealed and the report circulated that they would not leave before the middle of this week, in order to avoid any possibility of trouble, it having been rumored that Kid's band would attempt a rescue." [57]

Listing Lockhart as a posse member was an error; he was not one of the men taking Billy to Lincoln, according to county payment records.

There was plenty of moonlight for the trip, as the moon had risen at 9:30 p.m.[58]

Newman in *Newman's Semi-Weekly* reported:

"[Billy] was hand-cuffed and shackled and chained to the back seat of the ambulance. Kinney sat beside him, Mathews facing Kinney, Lockhart driving, and Reade, Wood and Williams riding along on horseback on each side and behind. The whole party was armed to the teeth...." [59]

The editor also reported that the posse stopped in front of his office on the way out of town:

"We handed the Kid an addressed envelope and some paper and he said he would write us some things he wanted to make public. He appeared quite cheerful and remarked that he wanted to stay with the boys until the whiskey gave out, any way."

"Said he was sure his guard would not hurt him unless a rescue should be attempted and he was certain that would not be done, unless, perhaps, 'those fellows over at White Oaks come out to take me,' meaning, to kill him. It was, he said, about a stand-off whether he was hanged or killed in the wagon."

"The Mesilla jail was the worst place he had ever struck. The sheriff wanted him to say something good about it when he left, but he had not done so." [60]

In addition to the teasing comment about letters from Billy, Newman wrote:

"We have had two interviews with Kid and have learned from him certain facts regarding the Lincoln county war and his own connection therewith which will be made public at the proper time. Having obtained our facts from him under promise not to divulge them until the proper time, we cannot cater to the curiosity of our readers regarding this man until that time arrives. He has

Ruins of the St. Nicolas Ranch where Billy and his guards spent the first night on their trip to Lincoln. Owned at the time by David L. Wood and Daniel M. Reade. Located on the White Sands Missile Range. 2010 photo.

appealed to Governor Wallace for a pardon or a commutation of his sentence; and until the result of this appeal is known we shall be obliged to put our readers off with promises" [61]

What were the facts that Newman and Billy believed should not be made public? This mystery, plus any information Billy might have supplied in his letters, is lost to history, because shortly after these items were published, *Newman's Semi-Weekly* ceased publication. This must have been the same information that Billy hinted at in his March 2, 1881, letter to Governor Wallace?

"I have some matters which date back two years and there are parties who are very anxious to get them, but I will not dispose of them until I see you. (The full letter is given on page 44.) [62]

There was grave concern among Mesilla authorities that an attempt would be made to either free Billy or – more likely – lynch him before he could be delivered to Sheriff Pat Garrett in Lincoln County. To prevent this, the first night of the 5-day trip was spent at the remote St. Nicolas Ranch. The St. Nicolas Ranch was located on the east side of the San Andres Mountains at St. Nicolas Springs. The site was eighteen miles north of San Augustin Pass and twelve miles off the road to Lincoln. [63]

The ranch was a natural place to stop because it was owned by two of the posse members, David Wood and Daniel Reade. Wood and Reade were both California Column Civil War veterans and were married to sisters.[64]

The second day, the posse spent the night at Patrick Coghlan's house in Tularosa. Coghlan and Billy knew each other well. Marcos Barrio, the mail carrier between Mesilla and Tularosa, reported to *Newman's Semi-Weekly* that he spoke to Billy there. Prior to Barrio's report, a wild rumor had been circulating around Mesilla that Billy had killed his guards and escaped.[65]

The third day, the posse spent the night at Blazer's Mill. That must have brought back a few memories of better times.

Where they spent the night the fourth day is unknown. Perhaps they camped somewhere on the road.

The fifth day they reached Fort Stanton. The next morning, April 21, the posse delivered Billy into the hands of Sheriff Garrett, as Olinger certified in his bill to Dona Ana County for his services:

> *"I Robert Olinger [charged with] the special duty of conveying William Bonny alias Kid alias William Antrim from Mesilla jail in said county and Territory to the county of Lincoln and Territory of New Mexico and delivering the said William Bonny alias Kid alias William Antrim to the Sheriff of the county of Lincoln and Territory of New Mexico do here by certify that I have this 21st day of April AD 1881 delivered the said William Bonney alias Kid alias William Antrim to the sheriff of the county of Lincoln Territory of New Mexico."* [66]

Olinger's bill shows that the six posse members were paid two dollars a day plus ten cents a mile for delivering Billy to Sheriff Garrett. They were reimbursed at the rate of twenty-five cents a day for food expenses.

Territory versus Clark, Murder of Robert R. Mann

Frank C. Clark was convicted of killing of Robert R. Mann. Clark had come to New Mexico in October, 1879, to find work with the A.T. & S.F. railroad, which was then laying track between San Marcial and Colorado (now Rodey). He obtained a job on a grading crew. Mann was a grader on the same crew.

> *"When the work of grading reached Colorado in December Clark was still at work, and one night while in camp the mules belonging to his employer's outfit were stolen while in Clark's care. Clark acted in a queer manner, and many suspected him of having been connected with the stealing. Mann expressed the belief in Clark's guilt, and the latter having hearing (sic) of it swore he would shoot Mann on sight."* [67]

Clark left the grading crew after that accusation and travelled to Dona Ana, where he rented a building for a saloon, saying that while he did not have the money to pay the rent, an acquaintance would in a few days. Clark opened his saloon on New Year's Day. That evening he spotted Mann in town and invited him into the saloon.

> *"Mann never came out of the building alive, nor was the saloon ever opened for business after that day. The next morning Clark was gone and the dead body*

of Mann lay on the floor with six bullet holes in it, the clothing entirely burned off and the body so blackened and burned as to be scarcely recognizable."

"The witnesses to the murder, who were scarcely sober enough to realize what was going on about them, say that when Mann entered the saloon, Clark drew his revolver and fired three shots at his unsuspecting victim, all of which took effect. Mann fell and Clark ran out at the door, but returned in a moment, fired three more shots into Mann's prostrate body. It is supposed that one of the bullets in striking the fire-place, near which the body was laying, threw out the fire from which Mann's clothing caught fire." [68]

The *Mesilla News* noted:

"The strangest part of the whole affair is that the body was burned on the side opposite the fire...." [69]

Clark's defense in his trial was that he had fired the first three shots in self-defense. The last three were immaterial, as Mann was already dead. Further, Mann's clothes were set on fire by a former partner. All aspects of Mann's alibi were contradicted by prosecution witnesses.

Interviewed in jail on the day of his hanging, May 13, 1881, Clark said, *"I would kill Mann again under like circumstances."* [70]

"Sheriff Southwick... had charge of the arrangements of the execution. The gallows was a light structure erected in a little valley near the Rio Grande, about a quarter of a mile from this place. By the laws of the territory all executions must be public...." [71]

"Sheriff started from the jail with prisoner and guard about 1 p. m. Friday followed by a large number of people." [72]

Mary Doughty Henschel, who like Stoes was a student in the courtroom school at the time, wrote:

"Once there was holiday for a double hanging. We wept as we saw the black-robed nuns praying with them." [73]

People began gathering at the hanging site three hours before the scheduled execution. A reporter estimated the crowd size at 175, almost all men, but a few women.

"Soon the funeral car came down from the jail, bearing the condemned man seated on the coffin that was soon to receive all that was mortal of Clark. The team was a common farm wagon driven by Kinney the mail contractor. When the team was stopped near the gallows, Clark jumped out lightly, having on the shackles or hand-cuffs." [74]

"[Clark] asked the sheriff if he could 'go to say good-bye to the sisters [of the Loretio Academy].' Sheriff answered yes, and walked with him to the carriage of the 3 sisters. Notwithstanding their efforts tears came to their eyes, while Clark appeared to choke up so he could not speak, being the first time he had shown any unusual emotion; put his hand up to shake hands; one sister said 'we will pray for you; in a little while you will be in another home,' another said 'I'm sorry,' the last said 'step up (meaning on the scaffold) with a firm step.' C.

shook hands but could not speak; walked up on the platform with a firm step, followed by the sheriff and Rev. [Augustine] Morin."

"He looked at the rope; Rev. Morin said in a few minutes it will be all over with. C. replied, 'I am ready to go and willing to go.' The Rev. Father then asked him to kneel which he did, and he gave absolution, in a few words. C. arose when Father said 'all is now ready, goodbye,' shaking hands. C. said 'Goodbye.' The reporter of THE NEWS asked C. if he had anything to say. He replied 'no nothing. It will do no good.'"

"The Sheriff then stepped to him, when C. asked, 'How much drop you got?' Sheriff said 5 feet. C [said], 'I think that ought to be drop enough.'" [75]

The problem a sheriff faced when executing a person by hanging was how far the body should drop when the gallows' trapdoor was sprung. If the drop was too far, the head of the condemned was ripped off. That happened in a famous New Mexico case when Tom "Black Jack" Ketchum was executed on April 26, 1901.[76] If the drop was too short, the condemned did not break his neck, leading to a slow, cruel death by strangulation. Breaking the condemned's neck was the intended and most humane outcome, because it produced rapid unconsciousness.

A few years after Clark's execution, the British Government took a scientific approach to the question of hanging and created a "Table of Drops." The Table of Drops gave the recommended distance a condemned person should fall to achieve a broken neck, but not pull his head off, based on the person's weight.[77]

After Clark had mounted the scaffold, he was asked if he had any final words:

"Clark said that he was living under an alias but would not disclose his right name. He further stated that he had a wife and children but would not reveal the place of their residence, preferring that they should never hear of his end." [78]

The account by the *Mesilla News* continued:

"Sheriff stepped behind and tied his arms, and commenced to tie his legs above the knees when C. said 'Down a little lower Jim.' Sheriff said, 'No, I'll tie twice (meaning above and below the knees),' proceeding to do so. C. said, 'It is not necessary to tie them so tight.'"

"Sheriff on the side put the noose around his neck, drawing it tight; C. said 'that's right, put it right round my ear, so that when I drop it won't slip.' C. complained several times about getting the rope 'a little too tight.' Sheriff said no, it is not tight enough. C. then said 'There that will do.'"

"Sheriff then put on the black cap over his head and started to the steps and the same instant gave the signal by jerking his handkerchief out of his left breast coat pocket, when Dave Woods (sic) cut the rope the double door trap dropped, C. fell breaking his neck, and never moved or jerked once."

"Dr. Munger examined the body and found that the pulse ceased seven minutes after the fall, and after twenty-one minutes Dr. Vilas of Las Vegas pronounced the man dead and he was cut down." [79]

The newspaper report states that Clark's pulse *"ceased seven minutes after the fall."* How did the reporter know this so precisely? Court regulations required that a doctor be present when a condemned man (or woman) was hanged. The doctor's job was to certify that the condemned had died. The doctor did this by "pulsing" the condemned man. As soon as the body plunged through the trapdoor, the doctor began taking the man's pulse, recording it. When the pulse dropped to zero, he pronounced the man dead. For more on pulsing, see the next section.

Clark had joined the Catholic Church two weeks before his hanging and had received confession. Following his death, Clark's remains were placed in the coffin he had ridden to the hanging on, taken to the San Albino Catholic Church for a funeral service, and then buried in the Mesilla Cemetery.[80]

Billy, who read the Territorial newspapers whenever he could, probably read of Clark's hanging and felt great relief that he had avoided that fate.

Territory versus Barela, Murder of José Jojola

Santos Barela was convicted of killing José Jojola. Following his trial, it was revealed that Barela's real name was Santos Bermudes. He was 21 years old.

Barela, like Clark, was working on a grading crew for the railroad. On the evening of February 18, 1881, he went into Colorado to visit a friend who owned a house there. Shortly after Barela's arrival, José and his wife came to the house:

> *"After some hours spent in the company of Barela at the house of their mutual acquaintance Mr. and Mrs. Jojola took their leave and repaired to their own home only a few rods distant. Barela almost immediately left the house also and followed them....*
>
> *"The Jojolas reached home and the husband who was feeling somewhat indisposed lay down on the bed while his wife proceeded to light a candle. Jojola had but just lain down when... Barela entered. Noiselessly he approached the bedside of the unsuspecting Jojola and placing a 45 calibre pistol to his head blew out his brains"."* [81]

Mrs. Jojola ran from the house, screaming. Barela followed her and flung her to the ground a few yards from the house. As Barela was attempting to rape her, a man named Franco Guereno approached and helped Barela pin her down.

Mrs. Jojola's cries brought her to the attention of a passerby, who freed her from Barela's and Guereno's hold.

> *"Barela followed her and fired four shots at her as she was entering an adjoining house."* [82]

Barela was arrested by the Colorado constable and taken to the Lynch Brothers Store, where he was confined overnight. A crowd gathered around the store, intending to lynch Barela, which was only prevented with great difficulty. The next morning he was handed over to Sheriff Southwick at Mesilla.[83]

When Barela was asked about the crime, he said, *"I killed him."* He added, *"I am a man; I like his wife; and have money to pay for it."* [84]

The same gallows that was used to hang Clark was used to hang Barela (but not the same rope, in respect for the hanged). However, as a result of criticism due to the presence of women at Clark's hanging, the scaffold was erected in the placita of the Mesilla jail, obscuring it from the public. Only *"reporters, physicians and a few others, probably 60 persons in all"* were permitted to observe the hanging. The date was May 21, 1881.

> *"Barela slept soundly on his last night on earth, and this morning partook of a hearty breakfast. The hour of execution was fixed at 1 o'clock, as in Clark's case. The morning was spent by the condemned man in prayer and consultation with Father Morin and the Sisters. At 10 o'clock he took some refreshment and appeared quite cheerful."*

> *"About 12 he drank a cup of coffee. At 12:45, his shackles were taken off and he was conducted from his cell to an outer room of the prison [the jailor's office], where the death warrant was read to him in the Spanish language by A. J. Fountain, Esq. The room was the same in which F. C. Clark had listened to the reading of a similar document a week before."* [85]

Stoes wrote of Barela's execution:

> *"As a little child of 8 years I sat in my seat in this court room and looked across the patio to see a man sitting behind the iron-barred door, sentenced to die on the gallows. Day after day he sat there... shackled hand and feet, reading his prayer book, and looking at the ground."*

> *"When the time came to build the scaffold in the patio we were dismissed. During his execution I stayed most of the time in my bedroom, praying for the poor man for whom my heart was so torn."* [86]

Barela faltered badly as he began to climb the scaffold. He was helped into position over the trapdoor by Father Morin.

> *"He was dressed in a black alpaca coat, black cloth pants, a new pair of shoes, bought for the occasion, and a broad brimmed black slouch hat, and wore on his breast a crucifix."*

> *"...he took off his hat and threw it on the scaffold in front of him, and kneeling down received Father Morin's last blessing."* [87]

Sheriff Southwick asked if he had any last words. Barela replied, *"No señor."*

> *"The sheriff then proceeded to bind his limbs and when he came to the arms Barela asked that they be tied so he could reach the crucifix with his hands. The rope was next adjusted, and as the black cap was drawn over his face the condemned man tottered to one side and would undoubtedly have fallen in another minute, but the sheriff quickly stepped from the trap and drew a white handkerchief from his pocket as a signal for his deputy to cut the rope which held the trap in place."*

> *"In a twinkling the trap doors parted beneath Barela's feet and his body shot downward its full length where with no sound save a dull thud it was caught by the rope and rebounded upward nearly a foot, then dangled at the end of the rope motionless and seemingly lifeless. Not a muscle moved after the drop."* [88]

The newspaper then published the result of pulsing Barela:

> *"The trap was sprung at precisely 12:52 o'clock. At 12:55 his pulse beat 60; at 12:58, 100; at 1:02, 32; ceasing at 1:05, exactly thirteen minutes after the fall."* [89]

It is relatively rare to see this ghoulish information published. None of the accounts mention where Barela was buried. He was probably buried in the Mesilla cemetery.

In both Clark's and Barela's cases, the hanging successfully broke the men's necks. When 17-year-old Damian Romero, mentioned in the "Grounds for Appeal" section of this chapter, was hanged, his neck did not break. As soon as Romero's body dropped through the trapdoor:

> *"The whole frame quivered, the muscles contracted, showing he was slowly but surely dying by strangulation. At one time the body was bent half double...."*

> *"The drop fell at 2:08 p.m. railroad time; pulse at 2:14 [was] 122; 2:15, 82; 2:16, 40; 2:17, no pulsation at the wrists or heart."*

> *"At 2:20 Romero was pronounced dead and the body taken down. It seemed that the most difficult part of the disagreeable proceeding had to be gone through with. This was getting the rope off the neck of the law's victim. Several persons tried to loosen it, but without avail. At last the sheriff lifted the head out of the coffin and placed it in his lap. Part of the rope was cut, and, after much pulling and twisting, it was taken from the neck of the dead boy."* [90]

Romero was hanged by San Miguel County Sheriff Bowman on January 31, 1883.

Chapter 9 | End of the Road

Escape

Sheriff Garrett gained custody of Billy on April 21, 1881. The following day Garrett had Billy imprisoned in the Lincoln County Courthouse.[1]

Because Lincoln had no jail at the time, two upstairs rooms in the County Courthouse were being used as the town's jail. Billy was confined alone in the smaller of the two jail rooms, which was considered the most secure.[2] The larger jail room contained five prisoners judged low-risk for escaping. Those prisoners were even permitted to retain their handguns![3] A third upstairs room served as Sheriff Garrett's office and a place *"where were kept surplus arms."*[4]

Billy's guards were Sheriff Garrett, Deputy Sheriff James W. Bell, and Deputy Marshal Robert Olinger. Garrett noted:

> *"During the few days the Kid remained in confinement, I [Garrett] had several conversations with him. He appeared to have a plausible excuse for every crime charged against him, except, perhaps, the killing of Carlyle."*[5]

> *"He expressed no enmity toward me for having been the instrument through which he was brought to justice...."*

> *"As to his guards, he placed great confidence in Bell and appeared to take a great liking to him. Bell had been in no manner connected with the Lincoln County War and had no animosity or old grudge against the Kid...."*

> *"As to Olinger, the case was altogether different. He and the Kid had met opposed in arms frequently during the past years of anarchy. Bob Beckwith, the bosom friend of Olinger, had been killed by the Kid at the close of the three days' fight in Lincoln. The Kid likewise charged Olinger with the killing of friends of his. Between these two there existed a reciprocal hatred and neither attempted to disguise or conceal his antipathy from the other."*[6]

Billy had a more immediate reason to despise Olinger. Olinger, by several accounts, continually bullied him during the trip from Mesilla to Fort Stanton.[7]

Notice that Garrett states that, in his opinion, Billy had a *"plausible"* (justifiable) reason for killing Sheriff Brady. Quite an admission!

On April 27, Garrett was obliged to leave Lincoln for White Oaks to collect county taxes, a regular duty of his sheriff's job. Bell and Olinger were left in charge of the prisoners.[8]

The next day, the *Las Vegas Gazette* published an astonishing interview with Governor Wallace:

> *"The conversation drifted into the sentence of 'THE KID.'"*

> *"It looks as though he would hang, governor."*

Lincoln County Courthouse. 1920's photo. Courtesy Maurice G. Fulton Papers, Special Collections, UA.

Lincoln County Courthouse. 1952 postcard. The white "x" marks the window from which Billy shot Deputy Marshal Robert Olinger.

"Yes, the chances seem good that the 13th of May would finish him."

"He appears to look to you to save his neck."

"'Yes,' said Gov. Wallace smiling, 'but I can't see how a fellow like him should expect any clemency from me.'"

"Although not committing himself, the general tenor of the governor's remarks indicated that he would resolutely refuse to grant 'the Kid' a pardon. It would seem as though 'the Kid' had undertaken to bulldoze the governor, which has not helped his chances in the slightest." [9]

Here is Governor Wallace making public his decision to not issue Billy a pardon. He also lets the reporter know that he resents Billy's efforts to remind him of his promise 773 days earlier. Whether the word "bulldoze" is his or the reporter's, it and the whole tenor of the interview expresses more than irritation – it conveys contempt that someone so obviously beneath Governor Wallace's social status – *"a fellow like him"* – could have the audacious temerity to keep reminding him, Wallace, that he had once given Billy his solemn word. It even suggests a bit of revenge on Billy for repeatedly reminding him of something he desired to forget.

Did Billy get a chance to see this interview in the *Gazette*? Or was he perhaps just told about it? The paper could easily have been delivered to Lincoln by mid afternoon. There was also telegraph service between Lincoln and Las Vegas to convey the news.

If Billy did learn of the interview, it would explain why he picked that particular day to escape.

That evening, about 5 p.m., Olinger took the prisoners from the larger jail room to Lilly's restaurant across the street for a meal – giving Billy precisely what he wanted – an ideal opportunity to escape.[10]

How Billy actually engineered the escape is unknown. Based on his investigation, Garrett gave the following account:

"At the Kid's request, Bell accompanied him down stairs and into the back corral [where the jail latrine was]. As they returned, Bell allowed the Kid to get considerably in advance. As the Kid turned on the landing of the stairs, he was hidden from Bell. He was light and active, and, with a few noiseless bounds, reached the head of the stairs, turned to the right, put his shoulder to the door of the room used as an armory (though locked, this door was well known to open by a firm push), entered, seized a six-shooter, returned to the head of the stairs just as Bell faced him on the landing of the stair-case, some twelve steps beneath, and fired. Bell turned, ran out into the corral and towards the little gate. He fell dead before reaching it." [11]

Several contemporary writers put forth an alternate explanation of the escape, based on Billy swinging his handcuffs as a bludgeon:

"[Olinger] had just gone to his supper, and Bell was sitting down on the floor, when 'Kid' approached him, talking in his pleasant way. Quick as lightning he jumped and struck Bell with his handcuffs, fracturing the skull. He immediately snatched Bell's revolver and shot him through the breast." [12]

Robert Ameredith Olinger. Undated photo. Courtesy Maurice G. Fulton Papers,
Special Collections, UA.

"*It seems the Kid had struck Bell over the head with the handcuffs and back of the ear also, breaking his skull and stunning him and then grabbing from Bell his revolver; and Bell, after partially recovering from the effects of the blow, started to run out of the hall and down stairs and Kid fired a shot at him which passed under Bell's arms and clear through his body. Bell ran towards the kitchen and old man Goss [Gottfried Gauss] was just coming out of it and Bell fell into his arms and expired without a word.*" [13]

A twist was added to this explanation by suggesting that Billy already had one hand free:

"*As time passes and further facts concerning the Kid's escape come in, the more wonderful and daring it appears. The hand-cuffs had been taken from his left hand, to allow him to eat supper. Watching an opportunity he dealt J. W. Bell a blow with the irons on his right hand. This broke his skull and as he fell the Kid grabbed his pistol and finished the work.*" [14]

"*At noon Olinger went to dinner and Bell exposed himself a little when 'Kid,' who could slip his handcuffs, seized Bell's pistol, knocked him down with it, and as he rose, shot him dead.*" [15]

Years later it was suggested that an unidentified accomplice had concealed a pistol in the outdoor latrine, which Billy retrieved and used to shoot Bell and escape. The fact that this theory was not suggested by any witness at the time, and the strong insistence in contemporary accounts that the gun that killed Bell was either seized from the jail armory or was Bell's own, casts serious doubt on this theory.

Gottfried Gauss, an eye-witness, offered the following account of what happened next:

"*That memorable day I came out of my room, whence I had gone to light my pipe, and was crossing the yard behind the court-house, when I heard a shot fired, a tussle up the stairs in the court-house, somebody hurrying down stairs, and deputy sheriff Bell emerging from the door running toward me. He ran right into my arms, expired the same moment, and I laid him down, dead....*"

"*...I saw the other deputy sheriff, Olinger, coming out of the hotel opposite, with the other four or five county prisoners where they had taken their dinner. I called to him to come quick. He did so, leaving his prisoners in front of the hotel. When he had come close up to me, and while standing not more than a yard apart, I told him that I was just after laying Bell dead on the ground in the yard behind, and before he could reply, he was struck by a well directed shot fired from a window above us, and fell dead at my feet.*" [16]

Olinger was shot with his own shotgun, which Billy had retrieved from Garrett's office. Another account of the shooting revealed just how intensely personal Olinger's killing was for Billy:

"*...Kid aimed at him through the window with a double-barreled shot gun and fired, hitting Olinger in the breast and after he fell emptied the other barrel, loaded with buck shot, in his shoulder. It is reported that the Kid then came out on the porch, broke the stock of the gun from the barrel and threw the pieces at*

Gottfried Gauss, eye-witness to Billy's escape from the Lincoln County Courthouse. Undated photograph. Courtesy Courtesy Archives and Special Collections, NMSU.

the corpse, at the same time saying, 'You will never follow me again with that gun.'" [17]

Gauss continued:

"...Billy the Kid called to me: 'Don't run, I wouldn't hurt you – I am alone, and master, not only of the court-house, but also of the town, for I will allow nobody to come near us. You go,' he said, 'and saddle one of Judge Leonard's horses, and I will clear out as soon as I can have the shackles loosened from my legs.' With a little prospecting pick I had thrown to him through the window he was working for at least an hour, and could not accomplish more than to free one leg, and he came to the conclusion to await a better chance, tie one shackle to his waist-belt, and start out. Meanwhile I had saddled a small skittish pony belonging to Billy Burt, as there was no other horse available, and had also, by Billy's command, tied a pair of red blankets behind the saddle...."

"When Billy went down stairs at last, on passing the body of Bell, he said, 'I'm sorry I had to kill him but couldn't help it.' On passing the body of Olinger, he gave him a tip with his boot, saying, 'You are not going to round me up again.'"

"We went out together where I had tied up the pony, and he told me to tell the owner of same, Billy Burt, that he would send it back next day. I, for my part, didn't much believe in this promise, but, sure enough, next morning, the pony arrived safe and sound, trailing a long lariat, at the court house in Lincoln." [18]

Various accounts report that Billy took as long as one hour to leave Lincoln. Yet no one attempted to block or restrain him. The *Las Vegas Daily Optic* published a letter signed simply "Durango" by a man who claimed to have watched Billy escape:

"The pusillamity (sic) of such conduct by a whole town, and that town the county seat, is almost incredible. Yet such is the fact. Mr. Lilly, the keeper of the restaurant opposite the court house, got down his gun and would have fired on Kid but was deferred by two men who were with him. Mr. J. H. LaRue got his gun down and was going to fire but was prevented by his wife. The balance of the population, whether friends or enemies to the Kid, manifested no disposition to molest him." [19] (Durango evidently did not feel any compulsion to draw a weapon himself.)

The news of Billy's escape was rapidly communicated to Garrett:

"On the 29th, I received a letter from John C. Delaney, Esq., of Fort Stanton, merely stating the fact of the Kid's escape and the killing of the guard. The same day Billy Nickey arrived from Lincoln and gave me the particulars." [20]

On April 30, Garrett returned to Lincoln. The day before a hastily-convened coroner's jury had formally ruled the two guards' killings an unjustified homicide, perpetrated by Billy the Kid. Garrett reconstructed the shooting of Bell as follows:

"It was found that Bell was hit under the right arm, the ball passing through the body and going out under the left arm. On examination it was evident that the Kid had made a very poor shot, for him, and his hitting Bell at all was a

scratch. The ball had hit the wall on Bell's right, caromed, passed through his body, and buried itself in an adobe on his left. There was other proof besides the marks on the wall. The ball had surely been indented and creased before it entered the body, as these scars were filled with flesh." [21]

Billy's escape was just 15 days before his scheduled hanging – Friday, May 13, 1881. On April 30, without knowing that Billy had escaped, Governor Wallace issued Billy's death warrant. The warrant was signed in Wallace's name by acting Governor William Ritch. [22]

The news of Billy's escape flashed across the territory, with the Santa Fe and Las Vegas newspapers the first to report the escape. But Billy's prior exploits had been reported nationally, and his escape was big news throughout the nation. Dozens of news-papers from California to New York reported the escape, in front page stories.

Garrett expressed his feelings about the escape as follows:

"[It] was a most distressing calamity, for which I do not hold myself guilt-less. The Kid's escape, and the murder of his two guards, was the result of mis-management and carelessness, to a great extent. I knew the desperate character of the man... that he was daring and unscrupulous, and that he would sacrifice the lives of a hundred men who stood between him and liberty, when the gallows stared him in the face, with as little compunction as he would kill a coyote."

"[I] now realize how inadequate my precautions were. Yet, in self-defense, and hazarding the charge of shirking the responsibility and laying it upon dead men's shoulders, I must say that my instructions as to caution and the routine of duty were not heeded and followed." [23]

The Hunt

When Billy rode out of Lincoln, he was armed with *"two new revolvers, four belts of cartridges, and a new Winchester,"* courtesy of Garrett's office armory. [24]

His first stop was at his old friend Yginio Salazar's family's ranch, west of Lincoln, where he was able to cut off the shackles that were still-attached to one leg. Billy knew that Salazar was just one of the many Lincoln County residents that he could rely on for help. As the Santa Fe newspaper put it:

"A man who came to Santa Fe yesterday from Lincoln county says that Billy the Kid has got more friends in that county than anybody. He gets all the money he wants, takes horses when he needs them, and makes no bones of going into and out of various towns." [25]

On learning of Billy's escape, Governor Wallace immediately issued a reward for his re-capture:

"$500 REWARD"

"I will pay $500 reward to any person or persons who will capture William Bonny (sic), alias the Kid, and deliver him to any sheriff of New Mexico. Satisfactory presents of identity will be required."

"Lew Wallace, Governor of New Mexico" [26]

Garrett's reaction was more sanguine:

"During the weeks following the Kid's escape, I was censured by some for my seeming unconcern and inactivity in the matter of his re-arrest. I was egotistical enough to think I knew my own business best, and preferred to accomplish this duty, if possible at all, in my own way. I was constantly, but quietly, at work, seeking sure information and maturing my plans of action." [27]

Meanwhile, Billy was also tracking Garrett's actions, as reported in the press:

"The Kid says he is among friends and is all right. His friends keep him provided with newspapers and he seems well satisfied in his present quarters." [28]

Instead of fleeing to Mexico, which Garrett thought his most probable (and smartest) action, Billy stayed in the Lincoln area, splitting his time between trusted sheep camps and ranches and fairly regular visits to Fort Sumner.

Within a few days of Billy's escape, the Territorial press began to publish wildly speculative reports about Billy. The *Daily New Mexican*, in a report that was picked up by almost all of the New Mexico newspapers, wrote that Billy had killed ex-sheriff Jacob Mathews. That story was later debunked.[29]

A few days later, the same paper reported that a Mr. Richard Dunham:

"...met the Kid at Stinking Springs and had a conversation with him. The Kid said then that he was going to Salt Lake [City] but that he intended being in Santa Fe on his trip." [30] (Like Billy would be hanging out at Stinking Springs!)

The *Las Vegas Gazette* reported:

"On Sunday he [Billy] was seen by quite a number of people in the neighborhood of [Fort] Sumner, and was talked with on that day by men who know him well. It is thought that Billy is on the lookout for Barney Mason, who was then in Sumner. 'The Kid' never had any great love for Barney, and especially since he assisted in the capture of Billy and party at Stinking Springs. He is said to have sworn to kill Mason, and will undoubtedly make an effort to work out his vengeance." [31]

The *Daily New Mexican* reported a *"man very well known in Santa Fe"* had encountered Billy in Chloride City:

"I slept with the Kid last night and did not know who he was. I see him across the street now." [32]

A few days later, the *Las Vegas Daily Optic* published this report by *"a gentleman from Fort Sumner:"*

"A few days ago [Billy] met Barney Mason and another man and, by throwing up his hands, led the men to suppose that he was disposed to be friendly. Barney, being more suspicious than his comrade, at once took to his heels, but his comrade approached 'Billy' and had a conversation with him. [33]

The *Las Vegas Daily Optic* followed that report with this one:

"'Billy, the Kid,' has been heard from again, this time near Roswell, in Lincoln county, and three more murders are set down against him."

"About dusk a few days ago he rode up to a cow camp of John Chisum, in which there were four men, three sitting around the fire engaged in preparing supper and the fourth some distance away hobbling horses. Approaching the last mentioned man he asked 'are you working for old John Chisum?' and receiving a reply in the affirmative he remarked, 'well, here is your pay' and killed him."

"The remaining three seeing their comrade thus ruthlessly murdered jumped to their feet, but, before they could draw their revolvers, the Kid had killed two of them, and leveling his pistol at the fourth one commanded him to throw up his hands; the order was promptly obeyed and, after informing him that his life had been spared so that he could deliver a message to Chisum, the Kid told him that he fought for Chisum all through the Lincoln county war and that Chisum had agreed to pay him therefore $5 per day and that he had never received one cent from him. 'Tell him I am living now to get even with my enemies; I shall kill his men wherever I find them and credit him with five dollars for each man I kill. Whenever I see him I will kill him and call the account square, said this incarnate fiend." [34]

The *Daily New Mexican* republished that story and added:

"While this story may be and probably is somewhat exaggerated, still it is certainly true in its main facts, so far as your correspondent by every investigation is able to ascertain." [35]

The *Las Vegas Morning Gazette* finally published an account that was based on hard information.

"Yesterday we took the opportunity to interview Barney Mason, who is in town, in reference to the whereabouts of Billy the Kid and what he has been doing since his tragic escape from Lincoln."

"Barney trailed him from Lincoln to Fort Sumner. He went first to or about the Agua Azul where he lost the horse taken from Lincoln. He laid down to sleep and in saddling the horse in the morning, the bronco broke away from him. He went from there down about Newcomb's cow camp. There he took a horse from one of his men and rode from there to the Consios Springs. There he slept again.... From there he made his way to Fort Sumner by the west side of the river."

"Mason is confident that Billy at present is about twelve miles above Sumner at the Segura ranch and that he is staying around in that vicinity at the sheep camps. The report that the Kid had killed three herders for Chisum is entirely false and without foundation." [36]

Newcomb is John Newcomb, the man who recovered Tunstall's body after his murder.

The fact that the horse Billy escaped on broke away from him the next morning while being saddled would explain why it showed up that day in Lincoln *"trailing a long lariat."* The animal's return was an accident, not the discharging of a promise, as inferred by Gauss.

Why Did Billy Not Leave the Area?

There were two reasons, one certain, one speculative.

It is certain that Billy had wide support among the Hispanic community of Lincoln County. The Lincoln County War had pitted a primarily Anglo faction against a mixed Anglo-Hispanic faction, although the leaders of both sides were Anglos. Most of Billy's Anglo friends had abandoned him by the time of his trial, while many Hispanics remained loyal, seeing him as someone who had fought with them against systematic Anglo oppression.

When Billy escaped the Lincoln jail, he had nothing but what he stole as he was leaving. Heading for Mexico with absolutely no money was risky and daunting. If he had truly been the ruthless outlaw his opponents portrayed him as, he would have turned to robbery for funds. But Billy had never robbed anyone in his life (rustling was viewed as a much lesser crime than armed robbery, even justifiable in some cases). When he was accused of holding-up Con Cosgrove's stage on October 16, 1880, (in his underclothes!) it was widely believed. Of course, later, Rudabaugh's jailhouse confession absolved Billy of any involvement in that crime (see page 29).

Between the perilous choice of striking out for Mexico and the known and agreeable choice of hanging out with his Hispanic friends and supporters, Billy chose the latter.

There is likely a second reason Billy did not leave the Lincoln county area – he wanted to remain close to a girlfriend.

Who Was Billy's Girlfriend?

Four main candidates have been proposed:

- Deluvina Maxwell, an adopted member of the Maxwell family
- Celsa (Martinez) Gutierrez, the sister of Sheriff Garrett's first wife
- Abrana (Segura) Garcia, possibly Deluvina's sister
- Paulita Maxwell, Pete Maxwell's younger sister

Deluvina Maxwell was a Navajo taken captive as a young child by Utes. When she was about nine years old, she was freed by Lucien Maxwell, probably by being purchased from her Native American captors. She then became a household servant and member of the Maxwell family.[37]

Undoubtedly, Deluvina had deep feelings for Billy, referring to him with endearments such as *"mi muchacho"* (my boy). [38] When asked about Billy not long before her death, she said, *"Billy the Kid was my compadre, my friend, poor Billy."* [39] But. at 33, she was more than ten years older than Billy, an obvious obstacle. Her oft-expressed affectionate feelings for Billy are the sole evidence for an <u>intimate</u> relationship. But Billy did cherish her friendship and loyalty, as exhibited by the fact that he gave her one of the four tintype plates of him known to have been made by the anonymous photographer at Fort Sumner. That tintype was later lost in a fire.[40] (See page 4.)

The candidate some historians have settled on is Celsa (Martinez) Gutierrez. If Celsa was Billy's girlfriend, there is a bizarre and concealed twist to this relationship. Celsa's maiden name was Martinez. Her father was Albino Martinez. Her sister was Juanita

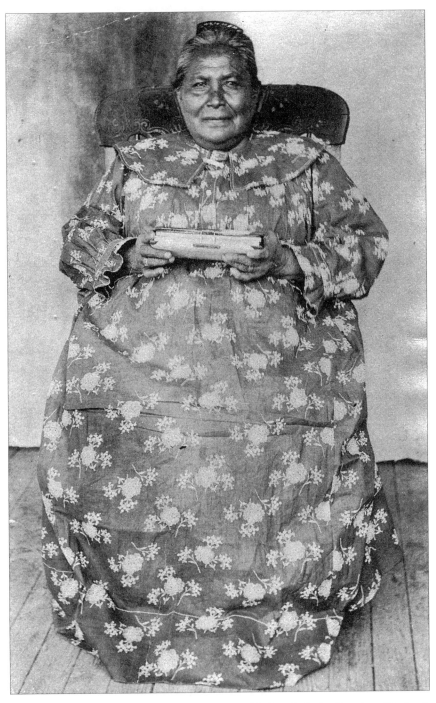

Deluvina Maxwell at her home in Fort Sumner. Undated photo. Courtesy Center for Southwest Research and Special Collections, UNM.

Paulita (Paula) Maxwell. Undated photo. Courtesy Arthur Johnson Memorial Library.

Martinez, who had married Pat Garrett in November, 1879. Juanita died within days of the marriage, after becoming violently ill during the marriage celebration.[41] She was buried in the Fort Sumner cemetery.

Within two months of Juanita Martinez's death, on January 14, 1880, Garrett married Apolinaria Gutierrez, daughter of José Dolores Gutierrez. At the time of his two marriages, Garrett was living in Fort Sumner. He was also serving as deputy sheriff of Lincoln County, having been appointed to that position just prior to his marriage to Juanita Martinez.[42]

Garrett's two witnesses in the wedding were Manuel Fernando Abreu and Alejandro Segura. Manuel Abreu was at Fort Sumner when Billy was killed and saw the body. Alejandro Segura was the Justice of the Peace on the coroner's jury that ruled Billy's killing justifiable homicide.[43]

How more intimate with and knowledgeable of the community around Fort Sumner could Garrett be?

He lived there, married the daughter of one Fort Sumner area family, and then when she died, married the daughter of a second Fort Sumner area family. In addition, his business as deputy sheriff was to know what was going on within the community.

In May, 1881 – when Garrett was hunting Billy – Celsa Martinez was Celsa (Martinez) Gutierrez, having married Sabal Gutierrez four years earlier. If Billy's girlfriend in Fort Sumner was Celsa (Martinez) Gutierrez, then Garrett was hunting for someone (Billy) who was in a likely intimate relationship with the sister of his deceased first wife – in an area Garrett knew well, among people he knew well – something he gave no hint of in his written account of searching for Billy.

One of Garrett's deputies at the time of the search, John William Poe, did allude to this undisclosed knowledge:

"Garrett seemed to have but little confidence in our being able to accomplish the object of our trip, but said that he knew the location of a certain house occupied by a woman in Fort Sumner which the Kid had formerly frequented...." [44]

Celsa (Martinez) Gutierrez was living with her husband Sabal Gutierrez, and they had a four year old daughter, Mauricia.[45] It seems unlikely that Sabal would tolerate a relationship of any degree of intimacy between his wife and Billy. In addition, Sabal was a loyal friend of Billy.

Note: There were two Celsa Gutierrez's in Fort Sumner in May, 1881. Numerous writers have confused the two. The first Celsa (Martinez) Gutierrez, Billy's possible girlfriend, was 23 in 1881. Her parents were Albino and Feliciana Martinez. Celsa Martinez becomes a Gutierrez by marrying Sabal Gutierrez.

The second Celsa Gutierrez was also 23 in 1881. Her parents were José Dolores Gutierrez and Feliciana (Valdez) Gutierrez. This Celsa Gutierrez, who has not been suggested as a girlfriend of Billy, was the sister of Apolinaria Gutierrez, Garrett's second wife. Thus, the often repeated statement that Billy's girlfriend was Garrett's wife's sister is correct only if the reference is to Garrett's deceased first wife – but usually it is intended to mean the sister of Apolinaria, his second wife.

The third candidate for girlfriend is Abrana (Segura) Garcia. Current descendents of Abrana report that, like Deluvina Maxwell, she was a Navajo who had been captured by Utes and then freed; she may have been a younger sister of Deluvina. She was raised by Fernando and Manuela Segura as Abrana Segura.[46]

In 1880, Abrana was 22 years old and married to Martin Garcia. Living with Abrana and Martin were three children, aged seven years, five years, and five months. The two oldest children were Martin's children from a previous relationship.[47]

There is a long tradition among the descendents of Abrana (Segura) Garcia that she was Billy's girlfriend, and even that she had a son by him.[48]

The last candidate, Paulita Maxwell, is the only one suggested by a contemporary public source:

> *"It is stated that Billy was hanging around Maxwell's place for the purpose of courting Maxwell's sister, who had captured his heart."* [49]

When, in later life, Paulita was asked if this was true, she denied it:

> *"An old story that identifies me as Billy the Kid's sweetheart... has been going the rounds for many years. Perhaps it honors me; perhaps not; it depends on how you feel about it. But I was not Billy the Kid's sweetheart. I liked him very much – oh, yes – but I did not love him."* [50]

This denial, printed in Walter Noble Burns' 1926 book, *"The Saga of Billy the Kid,"* was not questioned by Burns in his book, which led to its general acceptance by subsequent historians. But in recent years, Burns' original manuscript has become available. In the original manuscript, Burns preceded Paulita's denial with statements by several people affirming that she <u>was</u> Billy's girlfriend. These included Paulita's sister, Odila Maxwell Abreu, who stated:

> *"There is no secret about it. Billy the Kid was madly in love with Paulita."* [51]

Poe is quoted as telling Burns:

> *"Paulita Maxwell was awakened by the shot that killed her sweetheart. It was generally reported that she and the Kid were to be married and I was rather surprised that she showed little emotion when she stood beside his dead body."* [52]

Burns removed these statements from the published version of the book at the request of his publisher, who was concerned about liability for libel.

Additional evidence for the relationship is provided by a letter written by Sheriff Southwick. Southwick wrote that when Billy:

> *"...was in jail [in Mesilla] he showed me a letter from his girl a Miss Maxwell and that she was very much struck on Billy...."* [53]

In a second letter, he wrote *"I suppose the Miss Maxwell was the daughter of Pete Maxwell...."* [54] Sheriff Southwick meant, of course, the daughter of Lucien Maxwell (or the sister of Pete Maxwell).

After denying a "sweetheart" relationship with Billy, Paulita told Burns:

> *"Billy the Kid, after his escape at Lincoln, came to Fort Sumner, it is true, to see a woman he was in love with. But it was not I. Pat Garrett ought to have known who she was because he was connected with her, and not very distantly, by marriage."* [55]

This is a not-so-veiled reference to Celsa (Martinez) Gutierrez, Garrett's first wife's sister. This may be simple misdirection; or it may indicate that Billy had a second or earlier relationship.

Adelaida "Ida" Garrett

Following Billy's escape, the press complained that Garrett was only half-heartedly searching for Billy.

It was true; the reason was, Garrett and Apolinaria had just had a baby daughter. Adelaida "Ida" Garrett was born February 20, 1881, only two months before Billy escaped from the Lincoln jail. This previously unknown information was discovered by the author while researching *"Killing Pat Garrett, the Wild West's Most Famous Lawman – Murder or Self-Defense?"*

Garrett and Apolinaria were living in Lincoln at the Whortley Hotel, which Garrett had purchased from John N. Copeland on May 23 for $275. [56] With a new family and the responsibilities of a hosteller to attend to, Garrett probably prioritized his sheriff duties to those near to home so he could spend as much time in Lincoln as possible.

One of the tragedies of Garrett's and Apolinaria's lives was that Adelaida died when she was only 15 years old.[57]

Killed

Forty-four days after Billy's escape, on July 11, Garrett was motivated – finally – to visit the Fort Sumner area, to hunt for Billy. His reason was a letter from the same man whose snitching had lead to Billy's capture at Stinking Springs – Manuel Silvestre Brazil:

> *"Brazil's letter gave me no positive information. He said he had not seen the Kid since his escape, but, from many indications, believed he was still in the country. He offered me any assistance in his power to recapture him."* [58]

What was Brazil's motivation in volunteering such information? Hate? Revenge? Financial gain again? Whatever it was, he strongly wanted once again to get Billy captured (and killed).

Although Brazil's letter supplied nothing "positive," Garrett arranged to meet him three days later at Taiban Arroyo, an uninhabited site five miles south of Fort Sumner (and only a few miles from the Rock House at Stinking Springs where Billy had been captured), taking two deputies with him, John William Poe and Thomas C. McKinney.[59]

Brazil did not show at the meeting, so Garrett sent Poe into Fort Sumner to see what he could discover. Poe was the perfect choice for this task because he had only come to New Mexico from Texas a few weeks earlier and was practically unknown in Lincoln County:

"In pursuance of this plan, I [Poe] next morning left my companions and rode into town, where I arrived about ten o'clock...."

"When I entered the town, I noticed I was being watched from every side, and soon after I had stopped and hitched my horse in front of a store which had a saloon annex, a number of men gathered around and began to question me as to where I was from, where bound, etc. I answered with as plausible a yarn as I was able to give...." [60]

Poe spent some time in the saloon, bought himself a *"square meal,"* and sought to extract intelligence on Billy's whereabouts:

"...but was unable to learn anything further than that the people with whom I conversed were still suspicious of me, and it was plain that many of them were on the alert, expecting something to happen." [61]

His Fort Sumner mission a failure, Poe then visited the nearby town of Sunnyside, seven miles north of Fort Sumner. There, he met with Milnor Rudolph, who invited him to have supper at his ranch:

"After supper was over, I engaged in conversation with [Rudolph], discussing the conditions in the country generally, and after some little time, I led up to the escape of Billy the Kid from Lincoln, and remarked that I had heard a report that the Kid was hiding in or about Fort Sumner. Upon my making this remark, the old gentleman showed plainly that he was getting nervous; said that he had heard that such a report was about, but did not believe it...." [62]

Milnor Rudolph was the father of Charles Rudolph, who had helped Garrett capture Billy at Stinking Springs.

Leaving Milnor Rudolph, Poe rejoined Garrett and McKinney at Glorieta, a tiny settlement four miles north of Fort Sumner, as had been pre-arranged:

"I rode directly to the point where I had agreed to meet my companions, and, strange to say, as I approached the point from one direction, they came into view from the other, so that we did not have to wait for each other." [63]

Here Garrett's and Poe's accounts differ. Garrett says:

"[After hearing Poe's report] I concluded to go and have a talk with Pete Maxwell, in whom I felt I could rely." [64]

But Poe in his account claims the decision to question Pete Maxwell was his:

"I then proposed that, before leaving, we should go to the residence of Pete Maxwell, a man who up to that time I had never seen...." [65]

If Poe is correct, it shows Garrett's evident reluctance to pursue Billy at Fort Sumner.

"Garrett then proposed that we go into a grove of trees near the town, conceal our horses, then station ourselves in the peach orchard at the rear of [Pete's] house, and keep watch on who might come or go." [66]

It was about 9 o'clock at night, July 14, 1881, when the three men sneaked into Fort Sumner:

Maxwell residence at Fort Sumner. Formerly the officers' quarters for the fort. Pete Maxwell's room was in the front, left (southeast) corner. The visible figures are Maxwell family members. Undated postcard.

"We approached these houses cautiously, and when within ear shot, heard the sound of voices conversing in Spanish. We concealed ourselves quickly and listened; but the distance was too great to hear words, or even distinguish voices. Soon a man arose from the ground, in full view, but too far away to recognize.... With a few words, which fell like a murmur on our ears, he went to the fence, jumped it, and walked down toward Maxwell's house." [67]

Neither Poe nor McKinney had ever met Billy, so only Garrett was capable of identifying their target. The reason for the two deputies being present was simple – if Billy was found, Garrett expected a gunfight, and he wanted the odds weighed heavily in his favor.

After watching for about two hours, and seeing no indication of Billy, the three men approached the large, 12-room, adobe structure where Pete Maxwell, his mother, his sister Paulita, and other family members were living. The original purpose of the building was as officers' quarters. Pete's room was in the southeastern corner of the building. The door to his room opened onto a porch, which was fronted by a white picket fence.

"This is Maxwell's room in the corner. You fellows wait here while I go in and talk to him." [68]

In response to these instructions of Garrett's, Poe crouched on the edge of the porch and McKinney squatted on his heels just outside the fence. [69]

Garrett slipped soundlessly into Pete's room – the door was wide open:

> "...on account of the extremely warm weather." [70]

> "There were three windows in the room, all of which were raised. Through the open door and windows the moonlight streamed into the room." [71]

Inside the room, Garrett saw Pete "lying on the bed in the S. E. corner of the room." Garrett sat on the edge of the bed, positioning himself so he "was able to partially hide himself in the shadow." [72]

> "[I] had just commenced talking to [Pete] about the object of my visit at such an unusual hour, when a man entered the room in stockinged feet, with a pistol in one hand and a knife in the other." [73]

Outside, just seconds earlier, Poe had been startled by the stealthy approach of that same mysterious figure:

> "...my attention was attracted, from where I sat in the little gateway, to a man approaching me on the inside of and along the fence, some forty or fifty steps away. I observed that he was only partially dressed and was both bare-headed and barefooted, or rather, had only socks on his feet, and it seemed to me that he was fastening his trousers as he came toward me at a brisk walk." [74]

> "Upon seeing me, he covered me with his six-shooter as quick as lightning, sprang onto the porch, calling out in Spanish 'Quien es?' – at the same time backing away from me toward the door through which Garrett only a few seconds before had passed, repeating his query, 'Who is it?' in Spanish several times." [75]

In Pete's room, Garrett squinted at the silhouette in the doorway, starkly outlined by the moon, its features obscured in shadow:

> "He came and placed his hand on the bed just beside me, and in a low whisper [asked], 'who is it?'"

> "I at once recognized the man [from his voice], and knew he was the Kid, and reached behind me for my pistol, feeling almost certain of receiving a ball from his at the moment of doing so, as I felt sure he had now recognized me, but fortunately he drew back from the bed at noticing my movement, and although he had his pistol pointed at my breast, he delayed to fire, and asked in Spanish, 'Quien es? Quein es?' This gave me time to bring mine to bear on him, and the moment I did so I pulled the trigger and he received his death wound, for the ball struck him in the left breast and pierced his heart." [76]

Garrett fired a second time before he could see the effect of the first shot, but that shot missed its intended target, striking the room wall and glancing "off the headboard of a wooden bedstead." [77]

Outside, Poe:

> "...heard a groan and one or two gasps... as of someone dying in the room. An instant later, Garrett came out, brushing against me as he passed. He stood by me close to the wall at the side of the door and said to me, 'That was the

Deputy Sheriff John William Poe. Undated photo. Courtesy Maurice G. Fulton
Papers, Special Collections, UA.

Seated: Pete Menard Maxwell. Standing: Henry Leis. Undated photo. Courtesy
Arthur Johnson Memorial Library..

Kid that came in there onto me, and I think I have got him.' I said, 'Pat, the Kid would not come to this place; you have shot the wrong man." [78]

Garrett replied:

"I am sure that was him, as I know his voice too well to be mistaken." [79]

Pete, panic-stricken, had bolted out of the room on Garrett's heels, dragging *"his bedclothes with him."* [80]

Garrett's shots roused the members of the Maxwell household, who rapidly gathered outside Pete's room. Those present included Pete's mother Luz Maxwell, Pete's sisters Paulita and Odila Maxwell, Deluvina Maxwell, Pete's uncle Pablo Beaubien and his wife Rebecca, and Pablo Abreu. They were quickly joined by many others, including A. P. "Paco" Anaya, Jesus Anaya, Higinio Garcia, Jesus Silva, Sabal and Celsa Guiterrez, Martin and Abrana Garcia, Lorenzo and José Jaramillo, Vincente Otero, Isaac Sandoval, Frank Lobato, Marie Lobato, and George Miller (a Black soldier who was spending the night at Fort Sumner). [81]

No one in the crowd stepped forward to look inside Pete's room for fear that Billy was still alive and would shoot the first person he saw. Finally, someone produced a lit lamp – many sources say it was Deluvina Maxwell – which was placed on the ledge of one of the open windows. [82]

The light revealed Billy on the floor, on his back – *"a six-shooter lying at his right hand and a butcher knife at his left."* [83]

Initially, Poe and McKinney thought that Billy had fired once before he died, as they believed they had heard a third shot. On inspecting Billy's six-shooter, Garrett found that it was:

"...a self-cocker, calibre .41. It had five cartridges and one shell in the chambers, the hammer resting on the shell, but this proves nothing, as many carry their revolvers in this way for safety; besides, this shell looked as though it had been shot some time before." [84]

The "self-cocker" was one of the pistols Billy had taken from the Lincoln jail armory on escaping.

Fateful Choice

So why did Billy walk into his death, in Pete's room?

In describing his entrance into Fort Sumner, Garrett wrote:

"Soon a man arose from the ground, in full view, but too far away to recognize...." [85]

He later made the subject of his statement clear:

"Little as we suspected it, this man was the Kid." [86]

Garrett is implying that Billy had been having sex with his girlfriend in the orchard.

Reporting what he learned after the killing, Garrett wrote that after leaving the orchard, Billy:

"...went to the house of a Mexican friend, pulled off his hat and boots, threw himself on a bed, and commenced reading a newspaper. He soon, however, hailed his friend, who was sleeping in the room, told him to get up and make some coffee, adding – 'Give me a butcher knife, and I will go over to Pete's and get some beef; I'm hungry.'" [87]

Garrett does not name the "friend," but by adding that he was asleep, he suggests that the friend was the unwitting husband of Billy's girlfriend (who he had just been having sex with in the orchard).

Paco Anaya, who was present at the killing, and knew Billy well, gives a different account. He says that Billy was visiting the home of Jesus Silva, where Anaya spoke with him. Early in the evening of July 14, Billy and Silva left to water a horse that Billy had hidden at a nearby ranch (a very reasonable action). On returning to Fort Sumner, Billy went to the home of Sabal and Celsa (Martinez) Gutierrez, where Billy was staying.[88]

Then, quoting Celsa Gutierrez, Anaya writes:

"Billy entered the house, and he was carrying a bone. This was the hock of a leg, and when he had come in, he went straight to the kitchen, and returning to the room where we were, me and Sabal, Billy said to me, 'Celsa, I brought you some meat for you to make my supper.'" [89]

On checking the "bone," Celsa decided it was not worth cooking.

Billy then got a butcher knife and left the Gutierrez house, intending to cut some meat off a side of beef that was hanging on Pete's porch.[90]

A third, contemporaneous account, says:

"[Billy] had gone at once to the house of Manuela Bowdre, [the wife] of one of Billy's old compadres, Charlie Bowdre, who was shot when 'the Kid,' Rudabaugh, Tom Pickett and Billy Wilson were 'rounded up' at Stinking Springs...." [91]

The same account also notes:

"Since his escape, [Billy] had allowed his beard to grow and had attempted to disguise himself as a Mexican by darkening his skin by the use of some sort of root." [92]

A fourth account, based on stories told by descendents of Abrana (Segura) Garcia, says that Billy had spent the evening with Abrana, prior to crossing to the Maxwell house to obtain some meat for supper. This is the sole account that embraces a specific a person as Billy's girlfriend.[93]

All four accounts make it clear that Billy was among staunch friends, who certainly would have warned him if they had even the tiniest suspicion of danger close by.

So Billy's fateful choice to visit the Maxwell house, at the fateful moment that Garrett was in Pete's room, set up his death.

And then when Billy chose to ask *"Quien es?"* rather than retreat or shoot, he cinched his death.

Frank Silva, Jesus Silva's son, pointing with his left hand at where Garrett's errant
bullet entered the bedstead and with his right where it exited. The bench is the
bench on which Billy's body was laid. Undated photo. Courtesy Dolph Briscoe
Center for American History, UTA.

If Garrett had encountered Billy in any other way, the result would certainly have been a gunfight – and the consequence – unpredictable. Garrett recognized this:

"I went out contemplating the probability of being shot at, and the possibility of being hurt, perhaps killed; but not if any precaution on my part would prevent such a catastrophe...."

"Then, the 'lucky shot,' as they put it. It was not the shot, but the opportunity that was lucky, and everybody may rest assured I did not hesitate long to improve it." [94]

Justifiable Homicide

Once it was apparent that Billy was dead, Garrett re-entered the room:

"...and examined the body. The ball struck him just above the heart, and must have cut through the ventricles." [95]

The news of Billy's death was not received well by the large crowd gathered outside of Maxwell's room, as Poe noted:

"[Garrett, McKinney, and I were] keeping constantly on our guard, as we were expecting to be attacked by the friends of the dead man." [96]

Jesus Silva, with the help of others, lifted the body and took it into a hallway of the Maxwell house, and laid it on a long table. There, a thorough examination confirmed Billy was dead:

"Strange as it may seem, that wound did not bleed for two hours after he was shot." [97]

The body was then moved to a bench in a nearby blacksmith/carpenter shop.[98]

The Justice of Peace for Fort Sumner, Alejandro Segura, was sent for. He lived in Arenosa, a tiny settlement about seven miles away. When Segura arrived, he convened a coroner's jury consisting of Milnor Rudolph, Antonio Saavedra, Pedro Antonio Lucero, José Silva, Sabal Gutierrez, and Lorenzo Jaramillo – who all knew Billy well. Milnor, accompanied by his son Charles, travelled from Sunnyside to sit on the jury. Milnor was elected jury foreman by the other members.[99]

The coroner's jury report, written in Spanish, quoted the following evidence, supplied by Pete Maxwell:

"As I was lying down on my bed in my room about midnight the fourteenth (14th) of July, Pat F. Garrett entered my room and sat down on the edge of my bed to talk to me. Shortly after Garrett had sat down, Wm. Bonney entered and came over to my bed with a pistol in his hand and asked me 'Who is it? Who is it?' And then Pat F. Garrett shot two bullets at said William Bonney and the said Wm. Bonney fell to one side of my stove and I left the room. When I entered again 3 or 4 minutes after the shots, said Bonney was dead." (100) (English translation)

The jury then ruled:

"We of the jury unanimously find that Wm. Bonney has been killed by a bullet, fired from the pistol in the hand of Pat F. Garrett, in the left breast in

Milnor Rudulph. Rudulph served on the coroner's jury that ruled Billy's death *"justifiable homicide."* Photo taken in the mid-1880's. Courtesy Archives and Special Collections, NMSU..

the region of the heart, and our decision is that the deed of said Garrett, was justifiable homicide and we are unanimous in the opinion that the gratitude of the whole community is owed to said Garrett for his deed and that he is worthy of being rewarded." [101] (English translation)

Charles Rudolph's attendance at Billy's inquest and funeral meant that he, like Garrett, was present when Billy was captured and when he was buried.

Dead or Alive

Governor Wallace's $500 Territorial reward, issued following Billy's escape, was for *"any person or persons who will capture William Bonny (sic), alias the Kid, and deliver him to any sheriff of New Mexico."* [102] "Capture" obviously meant alive, but it was understood by all, including Billy, that the reward was good for a dead Billy also.

Five days after Billy's killing, in a surreal recapitulation of his actions following Billy's capture, Garrett went to Santa Fe to collect the reward. And, as then, William G. Ritch was acting as Territorial governor. And, as then, Ritch claimed he had not the authority to pay Garrett the reward:

"Yesterday afternoon Pat Garrett, accompanied by Hon. T. B. Catron and Col. M. Brunswick, called upon acting-Governor Ritch in regard to the reward offered by ex-Governor Lew Wallace for the Kid. The reward was fixed at five hundred dollars and the offer was published in the papers. Governor Ritch announced that he was willing to pay the amount, and would be glad to do so, but that he would have to look over the records first. He was not in the city when the offer was made, and had never received any notification of it, consequently did not know whether or not it was on record. In consequence of this state of affairs, the question of the reward was not settled." [103]

Acting Governor Ritch had replaced Governor Wallace on May 30, 1881.

After three days consideration, Governor Ritch decided that Wallace's offer of a reward was not legal, and refused to pay.

But, as before, public sentiment strongly supported rewarding Garrett. The White Oaks' *Golden Era* editor put it this way:

"It is not enough to be thankful and offer our sheriff congratulations only, we must give a stronger recognition. He must be amply rewarded. We must stand by our officers who do their duties so nobly, at such a great expense and at such great risks. Let every one subscribe and pay freely for this brave and commendable act, that Mr. Garrett may not only know that his services are appreciated, but that for them he is entitled to be rewarded in a monetary sense." [104]

The first person to start a collection for Garrett was Billy-hater James Dolan:

"Early yesterday morning Mr. James Dolan, one of the Lincoln county men with reason for congratulation upon the death of the Kid, started out with a subscription list in search of donations to the fund to be presented to Pat F. Garrett, sheriff of Lincoln county, and the slayer of the worst man the territory has known. Two men who are interested in property in the South headed the list with subscriptions of one hundred dollars each. These were followed by

donations ranging from twenty-five dollars down, and before night the sum had reached five hundred sixty dollars. The list was carried around in the afternoon and was also successful in securing subscriptions. It is hoped by those who have the matter in hand that the sum will be raised to at least six hundred dollars. Garrett deserves every cent of this and more, but if the other towns do as well he will receive a good round sum." [105]

In Mesilla, the editor of *Newman's Thirty-Four* (Newman) started a Garrett fund that collected more than $250. [106]

In Las Vegas:

"When the news of the killing of 'Billy the Kid' was brought to the city it was decided that Garrett should be handsomely remunerated for his trouble, and when THE OPTIC urged the same thing last night the matter was as good as settled. A fund was started and has reached nearly $1,000 already." [107]

This fund eventually reached more than $1,300. [108]

"Santa Fe will probably beat Las Vegas, although people, as a rule, are not subscribing as liberally as they should. There are some exceptions to this rule, of course, as some of the contributions were very handsome." [109]

A year and two days after Billy's killing, Garrett finally got the $500 promised by Governor Wallace. On July 18, 1882, the New Mexico Territorial Legislature passed a special act authorizing the payment of Garrett's reward:

"An Act For the Relief of Pat Garrett"

"The Territorial Auditor is hereby authorized to draw a warrant upon the Territorial Treasury of the Territory of New Mexico in favor of Pat Garrett for the sum of Five Hundred Dollars payable out of any funds in the Territorial Treasury." [110]

Between the collections and the legislative authorization, Garrett received as much as $7,000 in reward money for killing Billy.[111] Add the more than $1,500 Garrett received six and a half months earlier for capturing Billy and Garrett did right well in hunting Billy. Probably no other person in Wild West history ever made as much on one "outlaw" as Garrett did on Billy. One inflation calculator puts what Garrett earned on Billy at more than $220,000 in today's dollars. Some give numbers in the millions when comparing relative buying power.

Garrett was also given a gold sheriff's badge in the shape of a star. The front of the badge reads:

"Lincoln County"
"Sheriff"

The back of the badge reads:

"To Pat Garrett"
"With Best Regards of"
"A. J. Fountain"
"1881" [112]

Why is Colonel Fountain rewarding Garrett with a gold badge for killing his client? An engraved gold badge is not something one buys off the store shelf. It has to be custom made. As a lawyer, Colonel Fountain's sworn duty was to give his client the very best legal defense he was capable of. What kind of lawyer then rewards with gold the person who kills his client? That action would appear to be further evidence that Colonel Fountain gave Billy less than his best defense. It also explains why Colonel Fountain made no effort to file an appeal for Billy. Even though Billy had no money to pay for an appeal, if Colonel Fountain was passionate about Billy's unfair legal treatment – something obvious – a sense of justice should have motivated him to further represent Billy. Unequal justice is injustice, as all law students know.

Colonel Fountain could afford to buy Garrett a gold badge, but he could not afford to file an appeal for Billy? A few simple papers would have delayed Billy's hanging until the next meeting of the Territorial Supreme Court.

Poe and McKinney also received reward money, although the sources and amounts are unknown. It may be that Garrett shared a portion of his reward with his deputies.[113]

Press Response

Billy's death was reported in the national press, from California to New York, in over fifty newspapers. Even the *London Times* published a lengthy notice of his death.[114] The editorial tone of the Territorial newspaper coverage was predominantly celebratory, as in the following report by the Silver City newspaper:

> *"The vulgar murderer and desperado known as 'Billy the Kid' has met his just deserts (sic) at last.... Despite the glamour of romance thrown around his dare-devil life by sensational writers, the fact is he was a low down vulgar cutthroat, with probably not one redeeming quality."* [115]

The *Santa Fe Weekly Democrat* sneered:

> *"He is dead; and he died so suddenly that he did not have time to be interviewed by a preacher, or to sing hymns, or pray, so we cannot say positively that he has clumb the shining ladder and entered the pearly gates...."*

> *"No sooner had the floor caught his descending form, which had a pistol in one hand and a knife in the other, than there was a strong order of brimstone in the air, and a dark figure, with the wings of a dragon, claws like a tiger, eyes like balls of fire and horns like a bison, hovered over the corpse for a moment, and with a fiendish laugh said, 'Ha, ha, this is my meat' and sailed off through a window."* [116]

The *Las Vegas Daily Optic* thanked God and invoked vampires:

> *"A glorious God-send – the killing of 'the Kid.'"*

> *"If Pat Garrett is not paid a couple of thousand dollars for ridding the county of its worst vampire – 'Billy, the Kid' – the people are simply n. g. [no good]"* [117]

Replica of the first marker on Billy the Kid's grave. The original marker was made
from two pickets from the wood fence surrounding Pete Maxwell's residence.
Shortly after being erected, the marker was riddled with bullet holes, fired by a party
of drunken soldiers. 1930's photo.

The White Oaks *Lincoln County Leader* made the following compelling observation:

> *"The trouble with Bill was he talked before he shot. Always before that he shot first and talked afterward. That's the testimony of Pete Maxwell, eyewitness to the killing of William H. Bonney, known far and wide in the territory as Billy, The Kid."* [118]

The *Leader* was one of the few papers that had anything decent to say about Billy:

> *"Padre Redin at Anton Chico says, 'Billy did not have a bad heart, really. Most of his crimes were crimes of vengeance.'"* [119]

Billy's Burial

Early in the morning of July 15, 1881, the coroner's jury met over Billy's body in the Maxwell's blacksmith/carpenter shop. As noted, the jury's ruling was that Billy had been killed by Sheriff Pat Garrett with a bullet to the left breast and the killing was *"justifiable homicide."* [120]

The body was then prepared for burial by his true friend Deluvina Maxwell. Billy was dressed in:

> *"...a beige suit, a shirt, an undershirt, shorts, and a pair of stockings."* [121]

Garrett paid for Billy's burial clothes, just as he had for Thomas O'Folliard and Charles Bowdre. [122]

Jesus Silva recounted what happened next:

> *"...at 10 o'clock we buried Billy the Kid in the little cemetery near the old Fort, beside the bodies of Billy's former pals, Charlie Bowdre and Tom O'Folliard, who were killed by officers earlier."*

> *"I was chief pallbearer at Billy's funeral that morning. With me were Antonio Saavedra, Saval Gutierez [Sabal Gutierrez], Vincente Otero and a few others. We buried the Kid in a grave which had been dug by Vincente Otero."* [123]

Almost everyone who lived in Fort Sumner attended Billy's funeral. (124)

> *"The day after the funeral Pete Maxwell had his man pull a wooden picket from the parade-ground fence, saw off a foot or so, and nail it in a crossbar to the longer piece. Then he printed in crude letters BILLY THE KID, JULY 14, 1881."* [125]

Shortly after the hastily-made, wooden-picket marker was placed over Billy's grave it was riddled with eight bullet holes, fired by a party of drunken soldiers. [126]

Confirming Billy's Death

On July 18, 1881, the *Las Vegas Daily Gazette* reported the news of Billy's killing to its readers, writing in part:

> *"The last buckboard from Ft. Sumner brought news of the killing of the redoubtable Billy 'the Kid.' When this intelligence was noised abroad yesterday morning, there was intense excitement throughout Las Vegas. Many were inclined to doubt the truth of the report, but a half dozen business men and*

citizens produced letters from people resident in that country in support of the report...."

"Late in the forenoon Pat Garrett and several men from the neighborhood of Sumner arrived in the city. The tall, silent Garrett was the hero of the hour, and was lionized for the killing that was confirmed by personal testimony of him who has forever rid the Pecos country and Lincoln county of the intrepid outlaw...."

"From an interview with Mr. Garrett, advices from our special correspondent [Michael] Cosgrove, the mail contractor and other authentic sources, we are able to give the Gazette readers a full story of the death of the desperado, who while living under numerous aliases has been known the length and breath of the country as 'Billy the Kid....'"

"An inquest was held the next day, and as he was known to all the country, there was no doubt that 'the Kid' was really dead. The foreman of the jury [Milnor Rudolph], in a timely communication to the Gazette, says, 'This news is true, for I was foreman of the jury of inquest, and know it was 'the Kid's' body that we examined." [127]

Many people today believe that Billy was not really killed by Garrett. It is not possible to present the overwhelming evidence that Billy was killed by Garrett here. I have presented and addressed that evidence in *"Billy the Kid's Grave – A History of the Wild West's Most Famous Death Marker."* Strenuous efforts by historians have established that at least 46 persons saw Billy's dead body or attended his funeral.[128] Those people would have had to lie about that event for the rest of their lives if Billy had escaped death by Garrett's hand. No one who is known to have been present at Billy's death and funeral ever said it was not Billy who was killed.

Chapter	Epilogue
10	

Billy's Grave

In 1862, when Fort Sumner was established, a lot roughly one-half of an acre in size was set aside as a cemetery. Between 1862 and 1868, there were 22 military burials in the Fort Sumner cemetery, 21 soldiers and one civilian. Following the purchase of Fort Sumner by Lucian Maxwell in 1870, the cemetery became the accepted burial place for Fort Sumner residents.[1]

Billy's grave was marked by the hastily-made cross put up the day after his funeral by Pete Maxwell's handyman. That maker was stolen a few years later by a man named Chauncey and taken to Boston, supposedly to *"put it in a museum."* [2]

In October, 1905, Pat Garrett escorted Western author Emerson Hough to Fort Sumner. The men travelled by horse-drawn wagon from El Paso. Hough was writing about Garrett and wanted to see the site of Billy's killing. Hough wrote the following about their visit to the cemetery:

> *"...we learned when we entered the little barbed-wire enclosure of the cemetery where the Kid and his fellows were buried. There are no headstones in this cemetery, and no sacristan holds its records. Again Garrett had to search in the salt grass and greasewood. 'Here is the place,' said he at length. 'We buried them all in a row. The first grave is the Kid's, and the next to him is Bowdre, and then O'Folliard. There's nothing left to mark them.'"* [3]

The site of Billy's grave was briefly marked in 1927, but in the wrong location.[4]

In early April, 1930, four men – including three who had attended Billy's funeral – gathered in the Fort Sumner cemetery to locate Billy's grave: A. P. "Paco" Anaya, Jesus Silva, Vincente Otero, and Charles W. Foor. Foor was not present at Billy's burial, but he moved to Fort Sumner a few months later.[5]

The four men, after some arguing, agreed on the site. By mid-May, 1930, the construction of the current marker began with the laying of the cement curbing around the three graves. For a full, detailed history of Billy's grave, including an addressing of controversies such as whether the grave is in the correct location, whether it was washed away by the flooding of the Pecos River, and whether Billy is truly buried in the grave, see *"Billy the Kid's Grave – A History of the Wild West's Most Famous Death Marker."* [6]

"The True Life of Billy the Kid"

The first book written about Billy was *"The True Life of Billy the Kid"* by Don Jenardo. The book was published August 29, 1881 – forty-six days after Billy's killing! The 16-page book was issued by Frank Tousey, a New York publisher of what were nicknamed "Yellow Books." Yellow Books sold for five cents and had that label because traditionally they had yellow covers. Tousey tried to issue a new Yellow Book every week, effectively making the books a weekly magazine. The books generally recounted

Charles Wesley Foor. Undated photo. Courtesy Dolph Briscoe Center for American History, UTA.

Jesus Silva at Fort Sumner. Undated photo. Courtesy Maurice G. Fulton Papers,
Special Collections, UA.

Graves of Bowdre, O'Folliard, and Billy surrounded by a concrete curbing, The concrete slab is over Billy's grave. May, 1930 photo. Courtesy Maurice G. Fulton Papers, Special Collections, UA.

Charles Foor standing next to Billy, Bowdre, and O'Folliard's common grave marker. Foor collected the money to pay for the gravestone. 1931 photo. Courtesy Dolph Briscoe Center for American History, UTA..

the thrilling adventures of historical figures. *"The True Life of Billy the Kid"* was number 451 in Tousey's "Wide Awake Library."

Tousey, in his publicity, let it be known that Don Jenardo was the pen name of Illion Constellano, *"a Mexican, actively employed in the commercial and military service of his country."*

> *"He is known both in this country and in Europe as the most powerful of romance writers…. Added to a rich imagination and a mind of great originality, he possesses great experience. He has traveled all over the civilized world, and is master of a number of different languages."* [7]

Not true. The author's real name was Julius Warren Lewis. He had been writing stories for publication, often with his wife's help, since at least 1851.[8]

It is surprising that Lewis was able to whip out a Billy the Kid book so quickly. Lewis, although an American, was living in London at the time. He put his book together from New Mexico newspaper accounts, which would not have been easy to get in England.[9]

Considering Lewis' sources, the book is fairly accurate as to the major events of Billy's story. Lewis writes about the "war" between Murphy, Dolan & Co. and a group he calls John Chisum's cow-boys, the killing of Brady and Hindman (both men are shot by Billy while they are on horseback), the siege of McSween's fortified house in Lincoln (during which Susan McSween hysterically plays an Irish war song on her *"beautiful rose-wood"* piano), the arrival of Colonel Dudley with his troops, the burning of McSween's house (lighted with coal oil), and Billy's miraculous getaway just before being incinerated. In his escape attempt from the burning house, McSween is *"shot through the head"* and falls dead in his wife's arms.

Lewis writes about Governor Wallace's pardon proclamation, the killing of Chapman (by Silas Rodgers, an employee of Murphy, Dolan & Co.), Colonel Dudley's Court of Inquiry at Fort Stanton, the hiring of Ira Leonard by Susan McSween to help prosecute Colonel Dudley, and Dudley's acquittal. Garrett is hired to capture Billy, which he does *"in a small bottom."* Billy is taken to Mesilla, convicted, and sentenced to die. He is brought to Lincoln to hang.

Lewis explains the escape by having Billy hit Deputy Bell with his handcuffs and steal his gun while the two are walking down the street toward the Lincoln jail. Billy then shoots Bell dead. When Olinger comes running up, Billy kills him with a *"whole charge of buckshot… poured into the unfortunate man's heart."* He then *"galloped out of town, in the presence of the whole population."*

Lewis ends the book by having Garrett meet a snitch named Rias, who tells him that Billy *"sleeps to-night at the house of Pete Maxwell."* Garrett goes to Pete's *"deserted"* bedroom a bit before midnight and hides behind Pete's bed. A little after midnight, Billy walks into the bedroom, asking *"Quien es? Quien es?"* Garrett shoots him with a rifle:

> *"Billy the Kid, the terror of New Mexico, lay a lifeless corpse, while his blood dyed the dirt floor of Pete Maxwell's dark adobe hut."* [10]

The date, writes Lewis, was August 14, 1881.

Cover of *"The True Life of Billy the Kid"* by Don Jenardo, published August 29, 1881, by Frank Tousey. Don Jenardo was a pen name of Julius Warren Lewis. Courtesy Archives and Special Collections, NMSU.

Cover of Pat Garrett's book on Billy the Kid, published by the New Mexican Printing and Publishing Co. of Santa Fe, April 1, 1882. What event in Billy's life is this image supposed to represent?

In 1883, the U. S. Postmaster General issued new regulations for second-class mail that forbid the mailing of certain kinds of printed material, including so-called violent stories. As a result, Tousey withdrew *"The True Life of Billy the Kid"* and stopped listing it in his catalog. Very few original copies of the book exist today.[11]

"The Authentic Life of Billy the Kid"

On April 1, 1882, the New Mexican Publishing Co. of Santa Fe published *"The Authentic Life of Billy, the Kid, the Noted Desperado of the Southwest, Whose Deeds of Daring Have Made His Name a Terror in New Mexico, Arizona, and Northern Mexico"* by Pat Garrett. The book was priced at 50 cents.[12]

Garrett was helped in writing the book by his friend Ash Upson, although Upson's name does not appear on the book.

The Mesilla *Rio Grande Republican* newspaper favorably reviewed the book and noted:

> *"The book is selling very fast in this city. Nearly every 'old residenter' has purchased one. Our own copy has already been borrowed a dozen times, at least."* [13]

In spite of this generous press notice, the book did not sell well. The small Santa Fe publisher picked by Garrett had no national distribution. If Garrett's book had been published by one of the major New York publishers, such as Frank Tousey, the book would have sold many thousands of copies.

In the book, Garrett combines both oral background stories and his first-person accounts of his hunting, capturing, and killing Billy. The oral stories have not stood up to the test of history, but his accounts of his actual dealings with Billy are well collaborated by other sources.

Tunstall's Murder Site

In 1926, Walter Noble Burns published *"The Saga of Billy the Kid."* Burns' book was the first book-length biography of Billy since Charles Siringo's *"History of Billy the Kid,"* published in 1920. Burns' book was a huge success and stimulated lasting interest in Billy, who had been mostly forgotten by the public.

Motivated by the *"portrayal of Tunstall's death"* in Burn's book, in April, 1927, two nephews of Tunstall's travelled from London, England, to Lincoln, New Mexico, to *"investigate"* Tunstall's murder. They met with George Coe and others living in the Lincoln area who had known Tunstall. Coe took the two relatives to the spot where Tunstall had been murdered and they marked it with a pile of rocks topped by a stick cross. Those interested in Lincoln County War history owe a large bouquet of thanks to Coe and the two unnamed Tunstall relatives for this historically significant deed.[1]

In October of that year, New Mexico Representative James V. Tully met with Paul Walter of the New Mexico Historical Society and suggested that permanent plaques be placed on the various historical buildings in Lincoln identifying the parts they played in the Lincoln County War. Tully, who lived on a ranch in Glencoe, told Walter:

> *"There should be a marker for the spot back of my ranch on the so-called Tunstall Trail, nailed on a juniper tree to show where he was slain. This is now nearly forgotten."* [2]

Tully added:

> *"'Here Tunstall lies buried' should indicate the grave in the corral yard near the McSween store. It has no mark of any kind now."* [3]

In the fall of 1929, Dr. W. A. Osborne, Dean of the Medical School of Melbourne University, Australia, travelled to Lincoln to research the Lincoln County War. His interest:

> *"...was aroused because Tunstall, the first victim of the range war, was an Englishman."*

> *"[Dr. Osborne] made an extensive study of early day conflicts in Lincoln county, visited the haunts of 'Billy the Kid,' and talked to old timers of the section for detailed information."* [4]

Stimulated by the publicity generated by Dr. Osborne's visit, the U.S. Forest Service erected an official monument at the murder site in December, 1929.[5] The monument location is thickly forested today and it is challenging to mentally picture what it looked like on that fateful Monday, February 18, 1878.

The canyon where Tunstall was killed descends from a relatively flat plateau. Calling it a valley is perhaps a better description. Tunstall's party, made up of himself, Billy, Widenmann, Brewer, and Middleton, had just reached the mouth of the canyon, or the *"brow of the hill"* as Billy described it, when they sighted the chase posse riding *"at full speed"* behind them. Billy and Middleton were trailing some distance behind the other three, who were not riding together. Brewer and Widenmann were 200 to 300 yards to

The spot where Tunstall was murdered by Tom Hill and Buck Morton. The stones and cross were erected by George Coe and two unidentified Tunstall relatives in April, 1927. Courtesy Maurice G. Fulton Papers, Special Collections, UA.

George Coe standing next to the marker erected by the U.S. Forest Service in December, 1929, to mark the location of Tunstall's murder. Courtesy Maurice G. Fulton Papers, Special Collections, UA.

Tunstall's murder site today. 2017 photo.

Close-up of the plaque erected by the Lincoln County Historical Society on
February 18, 1978. 2017 photo.

Tunstall's left, off the trail. Tunstall apparently was riding about 100 yards to the right of
the trail, in front of his horses, who were following the trail.

Billy and Middleton raced forward to warn those riding ahead. The two had just
reached Brewer and Widenmann when the posse began firing. The lead men in the
posse were Hill and Morton, who were some distance in front of the main body. Billy,
Widenmann, and Brewer turned their horses left and rode *"over a hill towards another
which was covered with large rocks and trees in order to defend themselves and make a
stand."* Middleton raced toward Tunstall, screamed a warning, and then veered left and
joined Billy, Widenmann, and Brewer.

Hill and Morton, sighting Tunstall, their target, with no men near him, galloped
toward him. Tunstall stopped, turned, and faced them. Hill shouted to Tunstall to
approach, that he would not be hurt. At the same time, the two men stealthily drew their
weapons. Tunstall rode closer, expecting to talk. Without warning, *"Morton fired and
shot Tunstall through the breast, and then Hill fired and shot Tunstall through the head."*

With the other posse members now approaching, Hill and Morton probably thought
that with Tunstall positioned just in front of them, it would be harder for any witnesses to
know whether Tunstall had drawn on them. That was their planned alibi: he had shot first
and they returned fire in self-defense. After Tunstall fell from his horse, someone other
than Hill, probably Morton, shot the horse. To be certain of killing the horse, the killer

would have shot it in the head. Morton and Hill dismounted and just had time to remove two cartridges from Tunstall's pistol and drop it next to his body before the other posse members closed in. In a despicable act of mockery, someone, again probably Morton, placed Tunstall's hat under his horse's head and beat Tunstall's face with the butt of his gun.[6]

On February 18, 1978, the one hundredth anniversary of Tunstall's murder, the Lincoln County Historical Society placed a second commemorative monument at the site.

Graves of Roberts and Brewer

Andrew L. "Buckshot" Roberts was shot at Blazer's Mill on April 4, 1878, by Charles Bowdre. Roberts and Bowdre had fired at each other simultaneously. Bowdre's bullet entered Roberts' lower belly. Robert's bullet glanced off Bowdre's cartridge belt and took off George Coe's right index finger. Although mortally wounded, Roberts managed to get himself into Dr. Blazer's office. Roberts removed a Springfield rifle that was resting on pegs on the office wall. With ammunition found with the weapon, he positioned himself on a mattress in the doorway. Lying there, he could spot anyone approaching the entrance.

Richard Brewer, determined to finish Roberts off, worked his way to the Mill's sawmill building, located *"about 125 yards from the door of the room in which Roberts had taken shelter."* He crept to where he knew he had a clear view of the office doorway. The instant he glanced over the logs he was using for cover, Roberts saw him and fired. The bullet struck Brewer in his eye, killing him instantly.

Brewer was buried that same day *"in the south west corner of the little cemetery plat on the hill above"* the Mill. Whether Brewer was the first person buried there is unknown. His coffin was a home-made wooden *"box covered with black cloth and lined with white [cloth]."* It is highly likely that Roberts knew that Brewer's body was recovered from where he died. He may also have known that Brewer was being buried. If so, he likely took some morbid satisfaction from that knowledge.

Roberts died the next morning from his wound. He, too, was buried in a hand-made box in the cemetery on the hill above the Mill. The men were given a funeral service, with Dr. Blazer's sister Emma acting as minister.[1]

Roberts' and Brewers' graves were probably marked with wooden crosses. But by 1932, they had long been unmarked. On June 11 of that year, the Alamogordo Chamber of Commerce organized a marking of their graves. George Coe, who had earlier identified and helped mark Tunstall's murder site, and Almer Blazer, Dr. Blazer's son, were present at the marking ceremony.

> *"Nearly 100 automobile loads of persons from El Paso, Roswell, Silver City, Tularosa, [Alamogordo], and from mountain sections attended."* [2]

George Coe spoke to the gathering:

> *"[He] defended the Lincoln county settlers for forming the group headed by Billy the Kid. He said settlers were driven to desperation and he related injustices he said he suffered, which caused him to join the war. He said he resented Burn's book ['The Saga of Billy the Kid'] calling them outlaws in describing the mill fight. 'They were the finest citizens there, the same as in that section today,' he said."* [3]

Coe pointed out the irony of Roberts and Brewer being buried next to each other, *"to sleep eternally,"* as they were mortal enemies.

Almer Blazer spoke next. He noted that Coe's and his meeting at the ceremony was the first time they had seen each other in 34 years. He told the audience he was 13 years

The graves of Richard "Dick" M. Brewer and Andrew "Buckshot" Roberts in the Blazer's Mill Cemetery. 2017 photo.

old when the two men were killed, but he remembered it well. He related how his father with partners had founded the mill *"in the early 60s, furnishing lumber for building Old El Paso and Mesilla."*

> *"[Almer said] that few now realize how sparse the population was in those days; there being but two or three ranches in a distance of 25 miles along the Ruidoso.... He recalled that the first time he went to Roswell there were only three or four houses."* [4]

The group marked the graves with temporary markers. The Chamber told those present that the temporary markers would later be replaced by permanent stones:

> *"Mr. Blazer, who was at the burial in 1878, [knew] the exact location of the graves. A good sized cedar tree was growing directly over the graves."* [5]

In spite of the commitment to put permanent stone markers on the graves, it was never done. By the 1950s, the locations of the graves were forgotten.

In 1989, James H. Earle found a 1927 photo of the plot in which the two men were buried. The photo showed that the plot was 14 feet square and fenced with horizontal rails. There were no grave markers within the plot. With the photo as a guide, and the evidence of the fence, Earle was able to locate the plot in the Blazer's Mill Cemetery. The fence, although deteriorated, was still standing. Growing in the corner of the plot was the *"good sized cedar tree"* mentioned by Coe in his 1932 talk.[6]

In 1992, Albuquerque resident Harry Leighton decided to provide Brewer with a stone marker. With the support of interested Brewer relatives, $680 dollars were raised to pay for the gravestone. On July 11, 1992, at a dedication ceremony at the grave site, a granite stone was placed over the grave. It was engraved with Brewer's name and the dates 1850-1878. The 1850 birth date is probably off by a year or two. Five of Brewer's relatives attended the ceremony. The installation of the stone was delayed briefly because the monument supplier shipped the stone to Billy the Kid's grave in Fort Sumner by mistake.[7]

The burial location was estimated based on the Coe's description of it being next to the cedar tree.

A few years later, Buckshot Roberts' burial was commemorated by a Confederate States of America veteran's marker.

Cast of Characters

Here are brief biographies of the most important persons appearing in this book, with an emphasis on their roles in the events related in the book.

Allen, John J. "Jack." Real name may have been John Lewelling. Also known as "Little Allen." Born in Atlanta, Georgia. Allen's early life is unknown. On November 10, 1871, in Topeka, Kansas, he was convicted along with Jessie Evans of passing counterfeit 50-cent notes. He was sentenced to one year in the state penitentiary. He shows up next in Las Vegas in 1879 working as a mechanic. He and Rudabaugh became good friends. On April 2, 1880, the two men visited the Las Vegas jail with the intention of breaking out John J. Webb. Webb, a friend of Rudabaugh's, was accused of killing Michael Kelliher. Webb, who had not killed Kelliher, expected to be acquitted, so he refused to be sprung. During the freeing attempt, Allen shot and killed jailor Antonio Lino Valdez. Both Rudabaugh and Allen were indicted in absentia for Valdez's murder. The *Las Vegas Daily Gazette* reported on February 26, 1881, that while the two men were on the run, Rudabaugh murdered Allen because he was scared he might inform on him. Allen was buried at Martin's Well in the Jornada del Muerto (Journey of Death) north of Las Cruces.[1]

Angel, Frank Warner. Born May 28, 1845, in Watertown, New York. Angel obtained a law degree in 1869. He was appointed special investigator for the U.S. Department of Justice April 15, 1878, charged with investigating Tunstall's murder and corruption in Lincoln and Colfax Counties. He submitted his report on Tunstall's murder to the Justice Department on October 3, 1878, which charged Territorial Governor Axtell with 12 acts of corruption, fraud, and mismanagement that contributed directly to the death of Tunstall. His interviews with the participants in the Lincoln County War are of immense value to historians. Angel died March 15, 1906.

Axtell, Samuel Beach. Born October 14, 1819, in Franklin County, Ohio. Axtell was elected to the U. S. Congress in 1860, serving two terms. He was appointed governor of Utah in 1874, but removed after only one year in office due to extensive public criticism. He was appointed governor of New Mexico in 1875. He was removed as governor September 4, 1878. He was appointed chief justice of the New Mexico Territorial Supreme Court in 1882. He resigned from the court in 1885. Axtell died August 6, 1891.

Baca, Bonifacio "Bonnie." Born April 26, 1857 in Ceboletta, New Mexico. Bonifacio was the son of Saturnino Baca. Lawrence Murphy paid for Bonifacio to attend Notre Dame University. Bonifacio testified for the prosecution in Billy's trial in Mesilla. He died January 19, 1913.

Baca, Saturnino. Born November 30, 1830, in Ceboletta, Nuevo Mexico, Mexico. Saturnino fought for the Union during the Civil War, serving in Company E, First N.M. Cavalry, under Kit Carson. He participated in the Battle of Valverde and attained the rank of Captain. As a member of the Territorial Legislature in 1869, he introduced the bill that created Lincoln County and picked the name. He was probate judge of Lincoln County in 1872. He served as county sheriff for three terms. During the Lincoln County War, he owned the Torreón and was renting a nearby adobe house from McSween. Saturnino lost the use of his left arm on July 11, 1889. He was camped out with some sheep herders when:

> *"They were fired upon by unknown parties, nine shots being fired, two of which took effect on the body of Mr. Baca, one shattering the left elbow joint in such manner as to permanently disable the arm...."*

> *"The herders fled incontinently, and it required some time for Mr. Baca to find one of them to saddle his mule for him, after which he was obliged to ride eighteen miles to his home in Lincoln in this mutilated and excruciatingly painful condition...."* [2]

The perpetrators of the crime were never caught. Saturnino died March 7, 1925, in Lincoln.

Grave of John Dow Bail, Memory Lane Cemetery, Silver City, New Mexico. 2010 photo.

Bail, John Dow. Born July 24, 1825, in Brainbridge, Ohio. Bail studied law in Springfield, Ill, where he became good friends with Abraham Lincoln. He served in the Mexican-American War under General Scott and participated in the capture of Mexico City. He fought in the Civil War for the Union and was severely wounded at the siege of Vicksburg. He came to New Mexico in 1866. He served several times in the New Mexico Territorial Assembly. Bail died June 21, 1903, in Silver City, New Mexico. [3]

Baker, Frank. Real name Frank Johnson. Baker may have been born in New York. He came to New Mexico from Texas in the mid-1870s and joined a gang of outlaws and cattle rustlers known as "The Boys." He was suspected of several unsolved murders. He was arrested by Sheriff Brady for robbery and livestock stealing, but permitted to escape. He was one of the members of the chase posse that killed Tunstall. Baker was arrested for Tunstall's murder by a posse led by Richard Brewer using warrants issued by Justice of the Peace Wilson. While being taken to Lincoln on March 9, 1878, Baker tried to escape and was shot and killed.

Barela, Santos. Real name Santos Bermudes. Barela was tried at the April, 1881, session of the Third District Court in Mesilla and convicted of murdering José Jojola. He was hanged in the Mesilla courthouse placita on May 21, 1881. He was 21 years old. He was probably buried in the Mesilla Catholic cemetery.

Barnes, Sidney M. Born May 10, 1821, in Irvina, Kentucky. Barnes was admitted to the bar at age 21. He fought for the Union in the 8th Kentucky Volunteers during the Civil War and participated in the battles of Chickamauga, Lookout Mountain, and Murfreesboro. He was appointed New Mexico Territorial Attorney General Dec 21, 1878. Barnes died May 19, 1890, in Carthage, Missouri.[4]

Memorial marker for James W. Bell, Cedarvale Cemetery, White Oaks, New Mexico. 2007 photo.

Bell, James W. "Long Bell." Born in Maryland about 1853. Bell was a Texas Ranger before moving to New Mexico. He was one of the two deputies that Garrett left guarding Billy when he went to White Oaks. Bell was shot with his own pistol (probably) by Billy on April 28, 1881, during Billy's escape. He was buried originally in Lincoln, but now has a memorial marker in the Cedarvale Cemetery in White Oaks.

Blazer, Joseph Hoy. Born August 20, 1829, in Washington County, Pennsylvania. Blazer trained as a dentist. When the Civil War started, he joined the First Iowa Cavalry. He was discharged with a combat injury disability before the war ended. At the end of the Civil War, using ten six-mule wagons, he hauled a load of freight from Dallas to El Paso. He stayed in El Paso, freighting between El Paso, Tularosa, and Fort Stanton. In 1867, Blazer and three partners homesteaded a site on the Rio Tularosa and built a lumber mill. The mill burned down and was rebuilt in 1869. In 1876, Blazer became the sole owner. A flour mill was added in 1882. He died October 31, 1898, from stroke and heart failure. He was buried in the Blazer's Mill Cemetery.[5]

Bond, Ira M. Born about 1851. Bond became co-publisher and editor of the *Mesilla News* in 1874. He was a bitter enemy of Colonel Albert Fountain. He died April 2, 1931, at Takoma Park, Maryland.

Bousman, Louis Philip "The Animal." Born January 4, 1857, in Kanawha County, Virginia. Bousman moved to Tascosa, Texas, at the age of twenty where he worked as a cowhand. He was one of the LX ranch hands who joined Garrett's posse hunting Billy, who he had met previously in Tascosa. He was a deputy sheriff during the Panhandle Cowboy Strike in 1883, and killed one of the strikers. Bousman died January 2, 1942, in Waurika, Oklahoma.[6]

Bowdre, Charles. Born about 1848 in Mississippi. Bowdre married Manuela Herrera, the younger sister of Doc Scurlock's wife, about 1879. At the fight at Blazer's Mill, Bowdre fired the shot that fatally wounded Buckshot Roberts. During the Lincoln war, he was stationed in the Ellis home. He was killed December 23, 1880, at Stinking Springs by Garrett's posse. Bowdre was buried the next day in the Fort Sumner Cemetery, in a new suit paid for by Garrett.

Bowdre, Manuela Herrera. Her parents were José Fernando Herrera and María Juliana Martin. Manuela was the wife of Charles Bowdre. She was 14 when Bowdre was killed. Manuela married three times after Charles' death: to José Portillo, Maximiano Corona, and James Salsberry. She died February 13, 1939.[7]

Boyle, Andrew. Born November 22, 1838, in Scotland. Boyle may have served in the British army. He was a deputy under Sheriff Peppin during the Lincoln war. He testified at the Dudley Court of Inquiry that he set the fire that burned down the McSween home during the Lincoln war. He died May 14, 1882.[8]

Brady, William. Born August 16, 1829, in Ireland. Brady immigrated to the U.S. and joined the U.S. Army in 1851, serving two five-year terms. He joined the 2nd N.M. Volunteer Infantry August 19, 1861. He was promoted to Brevet Major and appointed commander of Fort Stanton April 29, 1864. He was replaced at Fort Stanton in October, 1865, by Emil Fritz and appointed commander of Fort Selden. He was transferred to Fort Sumner in May, 1866. He was discharged from the army October 8, 1866. In 1868, he purchased a large ranch east of Lincoln. He became a U.S. citizen July 20, 1869. He was elected sheriff of Lincoln County September 6, 1869. After serving two years, Brady was elected to the Territorial House for one term. In November, 1876, Brady was re-elected sheriff of Lincoln County. He was killed April 1, 1878, by shots fired from Tunstall's horse corral.[9]

Grave of Manuel Silvestre Brazil, Greenwood Cemetery, Hot Springs, Arkansas.
2011 photo.

Brazil, Manuel Silvestre. Born June 12, 1850, in Rosais, Sao Jorge Island, Azores Archipelago. Brazil came to the U.S. about 1865 and to the Fort Sumner area about 1871. He began ranching at a spring that became known subsequently as Brazil Springs, and he soon formed a ranching partnership with Thomas Wilcox. Brazil sold his ranch and moved to Las Vegas about 1893, then to Texas, and then to Hot Springs, Arkansas, where he died June 17, 1928.[10]

Brewer, Richard M. Born February 19, 1850, in St. Albans, Vermont. Brewer arrived in Lincoln in 1870 and homesteaded a ranch on the Rio Feliz. In 1874, he bought a second ranch from James Dolan. When Tunstall arrived in Lincoln and began buying livestock, he hired Brewer as his ranch foreman. Brewer was with Tunstall when he was murdered by Tom Hill and Buck Morton. On April 4, 1878, Brewer was killed at Blazer's Mill by Buckshot Roberts. For details on his grave site, see Appendix B.[11]

Grave of Warren Henry Bristol, Cold Spring Cemetery, Lockport, New York. Bristol was buried originally in the Mountain View Cemetery, Deming, New Mexico. A few years later, at the request of his widow, Louisa Bristol, his remains were moved to the Lockport cemetery. 2012 photo.

Bristol, Warren Henry. Born March 19, 1823, in Stafford, New York. Bristol graduated from Wilson Collegiate Institute and studied law at Fowler's Law School. He practiced law in Minnesota from 1850-1872. He was appointed judge of the New Mexico Third District Court in April, 1872. He was a committed partisan ally of the Murphy-Dolan faction during the Lincoln County War. In January, 1883, he was strongly criticized for sentencing an eight-year-old boy to jail, for *"dealing in manufactured tobacco without a license."*

"The facts developed at the trial were that the lad had in his possession a small (ten cent) package of smoking tobacco; that he met a boy who had a jack knife which he coveted. The accused lad struck a trade with the other boy for the knife, giving him the package of tobacco, a nickel and some chewing gum, or something of that sort, to boot. This was the whole case against the lad...."

"The boy was convicted [by a jury] and all that his attorney could accomplish was to get his sentence down as low as six months imprisonment. So the poor lad was caged in the [Mesilla] Jail among criminals of the worst class, and passed his term of imprisonment with none to sympathize with him except the few humane people who were in the court room at the trial...." [12]

Judge Bristol resigned from the court in 1885 and died January 12, 1890.

Brown, Henry Newton. Born in 1857 at Cold Spring Township, Missouri. Brown left Missouri at the age of 17, drifted into Texas, and worked as a cowboy and buffalo hunter. He left Texas for Lincoln, New Mexico, in 1876, after reportedly killing a man. In Lincoln he worked for Murphy, then for John Chisum. When the conflict between Murphy and Tunstall started up, he aligned himself with Tunstall. Brown was behind the corral wall with Billy when Sheriff Brady was shot, and was indicted for the killing. He was with Billy and the other Regulators at Blazer's Mill when Buckshot Roberts was killed. During the Lincoln war, he was positioned in the Tunstall store along with the Ealys. Following the Lincoln war he returned to Texas briefly, then moved to Caldwell, Kansas, were he became assistant city marshal and then full city marshal. He resigned after 16 months, spent some time in Missouri, and was rehired as Caldwell marshal. On April 30, 1884, Brown, his deputy, and two other men tried to rob the bank in Medicine Lodge, Kansas, killing the city marshal in the process. They were caught and jailed. A mob of 300 gathered to lynch the men. As they broke into the jail, Brown escaped, but was killed by a shotgun blast. The other three men were lynched. [13]

Campbell, William W. "Billy." Campbell first appeared in Lincoln on December 6, 1876, charged with killing Thomas King. He was tried December 14 by Justice of the Peace Wilson and acquitted. Oddly, he was arrested again the next day and tried a second time, also acquitted. By 1878, he was working for Dolan. At the February 18, 1879, peace parley arranged by Billy with Dolan, Campbell was present. When the men encountered Chapman later in the evening, Campbell ordered Chapman *"to dance."* When Chapman refused, Campbell shot him in the chest, claiming he had promised Colonel Dudley he would kill him. Campbell was arrested by order of Governor Wallace, but escaped to Texas. On September 8, 1881, Campbell and Joseph Waters killed William Blanchard and Joe Barrett at a trading post at Sunset Crossing on the Little Colorado River, east of

Grave of John Simpson Chisum. Paris, Texas. 2007 photo.

Winslow, Arizona, in a murder-for-hire scheme. Campbell and Waters were caught and jailed at St. Johns, Arizona. They were lynched on December 18, 1881.[14]

Caypless, Edgar A. Born in 1852 in New York. Caypless practiced law in Colorado before moving his practice to New Mexico in 1881. Caypless was asked by Billy to recover and sell the mare that he may or may not have given away when he was captured at Stinking Springs. Billy wanted the money to pay for an appeal for his conviction for murdering Sheriff Brady. Caypless eventually did obtain $50.95 for Billy, but by the time he got the money, Billy was dead. In 1884, Caypless moved back to Denver. In 1899, he moved to Hawaii and served one term as mayor of Honolulu. In Hawaii, Caypless was a militant supporter of the Hawaiian Home Rule Movement. Caypless died June 8, 1917, in his sleep in Denver, Colorado.[15]

Chambers, Alonso "Lon." Born in 1849 in Texas. Chambers was one of the LX ranch men sent to capture Billy in November, 1880. He was with Garrett at Fort Sumner when Thomas O'Folliard was killed. On September 29, 1883, three men attempted to rob the east-bound A.T. & S.F. train at Coolidge, Kansas. The target was the express car. The train engineer was killed and the fireman seriously wounded. Chambers and two other men were arrested for the crime. Chambers at the time was described as having a *"hard reputation about Coolidge."* They were tried and acquitted. In 1886, the actual robbers were caught and convicted. In May, 1884, Chambers was hired by Garrett as a deputy sheriff during the Panhandle Cowboy Strike. His death date is unknown.[16]

Chapman, Huston Ingraham. Born April 28, 1847, in Burlington, Iowa. As a thirteen-old youth, Chapman lost his left arm in a self-inflicted gun accident. He came to New Mexico in the fall of 1878. Chapman was hired by Susan McSween to pursue criminal charges against Colonel Dudley for the murder of her husband. Dudley despised Chapman and according to sworn hearsay testimony, encouraged his murder by Campbell. On February 18, 1879, the one-year anniversary of Tunstall's murder, Chapman was murdered by Campbell and Dolan. The coroner's jury found two bullet wounds in Chapman's breast. Only two shots were fired: one by Campbell and one by Dolan. Dolan claimed he fired only *"to attract the attention of the party."* Charged with accessory to Chapman's murder, Dolan's case was dismissed by Judge Bristol.[17]

Chisum, John Simpson. Born August 15, 1924, in Hardeman, Tennessee. By 1873, he had a huge cattle operation in New Mexico. Many of the men who later fought in the Lincoln County War worked for Chisum at one time, as Billy did. Chisum sold most of his cattle holdings in 1875. The *Las Vegas Gazette* said of his ranch at the time of the sale: *"It contains 1,600 sections of land, on which Mr. Chisum has 80,000 head of cattle."* Chisum died in Paris, Texas, on December 22, 1884.

Clark, Frank C. Real name unknown. Born in Ohio. Clark was tried at the April, 1881, session of the Third District Court in Mesilla and convicted of murdering Robert R. Mann. He was hanged in the dry Rio Grande River bed at Mesilla on May 13, 1881. He was buried in the Mesilla Catholic cemetery.

Clifford, Frank "Big Foot Wallace." Real name John Menham Wightman. Born March 18, 1860, in Wales. In 1871, Clifford moved with his family to Cimarron, New Mexico. He left home at 17 and drifted to Tascosa, Texas. He was one of the EXE ranch hands sent to capture Billy in November, 1880. He died September 8, 1946.[18]

Coe, George Washington. Born December 13, 1856, in Washington County, Iowa. Coe was the cousin of fellow Regulator Frank Coe. He came to New Mexico in 1876. He was at Blazer's Mill when Buckshot Roberts was killed. During the confrontation with Roberts at Blazer's Mill, Roberts shot off Coe's right index finger. Coe said he never sought medical treatment for the injury. He used cold water to keep the swelling down and doctored it with *"balsam salve picked out of the trees."* During the Lincoln war, Coe was positioned in the Tunstall store. He left Lincoln after the war, but returned in 1884, and spent the rest of his life in the area. He did a great service to those interested in Lincoln County War history when he with two Tunstall relatives marked the location of Tunstall's murder site. He died November 14, 1941.[19]

Copeland, John N. Born in Kentucky. Copeland was in New Mexico by 1872, working as a butcher for the Mescalero Agency. He acquired a ranch in the Lincoln area. In February, 1873, Copeland killed two Hispanic ranch hands, justifying the killings by accusing the men of theft. After Sheriff Brady was killed, Copeland was appointed to replace him. He was not a Murphy-Dolan partisan. Copeland lasted 31 days as sheriff before he was replaced by George Peppin at the order of Governor Axtell. He sold the Wortley Hotel to Garrett on May 23, 1881. Copeland died June 26, 1903.

Corbet, Samuel R. "Sam." Born August 5, 1851, in North Carolina. By 1877, Corbet was in New Mexico working for Tunstall as his clerk. He saved Jim French from being captured and probably killed following the shooting of Sheriff Brady by sawing *"a hole*

Grave of James Joseph Dolan, Dolan Cemetery, Lincoln County, New Mexico.
Undated photo. Courtesy Maurice G. Fulton Papers, Special Collections, UA.

under a bed and [hiding French] there with a gun in his hand." Corbet tried unsuccessfully to prevent Tunstall's store from being robbed after McSween's killing in the Lincoln war. He testified at the Dudley Court of Inquiry saying he saw Colonel Dudley in the store. He also saw Jessie Evans go into the store wearing only his underclothes and steal a new suit. He later served as Lincoln postmaster and county clerk. In 1890, he was elected Lincoln County School Superintendent. He died January 1, 1923, in Texas.

Cosgrove, Cornelius "Con." Born June 1, 1840, in Jackson, Missouri. He owned the stage line that ran once a week between Las Vegas and Las Cruces, which he started in 1880. The *Weekly New Mexico* wrote of the line:

"Con Cosgrove's Line from Las Vegas to Las Cruces, 315 miles, furnishes mail and passenger facilities for dozens of settlements in the eastern portion of our Territory, and is of the utmost importance." [20]

In June, 1881, Con closed his transport service and *"moved east."* He returned to New Mexico in 1884 and opened a stage line between Hillsboro and Las Vegas. Con died February 14, 1889.[21]

Cosgrove, Michael "Mike." Michael was the brother of Con Cosgrove. He supervised the mail delivery for the Cosgrove Line. Michael was living in Fort Sumner when Thomas O'Folliard was killed and undoubtedly saw him buried. He donated new clothes to Billy, Rudabaugh, Pickett, and Wilson when they were jailed in Las Vegas following their capture at Stinking Springs. He helped Garrett transport Billy, Rudabaugh, and Wilson to jail in Santa Fe. Michael was also in Fort Sumner when Billy was killed and saw him buried. He was interviewed about Billy's death in the *Las Vegas Daily Gazette* and confirmed that it was, without any doubt, Billy who was killed. In 1886, he moved to Kingston and opened a store. He died in February, 1887.[22]

Davis, George. Real name Jesse Graham. Also used the alias Tom Jones. Davis may have been a cousin of Jessie Evans. He was a member of the chase posse that killed Tunstall. He was indicted for the killing of Tunstall. In 1879, he was indicted for killing C. C. Eden. On May 19, 1880, he, Jessie Evans, and others robbed several stores at Fort Davis, Texas, reaping over $9,000 in cash. On July 3, 1880, a company of Texas Rangers sent after the robbers:

"Came upon the gang, who began to retreat. A running fight for a mile drove the robbers to the rocks, where, being fortified, they made a bold stand. The rangers charged, giving them a hand-to-hand fight. The robbers fought desperately, but soon surrendered, with the loss of Jesse Graham, alias George Davis." [23]

Dolan, James Joseph. Born May 2, 1848, in Ireland. Dolan served in 17th Regiment, New York Zouaves during the Civil War. He reenlisted after the war and was discharged at Fort Stanton. He was hired by Murphy as a clerk. He became a Murphy partner in April, 1874. When Murphy retired in 1877, the company became Dolan & Co. He was the master mover behind the events that resulted in Tunstall's killing. He was also responsible for starting the war in Lincoln and guiding it to its fatal outcome. In the fatal confrontation with Chapman, he first lied about his presence. When that was proved a lie, he claimed he only fired his Winchester *"to attract the attention of the party."* On July 13, 1879, Dolan married Caroline Fritz, the daughter of Charles Fritz. His murder charges for killing

Grave of Nathan Augustus Monroe Dudley, Arlington National Cemetery,
Washington, D.C. 2009 photo.

Tunstall and Chapman were dismissed by Judge Bristol. After the Lincoln County War he purchased Tunstall's store and prospered financially. Dolan died February 26, 1898.[24]

Dudley, Nathan Augustus Monroe. Born August 20, 1825, in Lexington, Massachusetts. Dudley joined the army in 1855. In 1857, he participated in the "Mormon War" in Utah. In 1861, he was court-marshaled on the charge of lying to a fellow officer, but acquitted. During the Civil War he was promoted to both colonel and brigadier general. Following the Civil War, he served in Arizona, then in New Mexico. In 1877, at Fort Union, he was court-marshaled and convicted of being too drunk to perform his duties. He was given command of Fort Stanton on April 5, 1878, the same day Buckshot Roberts was killed. Dudley's intervention in the Lincoln war and subsequent court of inquiry are described in Chapters 5 and 7. Dudley retired from the army on August 20, 1889. He died April 29, 1910.[25]

Ealy, Taylor Filmore. Born September 12, 1848, in Schellsburg, Pennsylvania. Ealy attended a theological seminary and received a medical degree from the University of Pennsylvania in 1874. He came to Lincoln as a Presbyterian medical missionary and school teacher, arriving February 18, 1878, the day Tunstall was killed. After the Lincoln war, he relocated to the Zuni Pueblo and worked as a school teacher. Two years later, he and his wife gave up missionary work and returned to Schellsburg where he established a medical practice. Ealy died February 20, 1915.[26]

Ealy, Mary R. Born December 23, 1850. Mary trained as a teacher. She married Dr. Taylor Ealy October 1, 1874. She died May 31, 1935.

East, James Henry. Born August 30, 1843, in Kaskaskia, Illinois. East left home for Texas at the age of 16 and became a cowhand. He was working for the LX ranch when he joined the posse that captured Billy at Stinking Springs. He helped Garrett transport Billy, Rudabaugh, and Wilson to jail in Santa Fe. In 1882, he was elected sheriff of Oldham County, Texas. He served two terms. In 1903, he moved to Douglas, Arizona. There, he served as town marshal and later as municipal judge. East died May 14, 1930.[27]

Ellis, Isaac. Born in 1829 in Missouri. Ellis arrived in Lincoln in June, 1877, with his two grown sons, Ben and Will, and established the Ellis store, which was also the family residence.[28] Isaac witnessed the shooting of Sheriff Brady and Hindman and testified for the prosecution at Billy's trial in Mesilla. During the Lincoln war, his store was one of the buildings occupied by McSween men. On the third day of the war, Isaac's son Ben was shot by an unidentified Dolan man. Dr. Ealy was unable to treat the wounded man that day, but the next day:

> "[Dr. Ealy] took [our] baby in his arms and led our little Pearl, and we all walked down the street to Ellis'. He felt sure even such desperadoes would not hurt women and children. The wound was a bad one, and the man had lost much blood. As Dr. Ealy was dressing the wound, we learned that Ben Ellis had been shot while in the corral feeding his horses." [29]

Isaac moved to La Luz in 1890 and died there in obscurity in 1910.

Emory, Thomas "Poker Tom." Real name William Oscar Arnim. Born January 2, 1854, in Moulton, Texas. On May 23, 1876, Arnim was convicted of stealing an ox and sentenced to two years in the penitentiary at Huntsville. Nine months later he escaped.

Grave of William Oscar Arnim, alias Thomas "Poker Tom" Emory, Schulenburg City Cemetery, Schulenburg, Texas. 2012 photo.

He adopted the alias Arnim and relocated to Tascosa, Texas. He was working for the LIT ranch when he joined the posse that captured Billy at Stinking Springs. He helped Garrett transport Billy, Rudabaugh, and Wilson to jail in Santa Fe. After those events, he returned to Tascosa and to cowboying. In 1896, he was pardoned for the ox-stealing conviction and prison escape by the Governor of Texas. He died in Schulenburg, Texas, on May 26, 1914.

Evans, Jessie. Alias Jesse Williams. Real name may have been Will Davis. George Davis may have been a brother or cousin. Born in 1853, in Missouri. Evans evidently grew up in Kansas. On November 10, 1871, in Topeka, Kansas, Evans was convicted of passing counterfeit 50-cent notes and fined $500. Sentenced with him was John J. Allen. When Evans came to New Mexico, he worked for John Chisum as his foreman. On December 31, 1875, Evans, John Kinney, and several others killed three men at a dance at Fort Selden. No one was charged. On January 26, 1876, Evans killed Quirino Fletcher at Las Cruces. The killing was apparently a revenge killing. Fletcher had killed two Texans a few months earlier in Mexico, one of whom may have been a friend of Evan's. Fletcher's body lay in the street all night. When his father was informed of the killing, he responded, *"Well, he has killed two men, but will kill no more."* Evans was tried and acquitted of that crime.

Evans was in the chase posse that pursued and murdered Tunstall and was indicted for that killing. On March 14, 1878, he was badly wounded while trying to rob a sheep herder. His fellow robber Tom Hill was killed. Evans made his way to Shedd's ranch, where he was arrested and taken to Fort Stanton, then to Mesilla. In Mesilla, he was charged with the murder of Tunstall, but released on bond after his case was postponed to the next court session. That inexplicable action by Judge Bristol at the request of District Attorney Rynerson gave him his freedom just in time to permit him to return to Lincoln and fight in the Lincoln war for Dolan. Following the Lincoln war, he went to Texas where he, George Davis, and others attempted to rob several stores at Fort Davis. He was caught and sentenced to the Texas penitentiary. In May, 1882, he escaped and disappeared from history.[30]

Foor, Charles Wesley. Born December 12, 1850, in Lebanon, Kentucky. Foor moved to Texas in 1873, where he worked as a cowboy. He spent 4 years at Fort Griffin, Texas, beginning in 1877. He moved to Fort Sumner in October, 1881, a few months after Billy's death. He ran a saloon for a few years and then took a job as a ranch hand. In 1887, he opened a hotel in Fort Sumner. In 1891, he became the Fort Sumner postmaster. In 1905, Foor opened a hotel in Sunnyside. When that failed he acquired a small ranch southeast of Fort Sumner. Foor acquired the Billy the Kid tintype that Billy gave to Deluvina Maxwell from the estate of John Legg. That tintype was lost when Foor's house burned down. In April, 1930, Foor and Jesus Silva, Vincente Otero, and A. P. Anaya gathered in the Fort Sumner cemetery to locate Billy's grave. The grave had been unmarked for 44 years. The site they eventually agreed upon was shown in *"Billy the Kid's Grave – A History of the Wild West's Most Famous Death Marker"* to be within a foot of Billy's grave's location as marked on a map made of the cemetery in 1905. He died January 20, 1940, and was buried in the Fort Sumner cemetery.[31]

Fountain, Albert Jennings. Original name Albert Jennings. Born October 23, 1838, in Staten Island, New York. Fountain's father was a sea captain, which was probably

222 ~ Appendix C

what inspired him to take a sea voyage to the Far East as a young man. He ended up in California in 1854. In California, he worked as a reporter for the *Sacramento Union*, and was dispatched as a war correspondent to Nicaragua to cover the Filibuster War (or Walker Affair). William Walker, an American mercenary, usurped the presidency of Nicaragua in July, 1856, and ruled until May 1, 1857. On quitting the newspaper, he studied law. In August, 1861, Fountain joined the California Column. He mustered out of the service in November, 1866. He served one term in the Texas Legislature. When Texans regained control of their state from the "carpetbaggers," he moved to Mesilla. In 1877, he co-founded and edited the *Mesilla Valley Independent*. Colonel Fountain defended Billy in his trial for killing Sheriff Brady. He and his eight-year-old son disappeared February 1, 1896, on his way home from attending court in Lincoln. No bodies were found. For more details on their presumed murders, see *"Killing Pat Garrett, the Wild West's Most Famous Lawman – Murder or Self-Defense?"* and *"The Stolen Pinkerton Reports of the Colonel Albert J. Fountain Murder Investigation."* [32]

French, Jim. Little is known about French. French was working for Tunstall when the Lincoln County War began. He was behind Tunstall's corral wall with Billy when Sheriff Brady and Hindman were killed. He and Billy ran out after the shooting and attempted to recover something from Brady's body. French was wounded in the thigh in that action. He was saved from capture by Sam Corbet hiding him under a bed. He was at Blazer's Mill when Buckshot Roberts was killed. He was in McSween's house with Billy during the Lincoln war and escaped with Billy successfully. There is no record of French after the Lincoln war.

Fritz, Emil Adolf. Born March 3, 1832, Egolsheim, Germany. During the Civil War, Fritz served in the California Column. He reenlisted after the war ended and served as commander of Fort Stanton, leaving the service to become a partner with Murphy. On a return trip to Germany, he died June 26, 1874. McSween was hired to collect Fritz's $10,000 life insurance policy benefit from the Merchants Life Assurance Company. McSween only succeeded in collecting about $7,000 of the benefit. After McSween charged his commission and expenses, less than one third remained for Fritz's heirs, which led to a lawsuit against McSween and, unfairly, against Tunstall. That lawsuit led to the confiscation of Tunstall's property, which was the incident that began the Lincoln County War.

Garcia, Abrana (Segura). Born in 1858, probably in San Miguel County, New Mexico. Abrana may have been the younger sister of Deluvina Maxwell. If she was, she was a Ute. She was raised by Fernando and Manuela Segura as Abrana Segura. In 1880, Abrana was 22 years old and married to Martin Garcia. When Billy was killed, she and Martin were living in Fort Sumner and had three children. The two oldest children were Martin's children from a previous relationship. Abrana died in 1925 and was buried in the Fort Sumner Cemetery.[33]

Garrett, Patrick Floyd Jarvis. Born June 5, 1850, in Chambers County, Alabama. Garrett was the Lincoln County sheriff at the time he captured and killed Billy. After leaving Lincoln, he lived in Roswell and then Uvalde, Texas. He returned to Las Cruces, New Mexico, February 23, 1896, after being hired to investigate the apparent murder of Colonel Fountain and his son. He served two terms as Dona Ana County sheriff and one

Grave of Alexander Grzelachowski, Nuestra Senora de Rufugio Cemetery, Puerto de Luna, New Mexico. 2009 photo.

term as El Paso Customs Collector. Garrett was killed by Jesse Wayne Brazel on Leap Day, February 29, 1908.[34]

Gauss, Gottfried G. Born in Germany about 1825. Gauss immigrated to the U.S. in 1853. He served thirteen years in the U.S. army, the last two during the Civil War. After arriving in Lincoln, he worked for Murphy. He was working for Tunstall when the Lincoln County War started. He was an eye-witness to Billy's escape from the Lincoln courthouse jail. He heard Billy shoot Bell. Bell then ran out of the courthouse and fell into Gauss' arms. He saw Olinger emerge from the Wortley Hotel and get shot by Billy. The likely reason he was outside and able to observe Billy's escape was because he was taking care of a large garden on land behind the courthouse. Gauss left Lincoln in the late 1890s, and may have died in 1902.

Gomez, Francisco. Saturnino Baca's son-in-law. Gomez submitted a signed deposition to the Dudley Court of Inquiry saying:

> "That he believed the said Mrs. McSween to be a respectable woman when he first became acquainted with her. That soon after... she began to make improper advances to him.... That the said Mrs. McSween persisted in these advances in such a palatable and lascivious manner, that [he] had sexual intercourse with the said Mrs. McSween.... That their sexual acts were committed at various places, chiefly in the brush near the river...." [35]

Grave of Ira Edwin Leonard, Columbia Cemetery, Boulder, Colorado. 2012 photo.

Grzelachowski, Alexander "Alejandro." Born in 1824 in Poland. Grzelachowski came to New Mexico in 1851 and to Puerto de Luna in 1873. When Grzelachowski arrived in the United States, he was a practicing Catholic priest. He served as a priest from his arrival in the U.S. in 1850 to 1862. In February, 1862, he joined the 2nd Regiment of the New Mexico Volunteers as a chaplain. After participating in the Battles of Glorieta Pass and Valverde, Grzelachowski left the priesthood and became a shopkeeper, first in Las Vegas, then in Puerto de Luna. When Guadalupe County was created February 26, 1891, and Puerto de Luna was made the county capital, Grzelachowski donated the land for the capital building. Grzelachowski died May 24, 1896, as a result of being thrown from of a horse-drawn wagon. Because he had left the priesthood, he was buried outside of the boundary line of the Puerto de Luna Catholic cemetery.[36]

Gutierrez, Celsa (Martinez). Born in 1858 in San Miguel County, New Mexico. Celsa parents were Albino and Feliciana Martinez. She was a younger sister of Garrett's first wife, Juanita Martinez. Celsa Martinez became Celsa (Martinez) Gutierrez by marrying Sabal Gutierrez. When Billy was killed, they were living in Fort Sumner and had a four year old daughter, Mauricia. She died July 25, 1923.[37]

Gutierrez, Sabal. Born about 1850. Sabal was the husband of Celsa (Martinez) Gutierrez. In 1880, he gave his occupation as sheepherder. Sabal was on the coroner's jury that ruled Billy's killing justifiable homicide. His death date is unknown.

Hall, Lee. Real name Lee Hall Smith. Hall may have been born in Texas. He may have been gored to death by a bull in 1882.

Herrera, José Fernando. Born in 1836 in Santa Cruz de la Canada. By the mid-1870s, Herrera had a farm in the Ruidoso Valley. He joined the Regulators after the killing of Tunstall. During the Lincoln war he was in Montaño's store. On the third day of the war, he mortally wounded Dolan man Charlie "Lallacooler" Crawford on the hill south of Lincoln. Tradition says it was a shot of 900 yards. Crawford lay where he fell until the next day when he was taken to Fort Stanton. He died a week later. Herrera's daughter Antonia Miguela married Doc Scurlock and daughter Manuela Herrera married Charlie Bowdre. José Herrera died December 13, 1915.[38]

Hill, Tom. Real name Tom Chelson. Hill arrived in New Mexico in the mid-1870s. He began riding with the outlaw group known as "The Boys." He was in the chase posse put together by Deputy Mathews to pursue Tunstall. He and Buck Morton murdered Tunstall and defaced his body. Hill was killed March 14, 1878, when he and Jessie Evans attempted to rob a sheep herder.

Hindman, George. He arrived in Lincoln in 1875. Hindman was crippled, having been mauled in earlier life in both the arms and legs by a bear. He and Sheriff Brady were killed April 1, 1878, by firing from behind Tunstall's corral wall.[39]

Leonard, Ira Edwin. Born March 25, 1832, in Batavia, New York. Leonard obtained a law degree and moved to Watertown, Wisconsin. After ten years, he moved to Jefferson City, Missouri, where he served as a district judge. He was nominated for the state supreme court by the Republican Party, but lost the election, which led to his moving to Boulder, Colorado. In 1878, he relocated to Las Vegas, New Mexico. Leonard began representing Billy in April, 1879, when Billy presented his evidence to the Lincoln grand jury on the killing of Chapman. During the Dudley Court of Inquiry, he served as the main prosecutor. Leonard accompanied Billy when he was conveyed in irons from the Santa Fe jail to Mesilla. He represented Billy at his court appearance for killing Buckshot Roberts. Susan McSween hired Leonard to represent her in her lawsuit against Colonel Dudley for the unlawful killing of her husband and the destruction of their property. In a never-explained action that may have cost her the case, he failed to show up when the trial opened in Mesilla. In 1882, Leonard moved to Socorro. He practiced law and became part owner of the *Socorro News*. Leonard died July 6, 1889, in Boulder, Colorado.[40]

Lewis, Julius Warren. Born April 8, 1833, in Southington, Connecticut. Although he had almost no schooling, Lewis began writing at the age of 18. After reading an article by Harriet Newell O'Brien, he contacted her by mail, which led to their eventual marriage. He wrote under the pen names of Don Jenardo and Illion Constellano. Many of his stories were collaborations with his wife. Lewis died October 28, 1920.[41]

Long, Jack "John." Known variously as Frank Rivers, Barney Longmont, John Mont, and Frank Ridden. Long arrived in Lincoln in 1876 and went to work for John Chisum as a cowhand. He was appointed deputy by Sheriff Mathews. He was in the chase posse that chased and killed Tunstall. He was indicted for killing Tunstall, but his murder charge was dropped when he pled Governor Wallace's amnesty. He was walking down the street in Lincoln with Sheriff Brady when Brady and Hindman were killed and he was wounded slightly. He made the first attempt to burn down McSween's house at the orders of Sheriff Peppin. When fired upon by McSween's defenders, he jumped into the house's outdoor toilet hole, where he spent the remainder of the conflict. He testified at the Dudley Court of Inquiry. He served as Dolan's best man at Dolan's wedding to Caroline Fritz. Long left New Mexico for locations unknown a year or so after Dolan's wedding.

Mason, Bernard "Barney." Born October 29, 1848, in Richmond, Virginia. Mason arrived in New Mexico about 1876. He began hanging out with Billy, who considered him a trusted friend. On November 29, 1879, Mason killed John Farris who fired three shots at him first. About the same time he became friends with Garrett. On January 14, 1880, in Anton Chico, he married Juana María Madrid in a joint wedding with Pat Garrett, who married Apolinaria Gutierrez. The 1880 census shows him living at Fort Sumner with Juana, 17. When Garrett put together his posse to capture Billy, he included Mason, whom he deputized for the purpose. As Mason and Billy had been close friends, Garrett knew that Mason's intelligence on Billy would be invaluable. Secret Service Agent Azariah Wild hired Mason as a spy to help Garrett capture Billy. Mason helped Garrett transport Billy, Rudabaugh, and Wilson to jail in Santa Fe. In 1886, Mason was hired by the residents of Fort Sumner to go to Las Vegas and buy Christmas supplies. He was given a large sum of money. When he returned months later, he had no supplies. He claimed that after buying the supplies he stopped in Anton Chico and eventually lost everything gambling. On May 18, 1887, Mason was convicted of stealing cattle and sentenced to one year in the state penitentiary. It was a short year. On November 16, 1887, he was pardoned by Territorial Governor Edmund G. Ross. In 1903, he was charged and convicted of assault. In 1905, Mason was charged with bribing a guard in Albuquerque to help a prisoner escape. About 1910, he moved to California. Mason died April 11, 1916.[42]

Grave of Pete Maxwell, Fort Sumner Cemetery, Fort Sumner, New Mexico. 2010 photo. The stones lining the iron fence are from the fireplace in Pete's bedroom.

Mathews, Jacob Basil. Born May 5, 1847, in Woodbury, Tennessee. Mathews fought for the Confederacy during the Civil War, enlisting at 16 in the 5th Tennessee Cavalry. He came to New Mexico in 1867 attracted by news of a gold strike near Elizabethtown. After mining for several years, he moved to Lincoln and worked briefly for Murphy. With a partner, he began ranching at a site that later became the town of Roswell. After selling out at Roswell and ranching for a while on the Rio Penasco, he moved to Lincoln. When Murphy retired and Dolan took over his business, Mathews was brought in as a secret partner. Appointed by Sheriff Brady as a deputy, Mathews led the posse that confiscated Tunstall's cattle at his ranch and provoked Tunstall's fatal effort to flee to Lincoln with his horses. Mathews selected the members of the chase posse that murdered Tunstall. Mathews was one of the deputies walking down the street in Lincoln with Sheriff Brady when Brady and Hindman were killed by shots fired from behind Tunstall's corral wall. After taking cover, Mathews wounded Jim French when he and Billy ran out to recover Billy's rifle. Mathews was present when Chapman was killed and was indicted for that murder, but never tried. Mathews testified at the Dudley Court of Inquiry. Mathews testifid against Billy in his trial for killing Sheriff Brady and was a member of the posse that conducted Billy to Fort Stanton and turned him over to Sheriff Garrett for hanging in Lincoln. In 1893, Mathews moved to Roswell. He died June 3, 1904.[43]

Commercial Hotel
MRS. P. M. JARAMILLO, Prop's.
ROOMS by the DAY, WEEK,
or MONTH.
First Class Accomodations.

Ad for Commercial Hotel owned by Paulita Maxwell 1909-1918. July 24, 1909,
Fort Sumner Review.

Maxwell, Deluvina. Born February, 1848, according to 1900 census data. She was a Navajo taken captive as a young child by Utes. When she was about nine years old, she was freed by Lucien Maxwell by being purchased for $50 from her Native American captors. She then became a member of the Maxwell family. Deluvina died November 27, 1927.[44]

Maxwell, Lucien Bonaparte. Born September 15, 1818, in Kaskaskia, Illinois. Through his marriage to his wife, Maxwell acquired the land granted to his father-in-law Carlos Beaubien by the Mexican government. It became known as the Maxwell Land Grant. Maxwell sold the Grant in 1870. At that time he was probably the richest man in New Mexico. He purchased the grounds and buildings of Fort Sumner on October 17, 1870. Maxwell died July 25, 1875, and was buried in the Fort Sumner Cemetery.[45]

Maxwell, Paulita. Born in January, 1864, in Mora, New Mexico. On January 14, 1883, Paulita married José Felix Jaramillo. She was 18. In 1909, Paulita separated from José. She moved to the town of Fort Sumner (not the Fort) and purchased the Commercial Hotel, located near the train station. In 1918, she began offering the hotel for lease, calling it *"the best paying small hotel in New Mexico."* Some time prior to 1920, she sold the hotel. Paulita died December 17, 1929, of Bright's disease and was buried in the Fort Sumner Cemetery.[46]

Maxwell, Pedro Menard "Pete." Born April 27, 1848, in Cimarron, New Mexico. Pete was the oldest child of Lucien Maxwell and his wife. Pete married Sarah "Sadie" C. Lutes on November 29, 1884, the same day Charlie Foor married his wife. Nothing is known of their reported child. He died June 21, 1898, and was buried in the Fort Sumner Cemetery. Six months after Pete's death, Sarah Lutes married James F. Wade.[47]

McKinney, Thomas Christopher "Kip." Born March 19, 1856, in Tarrant County, Texas. McKinney grew up in Uvalde, Texas. Prior to his arrival in New Mexico, he was a U.S. Marshal. Garrett appointed him one of his deputies. On May 8, 1881, he killed Bob

Grave of Susannah Ellen (Barber) McSween, Cedarvale Cemetery, White Oaks, New Mexico. Note the misspelling of McSween. 2010 photo.

Edwards. Edwards was a notorious horse thief. In mid-April, 1881, McKinney learned that Edwards had stolen 21 head of horses from John Slaughter at Tombstone, Arizona. Learning that he was in the Seven Rivers area, McKinney went after him with a posse. They encountered Edwards at Rattlesnake Springs. Edwards sighted McKinney first and opened up with his Winchester. McKinney returned the fire. His second *"shot broke one of Edward's legs. Edwards dropped to the ground but continued firing. McKinney then sent a bullet through his brain...."* McKinney was with Garrett when he killed Billy. When the Spanish-American war broke out, McKinney enlisted in the army and attained the rank of Captain. He died September 21, 1915.[48]

McNab, Francis "Frank." He sometimes spelled his name MacNab. Birth date unknown. McNab was one of the men behind Tunstall's corral wall when Sheriff Brady and Hindman were killed. He was killed at the Fritz ranch April 29, 1878, by a party of Dolan men.[49]

McSween, Alexander Anderson. Born in 1843 in Canada. Surprisingly little is known about McSween's early years. He may have practiced as a Presbyterian minister. He did not finish his law training. Nevertheless, in 1873, he began practicing law in Eureka, Kansas, where he met his future wife Susan Ellen Hummer. The same year he was elected Justice of the Peace. He and his wife arrived in Lincoln on March 5, 1875. McSween was killed attempting to flee his burning house on July 19, 1878.

Grave of Lawrence Gustave Murphy, Santa Fe National Cemetery, Sante Fe, New Mexico. 2009 photo.

McSween, Susannah Ellen "Susan." She always gave her maiden name as Homer, but it actually was Hummer. Born December 30, 1845, in Adams County, Pennsylvania. She was raised as a Dunkard, a sect of the German Baptist Brethren. The denomination mandated conservative dress and banned the use of alcohol and tobacco. In 1863, a party of Confederate forces on their way to what would become the Battle of Gettysburg raided the Hummer farm, demanding food supplies and stealing two horses. When the battle began, the family took what shelter they could. They were close enough to the battle to experience house-rattling cannon fire. Following the battle, Susan ran away from home. The next ten years of her life are a mystery. She appears in April, 1873, in Eureka, Kansas. On August 13, 1873, she married Alexander Anderson McSween. The marriage license gives her name as Sue E. Homer. Two years after McSween's murder, she married George L. Barber. In 1885, they acquired the Three Rivers Ranch. The couple divorced on October 16, 1892. Following the divorce, Susan retained ownership of the ranch. She sold it in 1917 to Albert Fall and moved to White Oaks, where she died January 3, 1931.[50]

Middleton, John. Born about 1865 in Tennessee. Middleton began working for Tunstall in October, 1877. He was riding with Tunstall when Tunstall was killed and was the first of Tunstall's companions to see the chase posse appear behind them. He was one of the men behind Tunstall's corral wall when Sheriff Brady was killed and was indicted for the killing. He was at Blazer's Mill when Buckshot Roberts was killed. One of Roberts' shots struck Middleton in the chest. Middleton died of smallpox on November 19, 1882, at San Lorenzo. In a deathbed confession, he said he had killed two men in Texas. The newspaper reporting his death wrote:

> *"For this last murder the state of Texas offered a reward of $1200 for his capture, dead or alive, and before dying he advised those around him to take his body to the Lone Star state, to earn that reward; but nobody seemed anxious to take the trouble of taking a small pox corpse along the road for the sake of blood money."* [51]

Morley, J. F. Known as "Jumbo" from his *"size and shape."* Morley first appeared in New Mexico in 1880 as a postal inspector. In January of that year he was nearly killed in a fight at Close's Dance Hall in Las Vegas with "Texas Bill" Truelove and his girlfriend Mollie Deering. In October, 1880, he arrested and preferred charges against Fred Weston and Mrs. Deolatere for the October 16 mail robbery that Rudabaugh later confessed to. On December 27, 1880, when the train containing Garrett and his prisoners was surrounded by a mob, Morley rushed to Las Vegas at Garrett's request and piloted the train to Santa Fe. On January 15, 1881, Morley was sworn in as a Las Vegas constable. The remainder of his life was spent in law enforcement in various places. He died some time after 1922.[52]

Morton, William Scott "Buck." Born in 1856 in Charlotte County, Virginia. By early 1877, Morton was in Lincoln working for Murphy and Dolan as their ranch foreman. He was selected by Mathews to lead the chase posse ordered after Tunstall. Morton and Tom Hill reached Tunstall ahead of the other posse members. Morton shot Tunstall in the breast; Hill shot him in the head. Then Morton shot Tunstall's horse and put Tunstall's hat under his horse's head. One of the two smashed Tunstall's skull with his pistol. Morton was arrested for Tunstall's murder by a posse led by Richard Brewer using warrants

Grave of Anthony Neis, Calvary Cemetery, Fort Smith, Arkansas. 2013 photo.

issued by Justice of the Peace Wilson. While being taken to Lincoln on March 9, 1878, Morton tried to escape and was shot and killed.

Murphy, Lawrence Gustave. Born in 1831 in Ireland. By the age of 17, Murphy was in New York where he enlisted in the U.S. Army. He served two terms and was discharged a few days after the Civil War began. He travelled to New Mexico and joined the New Mexico Volunteers and served for one year, was out for a few months, then re-enlisted. For a while, during his last tour, he served under Sheriff Brady at Fort Stanton. In April, 1866, he was made commander of Fort Stanton. In late 1866, he left military service and opened a brewery and store in Lincoln with Emil Fritz as a partner. In April, 1869, they hired Dolan as a clerk. Their business, which was essentially a monopoly, did well. In 1874, they built a large, two-story store in Lincoln that became known as "The House." That building later became the Lincoln County Courthouse. Murphy died October 20, 1878.

Neis, Anthony "Tony." Born October 16, 1851, in Fort Smith, Arkansas. At the age of 17, Neis moved to Santa Fe *"on account of his health [tuberculosis]."* On January 1, 1881, he was appointed Deputy U.S. Marshal by Marshal John Sherman. On March 29, Neis and Frank Chavez escorted Billy to Mesilla for his trial. Some time in 1883, Neis started the Rocky Mountain Association, a detective agency that had offices in Santa Fe and Albuquerque. That enterprise failed after a year. For the next twenty years, Neis served as a city constable or deputy sheriff. At the age of 54, his tuberculosis developed into a fatal condition:

"Upon the sixth day of December [1905] Mr. Neis was brought to Fort Smith, as it was evident he had only a few months to live, and he expressed a desire that he should die among his relatives and at his own home." [53]

Neis died March 15, 1905; at Fort Smith, Arkansas.

Newcomb, Simon Bolivar. Born March 9, 1838, in Wallace, Nova Scotia. Newcomb immigrated with his parents to Austin, Texas, when one year old. In 1855, he returned to Canada to obtain a law degree. After graduation, he moved back to Texas. In 1871, he was appointed El Paso district judge, and served for three years. He moved to Las Cruces in 1875 and practiced law. In 1880, he was appointed District Attorney of the Third Judicial District and served for eight years. Newcomb died May 23, 1901, of blood poisoning.[54]

Newman, Simeon H. Born January 12, 1846, in Richmond, Kentucky. Newman left home at the age of twenty, ending up in Fort Union, New Mexico. Following work as a miner and a teacher, he took a job on the *Las Vegas Weekly Mail* as a translator. After eight weeks, he bought the paper from its owner, Marshall A. Upson. His anti-Santa-Fe-Ring editorials did not sit well with the Las Vegas political powers. He was accused of libel for a letter he published in his newspaper and was jailed. He edited the paper for awhile from his jail cell, then sold it. The new owner changed its name to the *Las Vegas Gazette*. After a stay in Colorado, he moved to Mesilla and established *El Democrata*. After a few issues, he changed its name to *Newman's Thirty Four*. After a few months, he moved the paper to El Paso and renamed it the *Lone Star*. Newman died March 2, 1915, in El Paso, Texas.[55]

O'Folliard, Thomas "Tom." Born in 1858 (or maybe 1854) in Uvalde, Texas. It has been suggested that his real name was "Folliard," but the evidence put forward to support that theory is in error. Little is known about his life prior to his appearance in New Mexico in 1873. O'Folliard was with Billy in the McSween house during the Lincoln war. Like Billy, he escaped unharmed. O'Folliard was killed December 19, 1880, when O'Folliard, Billy, Bowdre, Pickett, Wilson, and Rudabaugh rode into Fort Sumner, thinking that Garrett was in Roswell. That false information had been conveyed to Billy by Garrett in a note that Garrett had forced José Valdez to write. It was an ambush. O'Folliard, riding the lead horse, was shot in the chest, probably by Garrett. It took O'Folliard an agonizing 45 minutes to die. He was buried in the snow-covered Fort Sumner cemetery the next morning.

Olinger, Robert Ameredith "Bob." Born 1850 in Carroll County, Indiana. Robert joined his older brother John at Seven Rivers in 1876, arriving from Texas. Robert was appointed deputy sheriff there. He killed three men before his involvement in the Lincoln County War: Juan Chavez, shot in cold-blood while shaking hands, John Hill, shot without warning, and Bob Jones, shot while *"under arrest, unarmed and defenseless."* [56]

Although Robert's brother John was in the posse that chased and killed Tunstall, Robert was not. He was in Lincoln as a Dolan man during the Lincoln war, however. Robert was one of the men that rushed the McSween house right after the arrival of Colonel Dudley on the last day of the Lincoln war. Here is his testimony from the Dudley Court of Inquiry:

> *"**Question**: What position did you take on going up to the McSween house?"*
> *"**Robert Olinger**: The front window of the McSween house."*
>
> *"**Question**: Did you remain there any length of time?"*
> *"**Robert Olinger**: I remained there one hour or one hour and a half."* [57]

From the McSween window, Robert moved to the Stanley house. During the desperate attempt by the trapped men to flee from the burning McSween house, Robert saw Harvey Morris killed. During Billy's trial, Robert was appointed by the court to lead the posse that conveyed Billy to Sheriff Garrett at Fort Stanton. Robert was killed April 28, 1881, by Billy with his own shotgun when Billy escaped from the Lincoln jail. He was buried in the Fort Stanton cemetery.[58]

Otero, Vincente. Born in 1848, based on the 1885 census, which shows him and his wife raising two adopted children. Otero's obituary claimed he was 105 when he died, but that cannot be correct. He was at Fort Sumner when Billy was killed. He dug Billy's grave the next morning. In April, 1930, he, Foor, Silva, and Anaya gathered in the Fort Sumner Cemetery to locate Billy's grave. The grave had been unmarked for 44 years. The marker for Billy's grave in the Fort Sumner cemetery is located at the site they selected. Otero died February 6, 1935.[59]

Patron, Juan Batista. Born November 20, 1852, in Santa Fe, New Mexico. Juan was educated at Santa Fe's St. Michael's School (founded by Archbishop Lamy in 1859). In 1870, the Patron family moved to Lincoln. On December 20, 1873, Juan's father was killed at a baile (dance). The killing happened when a large group of men led by brothers Sam, Merritt, and Tom Horrell burst into the dance hall and began shooting at everyone present. This was the cumulating act of the "Horrell War," an armed conflict between the

Horrell family and Hispanics living in Lincoln. On September 15, 1875, Juan and John Riley got into an argument on the street in front of the Torreón. While Juan was turned away, Riley shot him in the back. Riley claimed self-defense and was not charged. In 1877, Juan was elected to the Territorial Assembly. During the Lincoln war, his house was occupied by Dolan men. He moved to Puerto de Luna in 1879. Patron was killed there on April 9, 1884, by Michael Maney. After drinking together all day, the two got into an argument, apparently provoked by Juan. Juan drew on Maney, but his gun got snagged in his trousers. Before Juan could get his gun untangled, Maney shot him. Juan was buried beneath the vestibule of the Puerto de Luna Catholic Church.[60]

Peppin, George Warden. Born in 1838 in Chittenden County, Vermont. Peppin was a California Column veteran, having joined the Fifth Regiment of the California Infantry at the start of the Civil War. He was mustered out at Mesilla in November, 1864. Trained as a stone mason, he moved to Lincoln and built several of the town's buildings, including McSween's house and the two-story Murphy-Dolan store that later became the Lincoln Courthouse. He was appointed deputy sheriff by Brady and was with Brady when Brady and Hindman were killed. He was appointed Lincoln County sheriff on June 14, 1878, by Governor Axtell at the recommendation of Rynerson. During the Lincoln war, Peppin was the person nominally in charge of the men fighting the McSween faction, although Dolan was the de facto leader. He and Dolan provided Colonel Dudley with the justifying political cover Dudley desired to order his troops to Lincoln. Peppin ordered the burning of McSween's house. He testified in the Dudley Court of Inquiry, praising Dudley's actions in Lincoln. He submitted a signed deposition to the court saying, *"that he was forced to witness the said Mrs. McSween's lascivious conduct toward Francisco Gomez and that the scene was too disgusting to relate."* He was removed as sheriff in February, 1879. In later years, he worked as a mason, Fort Stanton butcher, deputy, and, for a while, Lincoln jailor. Peppin died January 14, 1909.[61]

Perea, Alejandro. Born about 1848. Perea built the rock house at Stinking Springs where Billy and his companions were captured. The 1870 census shows Perea living at Rio Colorado, just south of Puerto de Luna. Perea, 22 in 1870, was the second richest man in Rio Colorado. His net worth was $4,756. Perea was a sheep raiser and the rock house was likely built for sheltering his sheepherders and storing forage. In 1884, Lon Reed visited the house and saw the *"bleached skeleton"* of the horse that Garrett shot when capturing Billy still lying in the doorway of the house. Perea's death date is unknown.[62]

Pickett, Thomas "Tom." Born May 27, 1856, in Wise County, Texas. Pickett was raised in a strong religious family (his father's middle name was Bible). On April 1, 1876, Pickett became a Texas Ranger. He was discharged August 31, 1877. In August, 1876, while still a Ranger, he was charged with stealing cattle. The case was dismissed. By the fall of 1879, he was working as a Las Vegas city constable. In May, 1880, he quit and left Las Vegas. When he was captured with Billy at Stinking Springs he had only been riding with Billy for a short time. After being jailed overnight with Billy in Las Vegas, Pickett was released on bond with no charges related to being captured with Billy. In January, 1884, he and Billy Wilson and two others killed four unarmed Hispanic men in cold-blood at Seven Rivers. One of the men fired at, but not hurt, was José Roibal, who Garrett had hired to spy on Billy at Fort Sumner. (Roibal's brother Juan was with

Grave of Calvin Warnell Polk, Holdenville Cemetery, Holdenville, Oklahoma. 2010 photo.

Garrett at Stinking Springs when Billy was captured.) One newspaper report said Pickett recognized José Roibal and fired upon him *"in retaliation for the aid he gave Garrett in capturing [him at Stinking Springs]."* No charges were ever filed. Pickett died May 14, 1935, at Pine Top, Arizona, of inflammation of the kidneys.[63]

Poe, John William. Born October 17, 1851, in Mason County, Kentucky. Poe left home at 19 and made his way to Fort Griffin, Texas, where he became a buffalo hunter. By his own account, in six years, he may have killed as many as 20,000 buffalo. In 1878, he was appointed Fort Griffin town marshal, followed by an appointment as U.S. marshal. A year later, he moved to Tascosa and worked as a cattle detective. He left there for New Mexico in May, 1881, and was hired by Garrett as his chief deputy. He was with Garrett when Billy was killed at Fort Sumner. When Garrett chose to not run for a second term as Lincoln County sheriff, Poe ran and was elected. He resigned the office on December 31, 1885, and moved to Roswell, where Garrett was also living. On June 8, 1887, Garrett's first son was born. To reflect his friendship for Poe, Garrett named the boy Dudley Poe Garrett. In 1890, Poe co-founded the Bank of Roswell and served as president. Ten years later, he organized the Citizens National Bank and served as its president. He died July 23, 1923, at the Battle Creek Sanitarium at Battle Creek, Michigan. Some sources say he died from suicide due to depression.[64]

Polk, Calvin Warnell "Cal." Born January 8, 1863, in Caldwell County, Texas. Polk began working as a cowhand at a very young age. He was only seventeen when he joined Garrett's posse hunting Billy. Some time later he moved to Holdenville, Oklahoma, where he entered law enforcement, serving as deputy U.S. Marshal and city marshal. On January 15, 1904, he was found alive lying on the floor of his house with a gunshot wound to his forehead. He died just after being found. Suicide was considered but ruled out. The revolver found at the scene had the handles removed. Five cartridges were also removed. Apparently he was cleaning the gun and did not think there were six rounds in it, as he was said to always only load five as a safety measure.[65]

Reade, Daniel M. Born in 1840 in Warren County, Illinois. Reade enlisted in the 5th Infantry of the California Volunteers (California Column) February 6, 1862 and mustered out April 2, 1865, at Las Cruces. Reade was one of the deputies in the sheriff's posse that escorted Billy from Mesilla to Fort Stanton after Billy's trial. The first night of that trip was spent at the Wood-Reade ranch at St. Nicolas Springs. Reade died June 14, 1890.

Reed, Lon. Born in 1863 in Waco, Texas. Arrived in New Mexico in 1884. In 1897, he helped tear down the Maxwell house at Fort Sumner:

> *"The timbers were used to support the roof of the old Pigpen Ranch house, built that year seven miles south of the present town of Melrose by Lonnie Horn. Reed helped Horn build it, and he says it's true that part of the house is arranged just like the building in which the Kid was killed."* [66]

Riley, John Henry. Born May 12, 1850, in Ireland. By 1874, Riley was living in Lincoln, working for Murphy. Two years later he was made a Murphy partner. Just before Tunstall was killed, Riley accidentally exposed Rynerson's personal letter to him and Dolan explicitly ordering violence against McSween and Tunstall. Following the Lincoln County War, he was highly successful financially, buying and selling large ranches in Colorado and New Mexico. Riley died February 10, 1916.

Ritch, William Gillett. Born in 1830 in Ulster County, New York. During the Civil War, Ritch served in the 46th Wisconsin Infantry. He moved to New Mexico because of his health. Ritch was appointed Territorial Secretary in 1873. He became New Mexico Governor on June 3, 1875, when Governor Marsh Giddings died in office. He served until July 30, 1875, when he was replaced by Samuel B. Axtell. In a strange twist, he was acting governor when Garrett sought the reward for capturing Billy, and, again, when Garrett sought the reward for killing Billy. Ritch wrote several books on N.M. history. He died September 14, 1904.

Roberts, Andrew "Buckshot." Alias Bill Williams. Birth unknown. He fought for the Confederacy during the Civil War. He got the nickname "Buckshot" from a load of buckshot he had taken in his right arm. His immobilized right arm left him unable to lift a rifle to his shoulder. Just prior to his killing at Blazer's Mill by Bowdre, he sold a small ranch. He was at Blazer's Mill on the fateful day of his killing, April 4, 1878, because the payment for the ranch was to be mailed to him there. He was buried in Blazer's cemetery. See Appendix B for details on his gravesite.

Rudabaugh, David "Dirty Dave." Born July 14, 1854, in Fulton County, Illinois. He or others spelled his name at various times as Raudenbaugh, Radenbaugh, Radabaugh, Rudebaugh, Rudenbaugh, Radenbaugh, or Redenbaugh. The name means ship or helm-builder in German. In late 1875, Rudabaugh began hanging out with John Henry "Doc" Holliday in Dodge City, Kansas. He was earning his living at the time by committing petty hold-ups and rustling cattle.

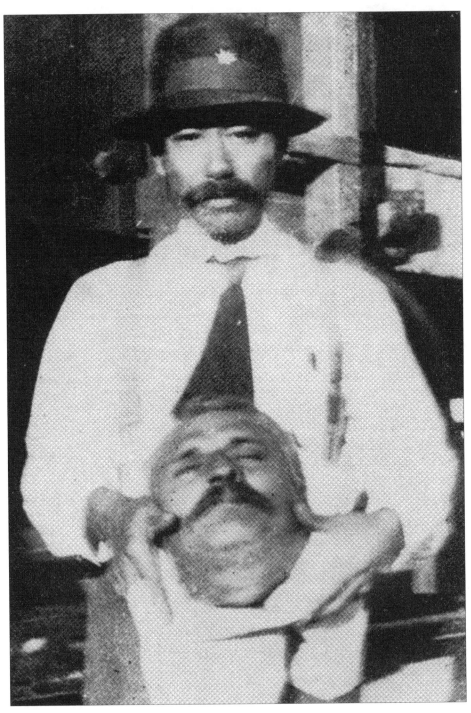

Head of David Rudabaugh. The man holding the head is probably "José," the man who killed and beheaded Rudabaugh.

Rudabaugh's head being paraded around the plaza in Parral, Mexico.

On January 27, 1878, Rudabaugh and five other men attempted to rob a train at Kinsley, Kansas. Rudabaugh was caught several days later. In the resulting trial, Rudabaugh turned state's evidence and testified against his accomplices. After the others were sentenced to five years in the Leavenworth penitentiary, Rudabaugh's case was dropped. Ordered out of Kansas, he moved to Las Vegas, New Mexico.[67]

Some time in early 1879, Rudabaugh was hired as a Las Vegas city constable. On August 14, 1879, Rudabaugh and two other men robbed the stage on the road between Las Vegas and Tecolote.[68] Rudabaugh was arrested for the crime, but released. He and his fellow constables engineered the conviction of three innocent men for the crime. Rudabaugh confessed to the crime 16 months later and the unjustly convicted men were released.

Learning from the mistakes of the unsuccessful Kinsley train robbery, on October 15, 1879, Rudabaugh and another man stopped a train *"in a deep cut"* north of Las Vegas and robbed $90 from the mail car. They were not caught. Rudabaugh later confessed to this robbery also.

On April 2, 1880, Rudabaugh and John J. Allen visited the Las Vegas jail with the intention of breaking John J. Webb from the jail. Webb, a friend of Rudabaugh's, was accused of killing Michael Kelliher. Webb, who had not killed Kelliher, expected to be acquitted, so he refused to be sprung. During the freeing attempt, Allen shot and killed jailor Antonio Lino Valdez. Both Rudabaugh and Allen were indicted in absentia for Valdez's murder.[69]

Rudabaugh was carrying the indictment for killing Valdez when he was captured at Stinking Springs with Billy on December 23, 1880.

Rudabaugh's trial for killing Valdez opened April 19, 1881, in Las Vegas. Rudabaugh testified in his own defense. He described how he and Allen went to the jail intending to free Webb, and how Allen unexpectedly shot the jailor while Rudabaugh's back was turned. Rudabaugh was convicted of first degree murder and sentenced to hang. His lawyer appealed the conviction, staying the execution until the appeal could be heard.[70]

On December 3, 1881, Rudabaugh and Webb and five others escaped from the Las Vegas jail.[71]

On February 18, 1886, Rudabaugh was killed by a Winchester rifle shot to the chest in Parral, Mexico, where he was living. He had been terrorizing the citizens of the small Mexican town for some time. The shooter was *a grocerman named José.* José then:

> *"Walked to the prostrate form which had been Rudabaugh and cooly severed the head from its shoulders with his boning knife. He placed the head on [a] broomstick and by this time all the lights in the town were on and the people were pouring out of their homes and shops into the middle of the plaza, many bearing torches...."*

> *"Dave's body was dumped in a hole at the edge of town. His head remained on the broom stick, in the Parral plaza, for several days."* [72]

Rudolph, Charles Frederick. Often spelled his name Rudulph. Born July 29, 1861, at Fort Union, New Mexico. Charles was Milnor Rudolph's son by his second marriage. Charles participated in the capture of Billy at Stinking Springs. Following that event, he returned to Sunnyside where his father was operating a school. When his father Milnor was summoned from Sunnyside to serve as foreman of the coroner's jury that ruled on Billy's death, Charles accompanied him. He saw Billy's body and attended the funeral. That made him and Garrett the only two people who were at Billy's capture and at his funeral. In 1881, he wrote a poem in Spanish about hunting and capturing Billy. The poem was titled, "La Campana Sobre Los Bilitos" (The Campaign Against Billy and His Gang). In 1883, he moved to Las Vegas where he opened a mercantile. On October 11, 1885, he was nearly killed by Charles Grover, a blacksmith. Grover, drunk, came into the mercantile and fell asleep in a chair. When he was asked to leave, he left and returned with a revolver:

> *"Grover drew his pistol and shot at [Charles] Rudolph, not standing more than three feet from him. Rudolph saved his life by quickly throwing up his hand and warding off Grover's hand containing the pistol just as it discharged, the bullet whizzing by Rudolph's ear in alarming proximity. Powder from the cartridge shell filled Rudolph's eyes and nearly blinded him."* [73]

Grover was acquitted of the charge of attempted murder, but found guilt of carrying arms and fined $10. In later years, Charles served as hotel manager, school teacher, county school superintendent, postmaster, probate clerk, store owner, and ranch manager. He died May 8, 1911, at Riciada.[74]

Grave of Yginio Salazar, Lincoln Cemetery, Lincoln, New Mexico. 2007 photo.

Rudolph, Milnor Louis. Born August 25, 1826, in Elkton, Maryland. Milnor left home at 16, spent 4 years in Memphis, Tennessee, then struck out for California, drawn by the discovery of gold. He got as far as Santa Fe, where he stopped, arriving in February, 1848. When the Civil War began, he joined the New Mexico Volunteers, enlisting on October 1, 1861. He mustered out in June, 1862. In 1870, he was elected to the Territorial Assembly and served as speaker for two years. In 1878, he moved to Fort Sumner. Three years later, he moved to Sunnyside, seven miles north of Fort Sumner, and started a school. He was the foreman of the coroner's jury that ruled Billy's death justifiable homicide. The day after the coroner's jury issued its official report, Milnor was interviewed by the *Las Vegas Gazette* and asked if Billy was really dead. He replied:

> *"This news is true, for I was foreman of the jury of inquest, and know it was 'the Kid's' body that we examined."* [75]

In 1884 or 1885, Milnor moved to Riciada, where he died November 11, 1887. [76]

Rynerson, William Logan. Born February 22, 1828, in Mercer County, Kentucky. In 1852, he travelled to California as one of the thousands attracted there by the gold discoveries. When the Civil War started, he enlisted in the First California Infantry, attaining the rank of Lieutenant Colonel. He was mustered out at Mesilla in November, 1866. He was elected to the Territorial Assembly in November, 1867, as a Republican. His election was disputed by the Democrats. When the legislative session opened, Rynerson introduced a resolution condemning Territorial Supreme Court Justice John P. Slough, who was a Democratic member of the Assembly. The two met in the billiard room of the Exchange Hotel in Santa Fe on December 14, 1867. Slough insulted Rynerson, calling him *"a son of a bitch and thief"* and suggesting that he wear a collar inscribed *"I*

Grave of Josiah "Doc" Gordon Scurlock, Eastland City Cemetery, Eastland, Texas. 2007 photo.

am Heath's dog" (Heath was Republican leader). The next day Slough and Rynerson met in the hotel's bar. Following a confrontation, Rynerson fatally shot Slough with a concealed derringer. (Slough did not know he was armed.) Rynerson was tried for the killing and acquitted. During the Lincoln County War, Rynerson was District Attorney of the Third Judicial District. In that capacity, he got Billy's murder trial moved from Lincoln to Mesilla. He was an unprincipled supporter of the Murphy-Dolan faction. He died September 26, 1893.[77]

Salazar, Yginio. Born February 14, 1863. Salazar was in the McSween house during the Lincoln war. He was fifteen years old. When the men inside made their break to escape the burning building, he was with the group that ran for the cover of the river. On exiting, he was shot in two places and knocked unconscious. He was left for dead by the Dolan men. When he woke hours later, he crawled 1,000 yards to his sister-in-law's house, leaving a trail of blood and reaching the house about midnight. In his sworn statement to J.P. Wilson the day after he escaped the burning McSween house, Yginio said that the reason he was in the house was because McSween said:

> *"...if I [Yginio] did not go with him, he would fine me fifty dollars, that he knew I had a good gun, and wanted me to go with him."* [78]

Salazar's parents' ranch was the first place Billy went after his escape from the Lincoln courthouse jail. There, the shackles that were still attached to one leg were cut off. Salazar died January 7, 1936, in Lincoln.

Scurlock, Josiah Gordon "Doc." Born January 11, 1849, in Talaposa, Alabama. Scurlock studied medicine in New Orleans. After a brief visit to Mexico in 1869, he travelled to Lincoln and began working for John Chisum. On September 2, 1876, he killed his friend Mike Herkins when his gun accidentally discharged. He married José Herrera's daughter Antonia Miguela October 19, 1876. He left New Mexico after the Lincoln war. The 1880 census shows him living at the LX Ranch headquarters on the Canadian River in Potter County Texas. After living in various cities in Texas, including Vernon, Cleburn, and Granbury, he moved to Eastland, Texas, in 1919. Throughout his life, he had a deep passion for writing. He wrote poems and book reviews. He joined the Theosophical Society. Scurlock died July 25, 1929, and was buried in Eastland, Texas.[79]

Sherman, John E. Jr. Born September 4, 1847, in Mansfield, Ohio. Sherman was the nephew of Civil War General William Tecumseh Sherman. Prior to his arrival in New Mexico, he worked for a law firm owned by Ulysses S. Grant, Jr., President Grant's son. He was appointed N.M. Territorial Marshal in March, 1876. When Special Agent Azariah Wild was investigating the murder of Tunstall, he asked Sherman for help in hunting down and capturing Billy. Sherman replied, *"I prefer not to do so."* By 1879, Sherman's professional and personal reputation was in a deep slide. In July, 1879, *Newman's Thirty-Four* reported:

"The indications seem to point unmistakably to the early removal of John Sherman, Jr., U.S. Marshal for this Territory. Serious charges have been made against him by the press almost from the beginning of his term of office, and the grand jury for this county at the term of court just closed has presented his case to the public and to the authorities in Washington in such a light as to compel his immediate removal, provided the powers that be are not determined to ignore the demands of justice, as has been done in former cases of a similar nature." [80]

Sherman resigned as U.S. Marshal on March 2, 1882, leaving behind office debts of $12,784.30 in 389 different accounts. After leaving New Mexico, he moved to Washington, D.C. and reentered the banking field. Sherman died May 31, 1890.[81]

Silva, Jesus Maria. Born October 13, 1853, in Bernalillo, New Mexico. Silva moved to Fort Sumner at age 20. He was Lucien Maxwell's ranch manager at Fort Sumner, and he continued in that position with Pete Maxwell after Lucien died. He was at Fort Sumner when O'Folliard was killed. Silva met with Billy early in the evening of July 14, 1881, the night that Billy was killed. Billy and Silva left to water a horse that Billy had hidden at a nearby ranch. On returning to Fort Sumner, Billy went to the home of Sabal and Celsa Gutierrez, where Billy was staying. When Billy was killed, Silva with the help of others, lifted the body and took it into a hallway of the Maxwell house, and laid it on a long table. From there it was moved to a bench in a nearby blacksmith/carpenter shop. Silva was chief pallbearer at Billy's funeral and burial the next morning. He was one of the four men who gathered in the Fort Sumner cemetery in April, 1930, to locate Billy's grave. Silva died June 3, 1941, and was buried in the Fort Sumner Cemetery. His son Luciano "Chano" Frank Silva was the last person buried in the cemetery. To be buried there, Frank was forced to obtain a court order. The order permitted his burial, but forbid any additional burials in the Fort Sumner Cemetery.

Grave of John Webster Southwick, Oak Ridge Cemetery, Springfield, Illinois. 2011 photo.

Siringo, Charles Angelo. Born February 7, 1855, in Matagorda County, Texas. Siringo went to work for the LX Ranch as a cowhand in 1877. He was a member of the posse for awhile that hunted Billy, although he was not at Stinking Springs when Billy was captured. He published his first book in 1885. In 1886, he became a Pinkerton Detective. He resigned from the Agency in 1907. In 1920, he published the *"History of Billy the Kid,"* the first full-length book on Billy's life. Siringo died October 19, 1928.

Smith, Henry A. "Beaver." Born about 1822 in Pennsylvania. When Billy was captured by Garrett, Smith was operating a grocery store and saloon at Fort Sumner. The well-known tintype of Billy is said to have been taken in Smith's saloon. The 1880 census shows him living with a 35-year-old housekeeper and her 20-year-old son. His death date is unknown.

Southwick, James Webster. Born April 21, 1847, in Springfield, Illinois. During the Civil War he served in Company E of the 114th Illinois Infantry and saw action in the Battles of Vicksburg, Jackson, Brandon, Guntown, Tupelo, and Mobile. He was discharged in August, 1865. When the Union Pacific railroad was built from Leavenworth, Kansas, to Ogden, Utah, he had the contract for furnishing the ties. He also bore the distinction of driving the golden spike which united Northern and Southern Pacific railroads into the Union Pacific. In November, 1880, he was elected Dona Ana County sheriff. The election was disputed by his opponent. On December 15, Judge Bristol ruled in his favor, awarding him the office. During Billy's trial in Mesilla, Southwick received two letters addressed to Billy from Paulita Maxwell, which he passed on to Billy. These letters are strong evidence that Paulita was Billy's girlfriend. When Frank Clark and Santos Barela were ordered hanged by Judge Bristol following their conviction for first-degree murder at the April, 1881, session of the Third District Court, Southwick carried out the sentences. In 1885, he returned to Springfield, Illinois, and opened a carpet shop. Southwick died March 23, 1922.[82]

Stewart, Frank. Real name John W. Green. Born October 23, 1852, in New York, New York. The original family name was Gruene. He moved to Kansas at a young age, probably about 1867. In July, 1880, Stewart was hired as a range detective by the Panhandle Cattleman's Association. In November of that year, Stewart led a group of men into New Mexico to recover stolen cattle. The foray was a failure. When Garrett was putting together his posse to capture Billy, Stewart joined him as one of the Texas contingent. He helped Garrett transport Billy, Rudabaugh, and Wilson to jail in Santa Fe. Newspaper reports show that in 1884 he was a Bernalillo County deputy sheriff. A couple of years later he was working as a ranch manager in the Las Vegas area. Some time after that he seems to have gone back to using John Green. Around 1916, he settled in Raton, where he worked in the A.T. & S.F. round house and engine shop until he retired. Stewart died May 11, 1935.[83]

Stoes, Katherine D. Maiden name Katherine Doughty. Born January 11, 1874, in Lake City, Wabasha, Minnesota. Stoes came to Mesilla as a child. She was attending school in the Mesilla courthouse when Billy, Frank Clark, and Santos Barela were tried. She may have witnessed the hanging of Clark. She was a prolific author of historical articles. Stoes died March 13, 1957.

Tunstall, John Henry. Born March 6, 1853, in London, England. Tunstall left England on August 18, 1872. His destination was Victoria, Canada. He arrived September 26, 1872. He got there by way of New York and San Francisco. His father with a partner had established a branch of their mercantile business in Victoria and Tunstall was sent there to learn the business. On February 18, 1876, he left Victoria for California. His goal was to make a fortune by establishing a sheep business. After investigating opportunities in California, he decided land was cheaper in New Mexico and business prospects were better. He left California August 14, 1876, for Santa Fe. In Santa Fe, he met Robert Widenmann, who convinced him that Lincoln, New Mexico, offered the golden opportunities he was seeking. He arrived in Lincoln November 6, 1876, and, with his father's money, began building his empire. He acquired a ranch on the Rio Feliz and stocked it with cattle and horses. He opened a general store and bank across the street from Murphy's store, enraging Murphy and Dolan and initiating the financial conflict that exploded into the Lincoln County War. Tunstall was murdered by Tom Hill and Buck Morton February 18, 1878.

Turner, Marion. He arrived in Lincoln County in 1872 and homesteaded near Roswell. On April 15, 1875, he murdered Juan Montoya in cold-blood. He was Peppin's chief deputy during the Lincoln war and was indicted for killing McSween. He pled Governor Wallace's amnesty. Turner disappears from Lincoln after 1885.

Waite, Frederick Tecumseh "Fred." Born September 23, 1853, at Fort Arbuckle, Indian Nation, now Chickasaw Nation, Oklahoma. Waite was maybe the best-educated man in Lincoln. As a graduate of Mound City Commercial College, St. Louis, Missouri, he had what would be called a Master's Degree in Business Administration today. He arrived in Lincoln in the fall of 1877, probably first taking a job as a cowhand with

John Henry Tunstall and unidentified older sister, in England, before leaving for Canada. Undated photo. Courtesy Maurice G. Fulton Papers, Special Collections, UA.

Grave of Frederick Tecumseh Waite, Pauls Valley Cemetery, Pauls Valley, Oklahoma. 2010 photo.

Grave of Lew Wallace, Oak Hill Cemetery, Crawfordsville, Indiana. 2012 photo.

John Chisum and then signing on with Tunstall. Waite was at Tunstall's ranch when Sheriff Mathews rode up with his posse and attempted to confiscate Tunstall's livestock. Mathews backed off after that first confrontation, but came back the next day with more men. Confronted a second time and convinced that Mathews' real goal was to murder him, Tunstall abandoned his ranch, taking only his string of beloved horses. Tunstall asked Waite to drive a wagon of supplies to Lincoln while he, Billy, Widenmann, Brewer, and Middleton herded the horses. By that quirk of fate, Waite was not with Tunstall when he was murdered. After leaving Lincoln, Waite returned to his family home in Himmonoah, Chickasaw Nation, Oklahoma. He was elected to the Chickasaw House of Representatives and later to the Chickasaw Senate. He was the leading candidate for president of the Nation when he died September 24, 1895.[84]

Waldo, Henry Linn. Born January 16, 1866, in Jackson County, Missouri. Waldo obtained his law license in California during the Civil War. He moved to Santa Fe in July, 1873, and joined the law firm of Elkins and Catron. He was appointed Territorial Supreme Court Justice in 1876. In 1878, he was appointed Territorial Attorney General. He served two years. During the Dudley Court of Inquiry, he defended Colonel Dudley. If the transcripts of that trial are any indication, he was an exceptionally nasty and wordy lawyer. Waldo died July 10, 1915.[85]

Wallace, Lewis "Lew." Born April 10, 1827, in Brookville, Indiana. By 1849, Wallace was practicing law. He was a Mexican-American and Civil War veteran. In the Civil War he attained the rank of major general. Beginning May 12, 1865, Wallace served as a judge on the military commission that convicted eight persons of murdering, conspiring to murder, and/or aiding the murder of President Abraham Lincoln. He was appointed New Mexico Governor on September 4, 1878. He arrived in Santa Fe 24 days later. On November 13, 1878, he issued a proclamation that extended amnesty to everyone in Lincoln County for any crime committed between two specified dates, except those who had been indicted already. On March 15, 1878, Billy wrote Wallace and asked for a secret meeting. Wallace agreed and they met March 17, 1879, at J.P. Wilson's home. Billy lived up to his end of the agreement that they made in the meeting. Wallace did not. Wallace resigned the governorship on March 17, 1881. He died February 15, 1905.

Webb, John Joshua. Born February 14, 1847, in Keokuk County, Iowa. His schooling in Iowa must have been almost non-existent, as he never learned to read or write. In 1862, Webb's family moved to Nebraska. Although only 15, Webb left home for Denver, Colorado. In 1875, he was in Ford County, Kansas, working as a teamster. In January, 1878, Webb was hired by Dodge City Sheriff Bat Masterson as a deputy. On the 27th of that month, Dave Rudabaugh and five other men attempted to rob a train at Kinsley, Kansas. They were caught and jailed by a posse led by Masterson that included Webb. The next year Webb participated in the Royal Gorge War on the side of the Denver & Rio Grande railroad. The D. & R.G. and the A.T. & S.F. railroads were racing to be the first to build track through the Coloradoan Royal Gorge. The competition became violent and both sides hired armed "guards," who were little more than gunmen and saboteurs. Webb was the D. & R.G.'s Chief of Guards.

When that ended, Webb moved to Las Vegas, New Mexico. He joined Rudabaugh as a city constable. On March 2, Michael Kelliher and two other men were in a Las Vegas saloon, acting wildly. Kelliher was armed in violation of city ordinance. Constables Webb,

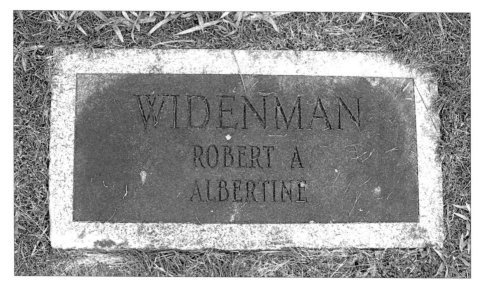

Grave of Robert Adolph Widenmann and his wife Albertine Seiler-Lemke, Mount Repose Cemetery, Haverstraw, New York. Note misspelling of Widenmann. 2012 photo.

Rudabaugh, and Dutchy (real name unknown) entered the saloon and asked Kelliher to surrender his weapon. He refused and drew on Webb. According to newspaper accounts, Webb then shot Kelliher in the breast and several more times as he fell to the floor. Webb was arrested, tried, and sentenced to hang on April 9, 1880. He appealed his case, delaying execution. On November 10, 1880, he escaped from the Las Vegas jail using a piece of wire to pick the cell door lock. He was captured by Sheriff Garrett on December 8 at Dan Dedrick's house at Bosque Grande. He was tried a second time. At this second trial, Rudabaugh testified that Webb did not kill Kelliher, Dutchy did. In spite of that testimony, Webb was sentenced to death again. On March 5, 1881, Governor Wallace commuted his death sentence to life in prison. On December 3, 1881, Webb, Rudabaugh and five others escaped from jail. Webb fled to Arizona, then Arkansas, where he died of smallpox on April 12, 1882, under the alias of Sam King.[86]

Widenmann, Robert Adolph. Born January 24, 1852, in Ann Arbor, Michigan. Widenmann's early life is obscure. He was in Santa Fe by August, 1876, when he met Tunstall. Although Tunstall liked and trusted him immediately, he told Tunstall only lies about his background. Widenmann followed Tunstall to Lincoln a few months after their Santa Fe meeting. He was with Tunstall at his Rio Feliz ranch when Sheriff Mathews' posse attempted to confiscate Tunstall's livestock. He was riding with Billy, Richard Brewer, and John Middleton when Tunstall fled to Lincoln with his horses and was murdered. He was behind Tunstall's corral wall with Billy when Sheriff Brady was shot. Afterwards, he claimed he was there only to feed Tunstall's dog and he saw and knew nothing of the shooting. He left New Mexico in October, 1878. In early 1879, Tunstall's father paid his expenses to travel to London, where he lived with (off) the family for six months. The ostensible purpose for the visit was to help Tunstall's father pursue legal action for his son's unjustified death. Widenmann real purpose was to share in any financial

Grave of David L. Anderson (Billy Wilson), Saint Mary Magdalene Cemetery,
Brackettville, Texas. 2008 photo.

settlement the Tunstalls received. Nothing came of Tunstall senior's efforts to obtain
compensation for Tunstall's death. On Widenmann's return to the U.S., he settled in
Nanuet, New York. In November, 1881, he married Albertine Seiler-Lemke. Sometime
after 1920, he moved to Haverstraw, now Stoney Point, New York, where he died April
15, 1930.[87]

Wild, Azariah Faxon. Born in 1835, in West Fairlee, Vermont. He served as a Union
soldier during the Civil War. On June 15, 1877, he was hired as a Special Operative by
the U.S. Secret Service. In late September, 1880, the Treasury Department dispatched
Wild to Lincoln County to investigate counterfeit bills being circulated in the area.
Convinced that Billy's "gang" were ringleaders in the distribution of the bills, Wild tried
to get Marshal Sherman to hunt and arrest the men. When Sherman declined, he convinced Garrett to take up the job. Garrett agreed to do it for no extra pay. During the hunt

for Billy, Wild hired Barney Mason as a spy to provide Garrett with intelligence on Billy. Wild died June 10, 1920, in New Orleans.

Wilson, William H. "Billy." Wilson was born November 23, 1860. Wilson was convicted of the crime of passing counterfeit bank notes on February 28, 1882, and sentenced to seven years in the penitentiary. Wilson had received the bills in payment for his White Oaks livery stable and passed them not knowing they were counterfeit. In May, 1882, Wilson got deathly ill:

> *"He is now sick, and although the disease was first pronounced the measles, it is now feared that he has the small pox. The authorities are at a loss to know what to do with him."* [88]

Wilson overcame his sickness and escaped from the pen on September 9, 1882. In January, 1884, he, Tom Pickett, and two others killed four unarmed Hispanic men in cold-blood at Seven Rivers. One newspaper described it as *"one of the most blood curdling crimes ever executed in frontier history."* The dead men were buried in a common grave. Wilson went to Texas and assumed the name of David L. Anderson, eventually becoming Terrell County sheriff. On August 25, 1896, thanks to the efforts of Pat Garrett and James J. Dolan, who had both testified at Wilson's counterfeiting trial, Wilson was granted a pardon for the 1882 counterfeiting conviction. In a letter supporting Wilson's pardon, Garrett wrote *"I have since 1891 known Billy Wilson in Texas as D. L. Anderson, where he has enjoyed the reputation of being a good, honest, and straight forward citizen... I know of nothing he has done which would be discreditable to him since his escape. He is a man of family, all of which command the respect of all the people with whom they come in contact."* Wilson died June 4, 1918, in Brackettville, Texas.[89]

Wilson, John B. Born about 1821 in Tennessee. Wilson's real name was Green Wilson. In January, 1875, he asked the Territorial legislature to change his name to Juan Bautista Wilson. The request was refused. On March 16, 1876, the *Daily New Mexican* reported:

> *"Since the 14th, Judge Wilson signed all his mandates John B. Wilson instead of Green Wilson."* [90]

When Wilson testified in the Dudley Court of Inquiry, he said he took John B. Wilson as a baptismal name in Albuquerque on January 20, 1859. The Ealy's always called him Mr. Green. When Tunstall was murdered, Wilson, as Justice of the Peace, issued arrest warrants for James J. Dolan, J. Conovar, Frank Baker, Jessie Evans, Tom Hill, George Davis, O. L. Roberts, P. Gilligos, F. Green, J. Awly, A. H. Mills, 'Dutch Charley,' Robert W. Beckwith, William Morton, George Harmon, and Jacob. B. Mathews. The warrants were issued February 19, 1878. Constable Antonio Martinez deputized Billy and Brewer to serve the warrants. On March 3, 1878, Governor Axtell nullified Wilson's J.P. office, effectively delegalizing the warrants. When Sheriff Brady and Deputy Hindman were killed by bullets from behind Tunstall's corral wall, Wilson was hit in the buttocks by a stray bullet. On the last day of the Lincoln war, Colonel Dudley personally ordered Wilson to issue an arrest warrant for McSween, saying if he did not, he would be put into *"double irons."* To enforce his order, Dudley sent several of his armed officers to Wilson's office. In the Dudley Court of Inquiry, Wilson testified that he wrote the warrant only because he feared for his life. The unlawful removal of Wilson by Governor Axtell did not sit well with Lincoln residents. He was re-elected to the office on June 15, 1878. In 1882, the *Las Vegas Gazette* reported that Wilson owned *"a large part of the town of Lincoln."* Wilson died in 1897.[91]

Wood, David L. Born September 13, 1835, in Douglas, Missouri. The 1850 census shows Wood at 16, along with hundreds of other single men, working as a gold miner at a mining camp on the Middle Fork of the American River. Gold was discovered there in 1848, setting off the California Gold Rush. On October 31, 1861, he joined the 1st Cavalry Regiment of the California Volunteers. He mustered out September 21, 1866, in Las Cruces. Wood was the bailiff during Billy's trial in Mesilla. During the trial he was appointed a deputy sheriff by Dona Ana County Sheriff Southwick. Wood was one of the deputies in the sheriff's posse that escorted Billy from Mesilla to Fort Stanton after Billy's trial. The first night of that trip was spent at the Wood-Reade ranch at St. Nicolas Springs. Wood as deputy participated in the hanging of Clark and Barela. When Sehero Gomez was tried for killing his wife, Wood testified for the prosecution that Gomez had confessed the killing to him and identified the murder weapon. That trial with its surprising outcome is discussed in Chapter 8. On May 24, 1899, Wood sold the Rock House Ranch to Garrett. That ranch played a key role in the events that led to Garrett's killing by Jesse Wayne Brazel. Wood died May 17, 1911, in Las Cruces, New Mexico.

"Billy the Kid," Joseph E. Lopez.

Notes

Introduction

1. Don Cline, *Antrim and Billy* (Creative Publishing Co., 1990), pp 44-47.

2. Cline, *Antrim and Billy*, p 49.

3. Cline, *Antrim and Billy*, p 59.

4. *Mining Life*, September 19, 1874.

5. *Arizona Republic* (Phoenix), Dec.30, 1951.

6. *Las Vegas Gazette*, Dec. 28, 1880

7. *Las Vegas Gazette*, Dec. 28, 1880

8. Joseph E. Lopez, interview with David G. Thomas, Aug. 9, 2014; Katherine D. Stoes, "Notes on the Jail," Katherine D. Stoes Papers, Archives and Special Collections, NMSU.

9. Anaya, *I Buried Billy* (Creative Publishing Company, 1991), pp 132.

10. Richard Weddle, "Shooting Billy the Kid," Wild West, August, 2012.

11. Weddle, "Shooting Billy the Kid."

12. *Albuquerque Journal*, April 4,1908.

13. Weddle, "Shooting Billy the Kid."

14. Emerson Hough, *The Saga of Billy the Kid* (Garden City Publishing, 1926), p 195.

1 – Capture

1. For details on Brazil's second snitching, see Chapter 9.

2. Garrett was elected sheriff Nov. 1, 1880, on the Democrat ticket, defeating incumbent sheriff George Kimbrell by 320 votes to 179 votes. He would take office as sheriff January 1, 1881. George Curry, *George Curry 1861-1947, An Autobiography* (Univ. of New Mexico Press, 1958), p 40.

3. The previous "reign of terror" was the Lincoln County War. *Santa Fe New Mexican*, July 7, 1880.

4. *Las Vegas Gazette*, Dec. 3, 1880.

5. Fifty men was large exaggeration. *Las Vegas Gazette*, Dec. 3, 1880.

6. William Bonney, letter to Lew Wallace, Dec. 12, 1880, Lew Wallace Collection, Indiana Historical Society.

7. John P. Wilson, *Fort Sumner, New Mexico* (Museum of New Mexico, 1974), pp 4-5.

8. Scott Smith, Letter to John Grassham, Sept. 4, 1997, Library Files, Fort Sumner Bosque Redondo Memorial Monument.

9. Lawrence R. Murphy, *Lucien Bonaparte Maxwell* (University of Oklahoma Press, 1983), p 111; Don McAlavy, "Along the Pecos," manuscript, March, 1976, Fort Sumner Public Library.

10. "Reports of U.S Secret Service Agents, 1875-1936," U.S. Treasury Department, Secret Service Division, NARA; Leon C. Metz Papers, C. L. Sonnichsen Special Collections, UTEP.

11. Wilson's full name was William H. Wilson. He was the victim of the phony bank notes, not the perpetrator. He received the counterfeit bills from W. H. West, who gave him the notes as payment for his ranch. Donald R. Lavash, *Wilson and the Kid* (Creative Publishing Company, 1990).

12. *The Sun* (N.Y., N.Y), Dec. 27, 1880.

13. Azariah F. Wild Report, Oct. 2, 1880, Leon C. Metz Papers.

14. During this time Wild was boarding in Garrett's house.

15. Roberts was shot April 4, 1878, but did not die until the next day. See Appendix B.

16. *Pampa Daily News*, Nov. 30, 1958; *Fort Worth Star Telegram*, Nov. 29, 1992.

17. John L. McCarty, *Maverick Town, The Story of Old Tascosa* (University of Oklahoma Press, 1988), pp 82-83.

18. Stewart never left an account of his actions in pursuing Billy. *Raton Range*, May 13, 1935.

19. McCarty, Maverick Town, pp 83-84.

20. Moore's full name was William C. Moore. Charles A. Siringo, *A Texas Cowboy, or Fifteen Years on the Hurricane Deck of a Spanish Pony* (Siringo & Dobson, 1886), p 198.

21. Ear cutting refers to knife cuts in an animal's ear as an aid to identification. Ear cutting does not constitute legal proof of ownership.

22. J. Evetts Haley, interview with James Henry East, Sept. 27, 1927, Panhandle Plains Historical Museum Research Center (PPHMRC).

23. There is some dispute as to who actually was in the expedition. This list comes from comparing the first-person accounts by Charles Siringo, James East, Cal Polk, Louis Bousman, and Frank Clifford. Siringo, *A Texas Cowboy*, pp 199-200; Haley, Interview with East, Sept. 27, 1927, PPHMRC; "The Life of C. W. Polk," given in James H. Earle, ed., *The Capture of Billy the Kid* (Creative Publishing Company, 1988), pp 16-18; "He Escaped Boot Hill to Help Capture Billy the Kid," interview with Louis Bousman, Aug. 14, 1938, *Amarillo Sunday News-Globe*; and Frank Clifford, *Deep Trails in the Old West, A Frontier Memoir* (University of Oklahoma Press, 2011), pp 80-81.

24 Siringo, *A Texas Cowboy*, pp 199-200.

25. "The Life of C. W. Polk," *The Capture of Billy the Kid*, p 19.

26. Clifford, *Deep Trails in the Old West*, pp xi-xii.

27. Biographical notes, E. A. Arnim Archives & Museum, Flatonia, Tex.

28. Clifford, *Deep Trails in the Old West*, pp 272-273.

29. James East, letter to W. H. Burges about Lee Smith, Herman B. Weisner Papers, Archives and Special Collections, NMSU; Clifford, *Deep Trails in the Old West*, p 272.

30 "The Life of C. W. Polk," *The Capture of Billy the Kid*, p 18.

31. Haley, Interview with East, Sept. 27, 1927, PPHMRC.

32. Siringo; *A Texas Cowboy*, p 200.

33. Haley, Interview with East, Sept. 27, 1927, PPHMRC.

34. "Land Grants," http://online. nmartmuseum.org/assets/files/Maps/ LandGrants.pdf, accessed Jan. 5, 2018.

35. Charles A. Siringo, *Riata and Spurs, The Story of a Lifetime Spent in the Saddle as Cowboy and Detective* (Sunstone Press, 2007), Facsimile of 1927 Edition, p 76.

36. Haley, Interview with East, Sept. 27, 1927, PPHMRC.

37. Clifford, *Deep Trails in the Old West*, pp 85-86.

38. Marriage Registry, Anton Chico Catholic Church. Copy in author's possession.

39. David G. Thomas, *Billy the Kid's Grave, A History of the Wild West's Most Famous Death Marker* (Doc45 Publishing, 2017), pp 8-9, 98; 1880 Fort Sumner Census Records, taken June, 1880.

40. *Santa Fe Daily New Mexican*, Dec. 29, 1879.

41. Wild Report, Oct. 2, 1880, Leon C. Metz Papers; Frank Warner Angel Report, Nov. 11, 1880, Interior Department Papers 1850-1907, RG 60, NARA.

42. John P. Wilson, ed., *Pat Garrett and Billy the Kid as I Knew Them, Reminiscences of John P. Meadows* (University of New Mexico Press, 2004), pp 43-44; Pat F. Garrett, *The Authentic Life of Billy, the Kid* (University of Oklahoma Press, 1954), pp 105-106.

43. *Santa Fe Daily New Mexican*, Dec. 29, 1880.

44. Siringo, *A-Texas-Cowboy*, p 203.

45. Clifford, *Deep Trails in the Old West*, p 86.

46. *Santa Fe Daily New Mexican*, Dec. 14, 1880.

47. *Las Vegas Daily Gazette*, Dec. 15, 1880.

48. *Las Vegas Daily Gazette*, Dec. 12, 1880.

49. Instead of riding straight through, Garrett says they camped after the first day. Haley, Interview with East, Sept. 27, 1927, PPHMRC; Garrett, *The Authentic Life of Billy, The Kid*, p 111.

50. Daniel Flores, *Alexander Grzelachowski, Puerto de Luna's Renaissance Man*, Vol I and II, no date, no publisher; C. Kajencki, Alexander Grzelachowski, Pioneer Merchant of Puerto de Luna, New Mexico, Arizona and the West, Vol. 26, No. 3, Autumn, 1984, p 258.

51. *Las Vegas Gazette*, Jan. 8, 1884; "Puerto de Luna," New Mexico Magazine, Jan., 1998.

52. Roibal is spelled Roybal or Roival by some sources. Rudulph (or Rudolph as it is written in many sources) wrote his account of the events in Spanish in the form of a poem. The quotes are from Branch's free translation of the poem. The two men who interrogated José were Tom O'Folliard and Tom Pickett. Louis Leon Branch, *Los Bilitos: the Story of "Billy the Kid" and His Gang, as told by Charles Frederick Rudulph* (Carlton Press, Inc, 1980), p 208.

53. Garrett, *The Authentic Life of Billy, The Kid*, p 113.

54. Garrett mistakenly uses "Gayheart ranch" throughout his account. The ranch was the Gerhardt ranch, located at Los Ojitos (little eyes), a tiny community that grew up around the spring at that location. Dr. John Gerhardt, the owner, was a medical doctor. Garrett, *The Authentic Life of Billy, The Kid*, pp 113-114.

55. Haley, Interview with East, Sept. 27, 1927, PPHMRC.

56. Author and researcher Richard Weddle argues convincingly that evidence within the tintype indicates that it was probably taken in the Fort Sumner dance hall instead of Beaver Smith's saloon. Richard Weddle, "Shooting Billy the Kid," Wild West, Aug. 2012, pp 59-62.

57. Haley, Interview with East, Sept. 27, 1927, PPHMRC.

58. *Santa Fe New Mexican*, Oct. 31, 1880; "Cosgrove Ad," Las Vegas Daily Gazette, Jan. 18, 1880.

59. The 1880 Fort Sumner Census taken June, 1880, shows Charles and Manuela Bowdre, William Bonney, A. B. Bennet (Bennett), and Willis Pruitt living in one room of the hospital building. Garrett, *The Authentic Life of Billy, The Kid*, p 115.

60 Garrett, *The Authentic Life of Billy*, The Kid, p 116.

61. Haley, Interview with East, Sept. 27, 1927, PPHMRC.

62. 1880 Fort Sumner Census, taken June, 1880.

63. Garrett, *The Authentic Life of Billy, The Kid*, p 116; Clifford, *Deep Trails in the Old West*, p 87.

64. Thomas F. Wilcox was half-owner of the Wilcox-Brazil ranch. The 1880 census shows him as a single man living with a (possibly adopted) stepson, 16-year old Juan Gallego (Gallegos), and a stepdaughter, one-year-old Dolores Padia.

65. Garrett, *The Authentic Life of Billy, The Kid*, p 117.

66. Garrett, *The Authentic Life of Billy, The Kid*, pp 117-118.

67. Haley, Interview with East, Sept. 27, 1927, PPHMRC.

68. Garrett says it was 8 pm; East says it was 11 pm. Haley, Interview with East, Sept. 27, 1927, PPHMRC; *Coconino Sun* (Flagstaff, AZ), Aug. 13, 1915.

69. Haley, Interview with East, Sept. 27, 1927, PPHMRC.

79. "The Life of C. W. Polk," *The Capture of Billy the Kid*, p 26.

71. Haley, Interview with East, Sept. 27, 1927, PPHMRC.

72. O'Folliard had been Billy's best friend and constant companion for three years. O'Folliard was with Billy in the McSween house when it was burned down during the Lincoln County War, and escaped when he, Billy, Jim French, Chavez y Chavez, Yginio Salazar, and Harvey Morris dashed from the building; Haley. Interview with East, Sept. 27, 1927, PPHMRC.

73. "The Life of C. W. Polk," *The Capture of Billy the Kid*, p 26; "East-Letter-to-Siringo"- The Capture of Billy the Kid, p 83; *Las Vegas Optic*, Dec. 27, 1880.

74. Garrett, *The Authentic Life of Billy, The Kid*, p 120.

75. Haley, Interview with East, Sept. 27, 1927, PPHMRC.

76. Harold L. Edwards, "Who Was Charles Bowdre," Outlaw-Gazette, Dec., 1995.

77. Geoffrey L. Gomes, "Manuel Brazil, A Portuguese Pioneer in New Mexico and Texas," Outlaw Gazette, Jan., 1995.

78. Garrett, *The Authentic Life of Billy, The Kid*, pp 121-122.

79. Garrett, *The Authentic Life of Billy, The Kid*, p 122.

80. Garrett, *The Authentic Life of Billy, The Kid*, p 122; Haley, Interview with East, Sept. 27, 1927, PPHMRC; McCarty, *Maverick Town*; Las Vegas Gazette, Dec. 27, 1880.

81. Garrett, *The Authentic Life of Billy, The Kid*, p 123.

82. Garrett, *The Authentic Life of Billy, The Kid*, p 122.

83. Garrett, *The Authentic Life of Billy, The Kid*, p 117.

84. Haley, Interview with East, Sept. 27, 1927, PPHMRC.

85. "The Life of C. W. Polk," *The Capture of Billy the Kid*, pp 26-27.

86. 1970 San Miguel County Census, taken Sept., 1870; Don McAlary, "Alejandro Perea Found Living in Township of Rio Colorado," Outlaw-Gazette, Nov., 1997.

87. Allen Barker, "I Refound Stinking Springs" True West, Feb., 1989.

88. Garrett, *The Authentic Life of Billy, The Kid*, p 123.

89. "The Life of C. W. Polk," *The Capture of Billy the Kid*, pp 27-28.

90. Garrett, *The Authentic Life of Billy, The Kid*, p 123.

91. Garrett, *The Authentic Life of Billy, The Kid*, p 125.

92. "The Life of C. W. Polk," *The Capture of Billy the Kid*, p 28.

93. *Las Vegas Gazette*, Dec. 27, 1880.

94. "Reminiscences of Louis Bousman," *The Capture of Billy the Kid*, p 53.

95. Haley, Interview with East, Sept. 27, 1927, PPHMRC.

96. Garrett, *The Authentic Life of Billy, The Kid*, p 125.

97. Haley, Interview with East, Sept. 27, 1927, PPHMRC.

98. Garrett, *The Authentic Life of Billy, The Kid*, p 125.

99. Haley, Interview with East, Sept. 27, 1927, PPHMRC.

100. "The Life of C. W. Polk," *The Capture of Billy the Kid*, p 30.

101. *Santa Fe New Mexican Review*, Jan. 11, 1884.

102. Branch, *Los Bilitos: the Story of "Billy the Kid" and His Gang*, p 213.

103. Garrett, *The Authentic Life of Billy, The Kid*, pp 126-127.

104. Haley, Interview with East, Sept. 27, 1927, PPHMRC.

105. Webb escape attempt, April 2, 1880. Captured December 8, 1880. *Public Ledger* (Memphis TN), April 3, 1880; *Dodge City Globe*, April 8, 1880; *Dodge City Globe*, Dec. 21, 1880.

106. Don Cline, "Tom Pickett, Friend of Billy the Kid," True West, July, 1997; Winslow Mail, May 18, 1934.

107. Lavash, *Wilson and the Kid*; Santa Fe New Mexican, Feb. 12, 1882; *Santa Fe New Mexican*, Sept. 15, 1882.

108. *Santa Fe New Mexican*, Oct. 31, 1880.

109. *Santa Fe New Mexican*, Oct. 31, 1880.

110. *Las Vegas Gazette*, Nov. 3, 1880; *Las Vegas Daily Optic*, March 3, 1881.

111. "The Life of C. W. Polk," *The Capture of Billy the Kid*, p 31.

112. Garrett, *The Authentic Life of Billy, The Kid*, p 127.

113. East says that Beaver Smith was present and protested when Billy gave him – not Polk – the Winchester: *"'Billy, I think you ought to let me have that Winchester as you owe me about $40 for ammunition and whiskey....' Billy said, 'Oh, give the old bastard the gun.'"* Haley, Interview with East, Sept. 27, 1927, PPHMRC; "The Life of C. W. Polk," *The Capture of Billy the Kid*, p 31.

114. Las Vegas Gazette, Dec. 27, 1880.

115. David G. Thomas, *Killing Pat Garrett, The Wild West's Most Famous Lawmn – Murder of Self-Defense?* (Doc45 Publishing, 2019), pp 207-210.

116. Haley, Interview with East, Sept. 27, 1927, PPHMRC.

117. "The Life of C. W. Polk," *The Capture of Billy the Kid*, p 31.

118. "Reminiscences of Louis Bousman," *The Capture of Billy the Kid*, p 56.

119. Rich Eastwood, *Nuestras Madres, A Story of Lincoln County NM* (Creative Space Independent Publishing, no date), pp 89, 92.

120. Lucien Maxwell married María de la Luz Beaubien on March 27, 1842. It is unlikely that the event described by East happened. Paulita was born in January, 1864; she was 16 years old in December, 1880. For an analysis of the (strong) evidence supporting the assertion that Paulita was Billy's girlfriend, see Thomas, *Billy the Kid's Grave*; "East Letter to Siringo," *The Capture of Billy the Kid*, pp 82-87.

121. Garrett, *The Authentic Life of Billy, The Kid*, pp 127-128; *Las Vegas Gazette*, Dec. 27, 1880.

122. East is referring to the shooting of Deputy Sheriff James W. Bell and Deputy Marshal Robert Olinger during Billy's escape from the Lincoln County Courthouse jail.

Haley, Interview with East, Sept. 27, 1927, PPHMRC.

123. Haley, Interview with East, Sept. 27, 1927, PPHMRC.

124. *Las Vegas Gazette*, Dec. 27, 1880.

2 – Jail

1. *Las Vegas Gazette*, Dec. 27, 1880, quoted in *Billy the Kid, Las Vegas Newspaper Accounts of His Career*, 1880-1881 (Morrison Books, 1958), p 5.

2. *Santa Fe New Mexican*, Dec. 28, 1880.

3. *Santa Fe New Mexican*, Jan. 31, 1880.

4. *Santa Fe Weekly New Mexican*, Jan. 31, 1880.

5. James West's real name was Anthony Lowe. John Dorsey's real name was Jim Dawson. Tom Henry's real name was Thomas Jefferson House.

6. *Santa Fe Weekly New Mexican*, Feb. 14, 1880.

7. *Las Vegas Daily Gazette*, Feb. 10, 1880.

8. *Las Vegas Gazette*, Dec. 28, 1880, quoted in *Billy the Kid, Las Vegas Newspaper Accounts of His Career*, 1880-1881, pp 12-14.

9. *Las Vegas Daily Optic*, Dec. 27, 1880.

10. Morley was the person who preferred charges against Weston and Mrs. Deolatere for the October 16 mail robbery. *Las Vegas Gazette*, Oct. 20, 1880.

11. Garrett, *The Authentic Life of Billy, The Kid*, p 129.

12. Albert E. Hyde, "The Old Regime in the Southwest," The Century Illustrated Monthly Magazine, Vol 63, March, 1902, p 699.

13. *Las Vegas Gazette*, Dec. 28, 1880.

14. *Santa Fe Daily New Mexican*, Dec. 29, 1880; *Arizona Weekly Citizen*, Jan. 1, 1881.

15. J. F. Morley, letter to James East, Nov. 29, 1922, James H. East Papers, 1882-1931, Dolph Briscoe Center, UT.

16. *Santa Fe Daily New Mexican*, Dec. 30, 1880.

17. The jail was located at the intersection of Water and Galisteo Streets. *Santa Fe Weekly New Mexican*, Aug. 16, 1880.

18. *Santa Fe Daily New Mexican*, Dec. 30, 1880.

19. *Santa Fe Daily New Mexican*, Dec. 30, 1880.

20. *Santa Fe Daily New Mexican*, Dec. 30, 1880; *Santa Fe Daily New Mexican*, Dec. 28, 1880.

21. *Santa Fe Daily New Mexican*, Dec. 30, 1880.

22. *Santa Fe Daily New Mexican*, Dec. 28, 1880; *Las Vegas Daily Optic*, Dec. 29, 1880; *Santa Fe Daily New Mexican*, Dec. 30, 1880; *Las Vegas Daily Optic*, Jan. 1, 1881.

23. *Las Vegas Daily Gazette*, Jan. 4, 1881.

24. *Las Vegas Daily Gazette*, Jan. 7, 1881.

25. *Las Vegas Daily Gazette*, Jan. 13, 1881.

26. "The Life of C. W. Polk," *The Capture of Billy the Kid*, pp 34-35.

27 Haley, Interview with East, Sept. 27, 1927, PPHMRC.

28. *Las Vegas Daily Optic*, Dec. 29, 1880.

29. *Las Vegas Daily Optic*, Dec. 29, 1880.

30. *Santa Fe New Mexican*, Dec. 30, 1880; *Las Vegas Daily Gazette*, Dec. 30, 1880.

31. Rudabaugh's fellow robbers were Las Vegas Constables Joe Carson and Jim Martin. Rudabaugh would later confess to also robbing the A.T. & S.F. train on October 13, 1879. *Las Vegas Daily Gazette*, Nov. 4, 1879; *Las Vegas Daily Gazette*, Feb. 27, 1881; *Santa Fe Weekly New Mexican*, Oct. 18, 1879.

32. Wm H. Bonney, letter to Lew Wallace, Jan. 1, 1881, Lew Wallace Collection, Indiana Historical Society.

33. The article credited Las Vegas Chief of Police E. Roberts for providing the photo source for the engraving. Roberts was not the Las Vegas chief or a Las Vegas policeman. The article was published a second time March 5, 1881; *Las Vegas Daily Optic*, March 5, 1881.

34. Robert A. Cameron, letter to D. B. Parker, Jan. 11, 1881, quoted in Los Angeles Division Newsletter, Spring, 1982, copy in author's possession.

35. Billy the Kid arrest warrant, Jan. 17, 1881, Mary Taylor Papers, Archives and Special Collections, NMSU.

36. Billy also had a younger brother named Joseph. For a long time historians believed that Joseph was an older brother. Joseph died unrecognized November 25, 1930. *Newman's Thirty-Four*, Jan. 19, 1881.

37. *Las Vegas Daily Gazette*, Jan. 20, 1881.

38. *Las Vegas Daily Optic*, Jan. 21, 1881.

39. *Las Vegas Daily Gazette*, Feb. 12, 1881.

40. *Las Vegas Daily Gazette*, Jan. 22, 1881.

41. *Santa Fe Weekly New Mexican*, March 15, 1880; *Santa Fe Daily New Mexican*, Jan. 6, 1881; *Las Vegas Daily Optic*, Feb. 25, 1881.

42. *Las Vegas Daily Optic*, March 5, 1881.

43. *Santa Fe Daily New Mexican*, March 1, 1881.

44. *Santa Fe Daily New Mexican*, March 1, 1881.

45. Albert E. Hyde, "The Old Regime in the Southwest," The Century Illustrated Monthly Magazine, Vol 63, March, 1902, p701.

46. Wm H. Bonney, letter to Lew Wallace, March 2, 1881, Lew Wallace Collection, Indiana Historical Society.

47. Wallace resigned March 17, 1881, but continued as acting governor until April 30, 1881. Wm H. Bonney, letter to Lew Wallace, March 4, 1881, Lew Wallace Collection, Indiana Historical Society.

48. *Las Vegas Daily Optic*, March 12, 1881.

49. John Houston Merrill, ed., *The American and English Encyclopedia of Law*, Vol. XX (Edward Thompson Company, 1892), pp 619, 1071, 1075, 1078.

50. *Las Vegas Daily Optic*, March 12, 1881.

51. Subpoena for Ellis, Mathews, and Baca, March 1, 1881, Fulton Papers, Special Collections, UA.

52. Change of venue and bonds of witnesses, June 4, 1879, Fulton Papers, Special Collections, UA.

53. *Newman's Thirty-Four*, March 5, 1881.

3 – Mesilla

1. *Santa Fe New Mexican*, April 11, 1957.

2. *Santa Fe New Mexican*, April 4, 1881, quoted in Robert N. Mullin, ed., *Maurice G. Fulton's History of the Lincoln County War* (University of Arizona Press, 1968), pp 387-388. The original is lost.

3. W Bonney, letter to Lew Wallace, March 27, 1881, Lew Wallace Collection, Indiana Historical Society.

4. *Santa Fe Daily New Mexican*, April 3, 1881; *Santa Fe Daily New Mexican*, Jan 4, 1881.

5. Leonard was also representing Susan McSween and Governor Wallace in matters arising from the Lincoln County War.

6. Mullin, *Maurice G. Fulton's History of the Lincoln County War*, p 388.

7. Mullin, *Maurice G. Fulton's History of the Lincoln County War*, p 388.

8. *Santa Fe Daily New Mexican*, April 3, 1881.

9. Mullin, *Maurice G. Fulton's History of the Lincoln County War*, p 388.

10. Mullin, *Maurice G. Fulton's History of the Lincoln County War*, p 388.

11. The Mexican-American War began May 13, 1946 and ended February 2, 1848. Mesilla was founded March 1, 1850. The mistaken border point was agreed to by the U.S. and Mexican border commissioners on April 24, 1851. The Gadsden Purchase, ratified April 25, 1854, moved Mesilla back into the United States. For details on the border commissioners' decision, the disputes it created, and the Gadsden Purchase, see David G. Thomas, *La Posta, From the Founding of Mesilla To Corn Exchange Hotel To Billy the Kid Museum To Famous Landmark* (Doc45 Publishing, 2013).

12. Ruling by Judge John Lemon, May 7, 1867, Mary Daniels Taylor Papers, Archives and Special Collections, NMSU.

13. Joseph E. Lopez's family owned the courthouse lot from 1905 to 1915. Joseph E. Lopez, interview with David G. Thomas, Aug. 9, 2014.

14. *Rio Grande Republican*, Sept. 24, 1881.

15. *Rio Grande Republican*, July 29, 1882.

16. *Rio Grande Republican*, July 29, 1882.

17. *Rio Grande Republican*, June 16, 1883.

18. 22. L. Bradford Prince, ed., *The General Laws of New Mexico* (W. C. Little & Co., 1880), Chapter LXVII, Section 1, p 358.

19. *Newman's Thirty-Four*, May 12, 1880.

20. *Rio Grande Republican*, July 29, 1882.

21. *Rio Grande Republican*, Oct. 21, 1882.

22. *Rio Grande Republican*, June 2, 1883.

23. *Las Vegas Gazette*, Jan. 22, 1882; *Rio Grande Republican*, June 16, 1883; *Rio Grande Republican*, Oct. 10, 1885.

4 – The Charges against Billy

1. Tunstall arrived in Lincoln November 6, 1876.

2. Lincoln County at the time was about the same size as Ohio. It contained an estimated 2,000 residents.

3. Alexander A. McSween, letter to Lawrence Lapoint, March 24, 1878, Fulton Papers, Special Collections, UA.

4. *Grant County Herald*, Jan. 9, 1878.

5. Eve Ball, ed., Lily Klasner, *My Girlhood Among Outlaws* (University of Arizona Press, 1988), p 274.

6. *Mesilla Valley Independent*, Supplement Issue, April 20, 1878.

7. *Mesilla Valley Independent*, Jan. 25, 1878.

8. *Mesilla Valley Independent*, Feb. 2, 1878.

9. *Cimarron News and Press*, April 2, 1878.

10. *Santa Fe Weekly New Mexican*, April 20, 1878.

11. George Peppin, affidavit on Tunstall store, April 18, 1878, Mary Daniels Taylor Papers, Archives and Special Collections, NMSU.

12. Angel Report, Interior Department Papers 1850-1907, NARA.

13. Mike Tower, *The Outlaw Statesman, the Life and Times of Fred Tecumseh Waite* (Authorhouse, 2007).

14. Elsie Widenmann, "Lincoln County Postscript, Notes on Robert A. Widenmann by his daughter Elsie Widenmann," New Mexico Historical Review, L:3, 1975, pp 211-230; *Santa Fe Weekly New Mexican*, July 27, 1878.

15. Also present at Tunstall's ranch were Widenmann, Waite, John Middleton, Gottfried Gauss, Martin Martz, Henry Brown, and William W. McCloskey. *Mesilla Valley Independent*, March 30, 1878; Billy the Kid deposition, Angel Report, Interior Department Papers 1850-1907, NARA.

16. *Mesilla Valley Independent*, March 30, 1878.

17. Billy the Kid deposition, Angel Report, Interior Department Papers 1850-1907, NARA.

18. *Mesilla Valley Independent*, Oct. 27, 1877.

19. *Mesilla Valley Independent*, Dec. 13, 1877.

20. *Santa Fe Weekly New Mexican*, Oct. 2, 1877.

21. Billy the Kid deposition, Angel Report, Interior Department Papers 1850-1907, NARA.

22. Billy the Kid deposition, Angel Report, Interior Department Papers 1850-1907, NARA.

23. *Mesilla Valley Independent*, March 30, 1878.

24. Billy the Kid deposition, Angel Report, Interior Department Papers 1850-1907, NARA.

25. William L. Rynerson, letter to friends Riley and Dolan, Feb. 14, 1878, Lew Wallace Collection, Indiana Historical Society.

26. Billy the Kid deposition, Angel Report, Interior Department Papers 1850-1907, NARA.

27. Jacob Mathews deposition, Angel Report, Interior Department Papers 1850-1907, NARA.

28. Gottfried Guass deposition, Angel Report, Interior Department Papers 1850-1907, NARA.

29. Panteleon Gallegos' real name was Sandoval.

30. Billy the Kid deposition, Angel Report, Interior Department Papers 1850-1907, NARA.

31. Angel concluded in his report that Jesse Evans might have witnessed the killing.

32. Albert Howe deposition, Angel Report, Interior Department Papers 1850-1907, NARA.

33. Richard Maxwell Brown, *No Duty to Retreat, Violence and Values in American History and Society* (University of Oklahoma Press, 1991).

34. Florencio Gonzales deposition, Angel Report, Interior Department Papers 1850-1907, NARA.

35. Quoted in Frederick W. Nolan, *The Lincoln County War*, Revised Edition (Sunstone Press, 2009), p 180.

36. Quoted in Frederick W. Nolan, *The Life and Death of John Henry Tunstall* (University of New Mexico Press, 1965), p 264.

37. *Las Vegas Gazette*, March 23, 1878.

38. Daniel Appel deposition, Angel Report, Interior Department Papers 1850-1907, NARA.

39. Albert Howe deposition, Angel Report, Interior Department Papers 1850-1907, NARA.

40. *Mesilla Valley Independent*, March 30, 1878.

41. Mary R. Ealy, letter to Maurice G. Fulton, undated, Herman B. Weisner Papers, Archives and Special Collections, NMSU.

42. Dr Ealy would eventually conduct thirty funerals, only one of which would be for a person who died a natural death. Mary R. Ealy, "Mrs. Ealy's Own Account," *New Mexico Sentinel*, Oct. 5, 1937.

43. Account of Tunstall Killing, undated, Herman B. Weisner Papers, Archives and Special Collections, NMSU.

44. Quoted in Nolan, *The Lincoln County War*, p 206.

45. Warrant for Tunstall killers, Feb. 19, 1878, Herman B. Weisner Papers, Archives and Special Collections, NMSU.

46. *Cimarron News and Press*, April 11, 1878.

47. Lewis Wallace, Proclamation by the Governor, November 13, 1878, Lew Wallace Collection, Indiana Historical Society.

48. *Cimarron News and Press*, April 11, 1878.

49. *Cimarron News and Press*, May 2, 1878.

50. McNabb was killed April 29, 1878. *Mesilla Valley Independent*, April 27, 1878.

51. *Mesilla Valley Independent*, May 4, 1878.

52. Edith Crawford, interview with Francisco Trujillo (translated by A. L. White), May 10, 1937, Federal Writers' Project, Library of Congress.

53. Nolan, *The Life and Death of John Henry Tunstall*, p 305.

54. M. R. Leverson, letter to President R. B. Hayes, April 2, 1878, quoted in Nolan, *The Lincoln County War*, p 246.

55. The torreón was built by Enricos Trujillo.

56. Nolan, *The Life and Death of John Henry Tunstall*, p 233.

57. *Mesilla Valley Independent*, quoted in *Sacramento Daily Union*, May 13, 1878; *Arizona Weekly Citizen*, April 26, 1878.

58. Mullin, *Fulton's History of the Lincoln County War*, p 163.

59. *Santa Fe Weekly New Mexican*, May 4, 1878.

60. *Santa Fe Weekly New Mexican*, April 20, 1878.

61. *Mesilla Valley Independent*, April 27, 1878.

62. *Mesilla Valley Independent*, April 27, 1878.

63. *Santa Fe Weekly New Mexican*, April 20, 1878.

64. Almer H. Blazer, "Dr. J. H.Blazer," undated manuscript, Tularosa Basin Museum of History.

65. Blazer, "Dr. J. H.Blazer."

66. Blazer, "Dr. J. H.Blazer."

67. Jeff Burton, ed., Philip J. Rasch, *They Fought for "The House,"* English Westerners' Society (The English Westerners' Society, 1971).

68. *Alamogordo Daily News*, July 21, 1932.

69. Almer Blazer, "Fight at the Blazer Mill," *Alamogordo News*, undated newspaper clipping, Tularosa Basin Museum of History.

70. Almer Blazer, "Fight at the Blazer Mill," *Alamogordo News*, undated newspaper clipping, Tularosa Basin Museum.

71. Frank Coe in his account says he talked with Roberts for some time before the shooting occurred. Almer Blazer, "Fight at the Blazer Mill," *Alamogordo News*, undated newspaper clipping, Tularosa Basin Museum of History.

72. Frank McArdle, "Frank Coe's Account Of Robert's Fight," *New Mexico State Tribune*, 1926, Tularosa Basin Museum of History.

73. Frank McArdle, "Frank Coe's Account Of Robert's Fight," *New Mexico State Tribune*, 1926, Tularosa Basin Museum of History.

74. *Alamogordo Daily News*, July 28, 1932.

75. *Mesilla Valley Independent*, April 13, 1878.

76. *Alamogordo Daily News*, July 28, 1932.

77. *Alamogordo Daily News*, Aug. 4, 1932.

78. *Cimarron News and Press*, May 2, 1878.

79. *Santa Fe Weekly New Mexican*, May 28, 1878.

80. *Mesilla Valley Independent*, April 20, 1878.

81. Grand Jury Indictment of Billy, April 18, 1878, Herman B. Weisner Papers, Archives and Special Collections, NMSU; Indictment

of Evans, etc., for killing Tunstall, April 18, 1878, Lewis A Ketring Papers, Archives and Special Collections, NMSU; Nolan, *The Lincoln County War*, p 269.

82. *Weekly New Mexican*, May 18, 1878.

83. *Mesilla News*, June 29, 1878.

84. *Mesilla News*, July 27, 1878.

85. *Mesilla News*, Aug. 3, 1878.

86. *Cimarron News and Press*, April 25, 1878.

5 – War in Lincoln

1. Mullin, *Fulton's History of the Lincoln County War*, p 249; Sue E. McSween testimony, Dudley Court of Inquiry Records, RG 153, NARA.

2. "Mrs. Ealy's Own Account," *New Mexico Sentinel*, Oct. 5, 1937.

3. Mullin, *Fulton's History of the Lincoln County War*, p 250; D. M. Appel, letter to Post Adjutant, July 15, 1878, Herman B. Weisner Papers, Archives and Special Collections, NMSU; *Las Vegas Gazette*, Sept. 4, 1877; George Peppin testimony, Dudley Court of Inquiry Records.

4. Mullin, *Fulton's History of the Lincoln County War*, pp 251-252, David M. Easton testimony, Dudley Court of Inquiry Records.

5. Mullin, *Fulton's History of the Lincoln County War*, p 251.

6. Baca's wife had a baby just three days earlier. Mullin, *Fulton's History of the Lincoln County War*, p 250.

7. "Mrs. Ealy's Own Account," *New Mexico Sentinel*, Oct. 5, 1937.

8. "Mrs. Ealy's Own Account," *New Mexico Sentinel*, Oct. 5, 1937.

9. Peppin had someone else write the note, he only signed it. Geo. W. Peppin, letter to Colonel Dudley, July 17, 1878, Herman B. Weisner Papers, Archives and Special Collections, NMSU; George Peppin testimony, Dudley Court of Inquiry Records.

10. Your Obdt. Servant (Colonel Dudley), letter to G. W. Peppin, July 16, 1878, Letters Received by the Office of the Adjutant General, 1871-1880, NARA.

11. "Mrs. Ealy's Own Account," *New Mexico Sentinel*, Oct. 5, 1937.

12. "Mrs. Ealy's Own Account," *New Mexico Sentinel*, Oct. 5, 1937.

13. Alexander Rudder testimony, Dudley Court of Inquiry Records.

14. Alexander Rudder testimony, Dudley Court of Inquiry Records.

15 James J. Dolan testimony, Dudley Court of Inquiry Records.

16. N. A. M. Dudley, report to Act. Asst. Adjutant General, July 20, 1878, Letters Received by the Office of the Adjutant General, 1871-1880.

17. No source gives a description of the howitzer. Probably it fired a 12-pound shot; James Bush testimony, Dudley Court of Inquiry Records.

18. N. A. M. Dudley, report to Act. Asst. Adjutant General, July 20, 1878, Letters Received by the Office of the Adjutant General, 1871-1880.

19. Martin Chavez testimony, Dudley Court of Inquiry Records.

20. Samuel Corbet testimony, Dudley Court of Inquiry Records.

21. David M. Easton testimony, Dudley Court of Inquiry Records.

22. Dudley, report to Act. Asst. Adjutant General, July 23, 1878, Letters Received by the Office of the Adjutant General, 1871-1880.

23. Marion Turner testimony, Dudley Court of Inquiry Records.

24. Sue E. McSween testimony, Dudley Court of Inquiry Records.

25. A. A. McSween, letter to Gen. Dudley, July 19, 1878, Letters Received by the Office of the Adjutant General, 1871-1880.

26. Dudley, report to Act. Asst. Adjutant General, July 20, 1878, Letters Received by the Office of the Adjutant General, 1871-1880.

27. Sue E. McSween testimony, Dudley Court of Inquiry Records.

28. Sue E. McSween testimony, Dudley Court of Inquiry Records; Mullin, *Fulton's History of the Lincoln County War*, p 265.

29. J. B. Wilson testimony, Dudley Court of Inquiry Records.

30. J. B. Wilson testimony, Dudley Court of Inquiry Records.

31. Peppin further claimed that Susan once told him, *"He [McSween] knows me to be a bad woman and thinks hard of me, but you do not know what is the matter between me and*

Mac." George W. Peppin, affidavit on Susan McSween, Exhibit No. 9, Dudley Court of Inquiry Records.

32. Sue E. McSween testimony, Dudley Court of Inquiry Records.

33. Sue E. McSween testimony, Dudley Court of Inquiry Records.

34. Issac (sic) Ellis testimony, Dudley Court of Inquiry Records.

35. Sue E. McSween testimony, Dudley Court of Inquiry Records.

36. John Long testimony, Dudley Court of Inquiry Records.

37. Doyce B. Nunis, ed., *George W. Coe, Frontier Fighter: The Autobiography of George W. Coe Who Fought and Rode with Billy the Kid* (R. R. Donnelley, 1984).

38. Andrew Boyle testimony, Dudley Court of Inquiry Records.

39. Andrew Boyle testimony, Dudley Court of Inquiry Records.

40. Mrs. T. F. Ealy, letter to Dr. Appel, Letters Received by the Office of the Adjutant General, 1871-1880.

41. Mrs. T. F. Ealy, letter to Lieut. Col. Dudley, Letters Received by the Office of the Adjutant General, 1871-1880.

42. The next day the Ealys went to Fort Stanton, never to return to Lincoln. D. M. Appel, statement on Saturnino Baca letter, July 20, 1878, Herman B. Weisner Papers, Archives and Special Collections, NMSU.

43. D. M. Appel, statement on Saturnino Baca letter, July 20, 1878, Herman B. Weisner Papers, Archives and Special Collections, NMSU; D. M. Appel testimony, Dudley Court of Inquiry Records.

44. Sue E. McSween testimony, Dudley Court of Inquiry Records.

45. William Bonney testimony, Dudley Court of Inquiry Records.

46. D. M. Appel, statement on Saturnino Baca letter, July 20, 1878, Herman B. Weisner Papers, Archives and Special Collections, NMSU.

47. Dudley, report to Act. Asst. Adjutant General, July 20, 1878, Letters Received by the Office of the Adjutant General, 1871-1880.

48. Robert Olinger testimony, Dudley Court of Inquiry Records; William Bonney testimony, Dudley Court of Inquiry Records.

49. William Bonney testimony, Dudley Court of Inquiry Records.

50. William Bonney testimony, Dudley Court of Inquiry Records.

51. Andrew Boyle testimony, Dudley Court of Inquiry Records.

52. Dudley, report to Act. Asst. Adjutant General, July 20, 1878, Letters Received by the Office of the Adjutant General, 1871-1880.

53. The coroner's jurors were Fellipe Marinda, José Garcia, Macimiano Chavez, Otaviano Salas, Fellipe Mes, and José Serna. Coroner's Report on deaths of A. A. McSween, Harvey Morris, Francisco Samora, Becinte Romera, and Robert Beckwith, July 20, 1878, Letters Received by the Office of the Adjutant General, 1871-1880.

54. Dudley, report to Act. Asst. Adjutant General, July 23, 1878, Letters Received by the Office of the Adjutant General, 1871-1880.

55. Yginio Salazar, statement of events in McSween house, July 20, 1878, Letters Received by the Office of the Adjutant General, 1871-1880.

56. D. M. Appel, statement on Saturnino Baca letter, July 20, 1878, Herman B. Weisner Papers, Archives and Special Collections, NMSU; Dudley, report to Act. Asst. Adjutant General, July 20, 1878, Letters Received by the Office of the Adjutant General, 1871-1880.

57 Dudley, report to Act. Asst. Adjutant General, July 20, 1878, Letters Received by the Office of the Adjutant General, 1871-1880.

58. "Mrs. Ealy's Own Account," *New Mexico Sentinel*, Oct. 5, 1937.

59. Dudley, report to Act. Asst. Adjutant General, July 23, 1878, Letters Received by the Office of the Adjutant General, 1871-1880.

60. Samuel Corbet testimony, Dudley Court of Inquiry Records.

61. Samuel Corbet testimony, Dudley Court of Inquiry Records.

6 – Governor Wallace's Amnesty Proclamation

1. General Lewis Wallace, letter to C. Shulz, September 11, 1878, Lew Wallace Collection, Indiana Historical Society.

2. *Las Vegas Gazette*, Sept. 14, 1878.

3. *Santa Fe New Mexican*, Sept. 14, 1878.

4. Angel Report, Interior Department Papers 1850-1907, NARA.

5. New Mexico had not seen the last of Axtell. He was appointed to the NM Territorial Supreme Court in 1882. Lew Wallace, letter to Sue (Mrs. Wallace), Oct. 3, 1878, Lew Wallace Collection, Indiana Historical Society.

6. Axtell served as Chief Justice from August, 1882, to May, 1885.

7. Lewis Powell, George Atzerodt, David Herold, and Mary Surratt were hanged on July 7, 1865. O'Laughlen died in prison. Samuel Arnold, Dr. Samuel Mudd, and Edman Spangler were pardoned by President Johnson on March 1, 1869. Christopher R. Mortenson, *Politician in Uniform, General Lew Wallace and the Civil War* (University of Oklahoma, 2019).

8. Wirz served as commander of the prison camp from April 1864 to April 1865.

9. Geo. W. McCrary, letter to Governor Wallace, Oct. 2, 1878, Lew Wallace Collection, Indiana Historical Society.

10. Lewis Wallace, Proclamation by the Governor, November 13, 1878, Lew Wallace Collection, Indiana Historical Society.

11. *Mesilla News*, Nov. 23, 1878.

7 – Governor Wallace's Pardon Betrayal

1. Dudley, report to Act. Asst. Adjutant General, February 19, 1879, Letters Received by the Office of the Adjutant General, 1871-1880.

2. *Mesilla News*, June 28, 1879.

3. *Lewiston Daily Teller* (Lewiston ID), March 21, 1879.

4. Accusations against Colonel Dudley, undated, Letters Received by the Office of the Adjutant General, 1871-1880.

5. Meeting notice posted by Huston Chapman, December 7, 1878, Letters Received by the Office of the Adjutant General, 1871-1880.

6. Accusations against Colonel Dudley, undated, Letters Received by the Office of the Adjutant General, 1871-1880.

7. *Mesilla News*, June 28, 1879.

8. *Mesilla News*, June 28, 1879.

9. *Newman's Thirty-Four*, March 5, 1879.

10. Byron Dawson, letter to Post Adjutant, Fort Stanton, February 19, 1879, Letters Received by the Office of the Adjutant General, 1871-1880.

11. *Newman's Thirty-Four*, Aug. 20, 1879; Accusations against Colonel Dudley, undated, Letters Received by the Office of the Adjutant General, 1871-1880.

12. *Mesilla News*, April 5, 1879.

13. *Mesilla Valley Independent*, March, 1879.

14. *Mesilla Valley Independent*, March, 1879. Maurice Kildare, "Murder at Sunset Crossing," *Oldtimers Wild West*, January 1975, p 38.

15. General Sherman, order for troops to protect Governor Wallace, March 18, 1879, Letters Received by the Office of the Adjutant General, 1871-1880.

16. Lew Wallace, letter to Colonel Edward Hatch, March 22, 1879, Lew Wallace Collection, Indiana Historical Society; *Santa Fe New Mexican*, March 22, 1879.

17. Lew Wallace, letter to Captain Juan Patron, March 3, 1879, Lew Wallace Collection, Indiana Historical Society.

18. Lew Wallace, letter to General Edward Hatch, March 7, 1879, Lew Wallace Collection, Indiana Historical Society.

19. Edward Hatch, Special Field Orders No.2, March 8, 1879, Lew Wallace Collection, Indiana Historical Society.

20. Wallace, letter to Capt. H. Carroll, March 10, 1879, Lew Wallace Collection, Indiana Historical Society.

21. W. H. Bonney, letter to General Lew Wallace, undated, but believed to have been delivered March 13, 1879, Lincoln County Heritage Trust Collection, Fray Angélico History Library.

22. Lew Wallace, letter to W. H. Bonney, March 15, 1879, Lew Wallace Collection, Indiana Historical Society.

23. *The Indianapolis News*, July 5, 1900.

24. *New York Times*, June 29, 1902.

25. Texas Jack was captured April 12, 1879. *Mesilla Valley Independent*, March 29, 1879.

26. W. H. Bonney, letter to Friend Wilson, March 20, 1879, Lew Wallace Collection, Indiana Historical Society.

27. Nolan, *The West of Billy the Kid*, p 196.

28. W. H. Bonney, letter to General Lew Wallace, March 20, 1879, Lew Wallace Collection, Indiana Historical Society.

29. Wallace, letter to Hon. Carl Schurz, March 31, 1879, Lew Wallace Collection, Indiana Historical Society; Paul L. Tsompanas, *Juan Patron, A Fallen Star in the Days of Billy the Kid* (Belle Isle Books, 2013).

30. "Statements by Kid, made Sunday night March 23, 1879," Lew Wallace Collection, Indiana Historical Society.

31. "Statements by Kid, made Sunday night March 23, 1879," Lew Wallace Collection, Indiana Historical Society.

32. Lew Wallace, letter to Hon. Carl Schurz, June 11, 1879, Letters Received by the Office of the Adjutant General, 1871-1880.

33. Surprisingly, Charles Fritz, the brother of Murphy ally Emil Fritz was on the grand jury. *Newman's Thirty-Four*, May 7, 1879; Indictment of Marion Turner and John Jones for shooting McSween, April 30, 1879, Herman B. Weisner Papers, Archives and Special Collections, NMSU; Report of the grand jurors for Lincoln County, April, 1879, Letters Received by the Office of the Adjutant General, 1871-1880.

34. Although requesting a pardon, the plaintiffs are *"not confessing [to any] alleged crime[s]."* Plea for a pardon for Jacob B. Matthews, Wm. B. Powell, John Long, and John Hurley by attorney S. B. Newcomb, May 1, 1879, Herman B. Weisner Papers, Archives and Special Collections, NMSU.

35. *Newman's Thirty-Four*, May 7, 1879.

36. *Newman's Thirty-Four*, May 7, 1879.

37. *Mesilla News*, April 26, 1879.

38. Third Judicial District Court records, April 21, 1879, Herman B. Weisner Papers, Archives and Special Collections, NMSU.

39. Dudley, letter to U.S. Attorney General Charles Devens, Sept. 16, 1879, Letters Received by the Office of the Adjutant General, 1871-1880.

40. Dudley, letter to E. D. Townsend, Adjutant General U.S. Army, April 20, 1879, Letters Received by the Office of the Adjutant General, 1871-1880/

41. Dudley, letter to U.S. Attorney General Charles Devens, Sept. 16, 1879, Letters Received by the Office of the Adjutant General, 1871-1880.

42. Brevet Major General Jno. Pope, letter to Adjutant General U.S. Army, Oct. 15, 1879, Letters Received by the Office of the Adjutant General, 1871-1880.

43. Charges against Colonel N. A. M. Dudley, Dudley Court of Inquiry Records.

44. Decision of the Court regarding evidence of conspiracy, Dudley Court of Inquiry Records.

45. Dudley Court of Inquiry Records.

46. Colonel N. A. M. Dudley testimony, Dudley Court of Inquiry Records.

47. Waldo's summation was submitted in hand-written form and ran to 75 pages. Argument Henry L. Waldo, Esq., Counsel for Lt. Col. N. A. M. Dudley, Dudley Court of Inquiry Records.

48. Ira E. Leonard, letter to Gov. Lew Wallace, June 6, 1879, Fulton Papers, Special Collections, UA.

49. Court statement of its finding of facts, Dudley Court of Inquiry Records.

50. Court statement of its ruling, Dudley Court of Inquiry Records.

51. *Las Vegas New Mexico Herald*, July 30, 1879.

52. Opinion of Brevet Major General Jno. Pope, Dudley Court of Inquiry Records.

53. Report on the proceedings of the Dudley Court of Inquiry by Judge Advocate P. T. Swain, Dudley Court of Inquiry Records.

54. *Las Vegas New Mexico Herald*, June 25, 1879.

55. William Bonney testimony, Dudley Court of Inquiry Records.

56. Dudley, letter to U.S. Army Adjutant General, March 8, 1880, Letters Received by the Office of the Adjutant General, 1871-1880.

57. E. Donald Kaye, *Nathan Augustus Monroe Dudley, Rogue, Hero, or Both?* (Outskirts Press, 2007),

58. Dudley, letter to U.S. Army Adjutant General, Nov. 4, 1879, Letters Received by the Office of the Adjutant General, 1871-1880.

59. Dudley, letter to U.S. Army Adjutant General, Nov. 4, 1879, Letters Received by the Office of the Adjutant General, 1871-1880.

60. Dudley, letter to the Assistant General Dept. of the Missouri, Dec. 9, 1879, Letters Received by the Office of the Adjutant General, 1871-1880.

61. Mesilla News, Dec. 6, 1879, quoted in Letters Received by the Office of the Adjutant General, 1871-1880.

62. Waldo summation, Dudley Court of Inquiry Records.

63. Sebrian Bates testimony, Dudley Court of Inquiry Records.

64. *Mesilla News*, Dec. 6, 1879, quoted in Letters Received by the Office of the Adjutant General, 1871-1880.

65. *The Indianapolis News*, July 5, 1900.

66. *New York Times*, June 29, 1902.

67. Lew Wallace, letter to W. H. Bonney, March 15, 1879, Lew Wallace Collection, Indiana Historical Society.

68. Wm. H. Bonney, letter to Gov. Lew Wallace, March 4, 1881, Lew Wallace Collection, Indiana Historical Society.

69. W. Bonney, letter to Gov. Lew Wallace, March 27, 1881, Lew Wallace Collection, Indiana Historical Society.

70. Criminal Docket Book, Third Judicial District Court, October Term, March Term, 1881, Territorial Archives of New Mexico, State Records Center and Archives, pp 289, 273.

71. *Santa Fe Weekly New Mexican*, July 26, 1879.

72. James and Caroline's first child, Emil Dolan, died June 4, 1882. *Santa Fe Weekly New Mexican*, July 26, 1879.

8 – Trial in Mesilla

1. *Illinois State Journal*, March 24, 1922.

2. *Rio Grande Republican*, July 22, 1882.

3. Robert N. Mullin, *An Item from Old Mesilla*, undated, no publisher given.

4. *Fort Worth Star-Telegram*, December 2, 1928.

5. Katherine D. Stoes, "Frontier School Held in Court Room of La Mesilla; Pupils Vow Never to Sin – Nor to be Hanged," *Las Cruces Citizen*, April 23, 1953.

6. David G. Thomas, *La Posta – From the Founding of Mesilla, to Corn Exchange Hotel, to Billy the Kid Museum, to Famous Landmark* (Doc45 Publishing, 2013), pp 39, 61.

7. Federal Registry, Book B, March Term, 1881, Denver, NARA.

8. *Newman's Thirty-Four*, March 30, 1881.

9. Civil Docket Book, Third Judicial District Court, March Term, 1881, Territorial Archives of New Mexico, State Records Center and Archives; Federal Registry, Book B, March Term, 1881, Denver, NARA.

10. Federal Registry, Book B, March Term, 1881, Denver, NARA.

11. *Newman's Semi-Weekly*, April 2, 1881.

12. *Newman's Semi-Weekly*, April 2, 1881.

13. *Newman's Semi-Weekly*, April 4, 1881.

14. Civil Docket Book, March Term, 1881, Territorial Archives of New Mexico, State Records Center and Archives; Federal Registry, Book B, March Term, 1881, Denver, NARA.

15. L. Bradford Prince, ed., *The General Laws of New Mexico* (W. C. Little & Co., 1880), Chapter LI, Section 1, p 257.

16. Prince, *The General Laws of New Mexico*, Chapter L, Section 1, p 257.

17 Prince, *The General Laws of New Mexico*, Chapter LVII, Section 23, p 289.

18. Prince, *The General Laws of New Mexico*, Chapter LVII, Section 24, p 289.

19. Prince, *The General Laws of New Mexico*, Chapter XV, Section 18, p 67.

20. Territory vs Edward M. Kelly, Charles H. Gildersleeve, ed., *Reports of Cases Argued and Determined in the Supreme Court of the Territory of New Mexico, 1880 to 1883* (Callaghan & Co, 1911), pp 292-307.

21. Territory vs Edward M. Kelly, Gildersleeve, ed., *Reports of Cases Argued*, pp 292-307.

22. Territory vs Edward M. Kelly, Gildersleeve, ed., *Reports of Cases Argued*, pp 292-307.

23. *Santa Fe New Mexican*, Oct. 15, 1880; *Las Vegas Gazette*, Feb. 18, 1882.

24. *Santa Fe New Mexican*, Sept. 11, 1893.

25. Prince, *The General Laws of New Mexico*, Chapter LVII, Section 30, p 290.

26. Joseph E. Lopez, interview with David G. Thomas, Aug. 9, 2014; Katherine D.

Stoes, "Notes on the Jail," Katherine D. Stoes Papers, Archives and Special Collections, NMSU.

27. *Las Cruces Citizen*, April 23, 1953.

28. 1880 Mesilla Census Reports, taken June 20, 1880.

29. Prince, *The General Laws of New Mexico*, Chapter LXVIII, Section 1, p 366.

30. "Subpoena to Isaac Ellis, J. B. Mathews, Saturnino Baca, and Bonny Baca," March 1, 1881, Herman B. Weisner Papers, Archives and Special Collections, NMSU.

31. Robert Popper, "History and Development of the Accused's Right to Testify," Washington University Law Review, Vol. 1962, Issue 4, pp 454-471.

32. Popper, "History and Development of the Accused's Right to Testify," pp 454-471.

33. Prince, *The General Laws of New Mexico*, Chapter XXXII, No Section Number, p 151.

34. Popper, "History and Development of the Accused's Right to Testify," pp 454-471.

35. *Rio Grande Republican*, Sept. 2, 1882.

36. *Mesilla Valley Independent*, April 27, 1878.

37. "Instructions asked by defendant," April 9, 1881, William A. Keleher Papers, Center for Southwest Research, UNM.

38. "Instructions to the jury," April 9, 1881, Mary Daniels Taylor Papers, Archives and Special Collections, NMSU.

39. *Newman's Semi-Weekly*, April 9, 1881.

40. *Newman's Semi-Weekly*, April 13, 1881.

41. "Death Sentence of William Bonney," April 13, 1881, William A. Keleher Papers, Center for Southwest Research, UNM.

42. *The Union Sun* (Lockport, NY), March 10, 1905.

43. *Rio Grande Republican*, May 17, 1901.

44. *Santa Fe Daily New Mexican*, April 15, 1881.

45. *Santa Fe Daily New Mexican*, April 16, 1881.

46. *Santa Fe Daily New Mexican*, April 19, 1881.

47. *Newman's Semi-Weekly*, April 2, 1881.

48. *Newman's Semi-Weekly*, April 2, 1881.

49. Wm H. Bonney, letter to Lew Wallace, March 4, 1881, Lew Wallace Collection, Indiana Historical Society.

50. William Bonney, letter to Edgar Caypless, April 15, 1881, Maurice G. Fulton Papers, Special Collections, UA.

51. Affidavit by Edgar Caypless, April 19, 1881, Herman B. Weisner Papers, Archives and Special Collections, NMSU.

52. William Bonney vs Winfield Scott Moore, April 18, 1881, Herman B. Weisner Papers, Archives and Special Collections, NMSU.

53. William Bonney vs Winfield Scott Moore, July 26, 1881, Herman B. Weisner Papers, Archives and Special Collections, NMSU.

54. Romine was hanged March 14, 1881, at Silver City. His last statement was, *"Well, it's pretty damned rough to have to croak so soon, but a good many better men that I am have gone the same road and I guess I can stand it."* Territory vs Richard Romine, Gildersleeve, ed., Reports of Cases Argued, pp 114-120; *Santa Fe New Mexican*, March 15, 1881.

55. Romero was hanged February 2, 1883, at Springer. Territory vs Damian Romero, Gildersleeve, ed., *Reports of Cases Argued*, pp 474-479; *Las Vegas Gazette*, Feb. 1, 1883.

56. Robert Olinger appointed deputy sheriff, April 15, 1881, William A. Keleher Papers, Center for Southwest Research, UNM.

57. *Newman's Semi-Weekly*, April 20, 1881.

58. http://aa.usno.navy.mil/cgi-bin/aa_rstablew.pl, accessed April 18, 2020.

59. *Newman's Semi-Weekly*, April 10, 1881.

60. *Newman's Semi-Weekly*, April 10, 1881.

61. *Newman's Semi-Weekly*, April 16, 1881.

62. Wm H. Bonney, letter to Lew Wallace, March 2, 1881, Lew Wallace Collection, Indiana Historical Society.

63. Eileen Hunt, "Incident At Las Cruces," *Old West Magazine*, Fall, 1977; *Santa Fe New Mexican*, Sept. 12, 1882.

64. Information supplied by Dean Reade, grandson of Daniel M. Reade.

65. *Newman's Semi-Weekly*, April 20, 1881.

66. "Olinger's bill for transport expenses," April 21, 1881, Herman B. Weisner Papers, Archives and Special Collections, NMSU.

67. *St Louis Globe Democrat*, May 15, 1881.

68. *St Louis Globe Democrat*, May 15, 1881.

69. *Las Vegas Daily Gazette*, May 18, 1881.

70. *Mesilla News*, May 14, 1881.

71. *Las Vegas Daily Gazette*, May 18, 1881.

72. *Mesilla News*, May 14, 1881.

73. Mary Doughty Henschel, "Saint James Mission," 1876-1880, Katherine D. Stoes Papers, Archives and Special Collections, NMSU.

74. *Las Vegas Daily Gazette*, May 18, 1881.

75. *Mesilla News*, May 14, 1881.

76. Ketchum's last words were, *"Good bye, please dig my grave very deep... all right, hurry up;"* The *Albuquerque Daily Citizen* reported, *"When the body dropped through the trap the half inch rope severed his head as cleanly as if a knife had cut it. The body pitched forward, the blood spurting from the headless trunk. Many spectators turned away in horror. Doctor Slack pronounced life extinct in five minutes."* Albuquerque Daily Citizen, April 28, 1901.

77. The British Medical Journal cautioned: *"There are various incidents necessarily occurring at every execution by hanging which are found to affect the energy of the drop. The principal of these are: The stretching of the rope, the springing of the beam, the tightening of the knot at the top of the rope, the constriction of the neck of the culprit."* James Barr, "Judicial Executions," quoted in Ernest Hart, ed., *British Medical Journal*, Vol. II for 1891 (British Medical Association, 1891), p 822.

78. *Las Vegas Daily Gazette*, May 18, 1881.

79. *Mesilla News*, May 14, 1881.

80. *Mesilla News*, May 14, 1881.

81. *Rio Grande Republican*, May 21, 1881.

82. *Las Vegas Gazette*, April 28, 1881.

83. Joseph E. Lopez, interview with David G. Thomas, Aug. 9, 2014.

84. *Las Vegas Gazette*, April 28, 1881.

85. *Rio Grande Republican*, May 21, 1881.

86. Katherine D. Stoes, "Notes on the Jail," Katherine D. Stoes Papers, Archives and Special Collections, NMSU.

87. *Rio Grande Republican*, May 21, 1881.

88. *Rio Grande Republican*, May 21, 1881.

89. *Rio Grande Republican*, May 21, 1881.

90. *Las Vegas Gazette*, Feb. 1, 1883.

9 – End of the Road

1. *Newman's Semi-Weekly*, April 20, 1881.

2. Pat F. Garrett, *The Authentic Life of Billy, the Kid, the Noted Desperado of the Southwest, Whose Deeds of Daring Have Made His Name a Terror in New Mexico, Arizona, and Northern Mexico* (University of Oklahoma Press, 1954), pp 132-133.

3. The five other prisoners were Marejildo Torres, John Copeland, Augustin Davalas, Alexander Nunnelly, and Charles Wall. Eddie Taylor, "Eye Witness Prisoners: April 28, 1881," *The Outlaw Gazette*, November 2001, Vol. 14, p 18.

4. Garrett, *Authentic Life*, p 132.

5. Billy did not kill James Carlyle, although he was present when Carlyle was killed; Garrett, *Authentic Life*, p 133.

6. Garrett, *Authentic Life*, p 134.

7. *Daily New Mexican*, April 20, 1881.

8. *Las Vegas Daily Optic*, May 3, 1881; Garrett, *Authentic Life*, p 140.

9. *Las Vegas Gazette*, April 28, 1881.

10. *Santa Fe Daily New Mexican*, May 3, 1881.

11. Garrett, *Authentic Life*, p 135.

12. *Santa Fe Daily New Mexican*, May 3, 1881.

13. *The New Southwest*, Supplement, May 14, 1881.

14. *Las Vegas Daily Gazette*, May 10, 1881.

15. *Tombstone Epitaph*, June 6, 1881.

16. *Lincoln County Leader*, March 1, 1890.

17. *Golden Era*, May 5, 1881.

18. *Lincoln County Leader*, March 1, 1890.

19. *Las Vegas Daily Optic*, May 3, 1881.

20. Garrett, *Authentic Life*, p 140.

21. Garrett, *Authentic Life*, pp 138-139.

22. "Death Warrant of William Bonney," William A. Keleher Papers, Center for Southwest Research, UNM; "Death Warrant Order," April 30, 1881, Leon C. Metz Papers, C. L. Sonnichsen Special Collections, UTEP.

23. Garrett, *Authentic Life*, pp 139-140.

24. *The New Southwest*, Supplement, May 14, 1881.

25. *Santa Fe Daily New Mexican*, June 16, 1881.

26. *Santa Fe Daily New Mexican*, May 5, 1881.

27. Garrett, *Authentic Life*, p 142.

28. *Santa Fe Daily New Mexican*, May 20, 1881.

29. *Santa Fe Daily New Mexican*, May 4, 1881.

30. *Santa Fe Daily New Mexican*, May 5, 1881.

31. *Las Vegas Gazette*, May 12, 1881.

32. *Santa Fe Daily New Mexican*, May 13, 1881.

33. *Las Vegas Daily Optic*, May 14, 1881.

34. *Las Vegas Daily Optic*, June 10, 1881.

35. *Santa Fe Daily New Mexican*, June 10, 1881.

36. *Las Vegas Morning Gazette*, June 16, 1881.

37. *Albuquerque Journal*, Nov. 29, 1927; J. Evetts Haley, "Interview with Deluvina Maxwell," June 24, 1927, PPHMRC.

38. *Dallas Morning News*, July 8, 1928.

39. J. Evetts Haley, Interview with Deluvina Maxwell, June 24, 1927, PPHMRC.

40. Richard Weddle, "Shooting Billy the Kid," *Wild West*, August 2012, p 61.

41. Anaya, *I Buried Billy*, pp 75-76; Walter Noble Burns, *The Saga of Billy the Kid* (Grosset & Dunlap, 1926), p 186.

42. Anaya, *I Buried Billy*, p 77; Leon C. Metz, *Pat Garrett, The Story of a Western Lawman* (University of Oklahoma Press, 1974), p 58.

43. "Marriage Registry," Anton Chico Catholic Church; Copy in author's possession.

44. John William Poe, *The Death of Billy the Kid* (Sunstone Press, 2006), pp 27-28.

45. 1880 Census for Fort Sumner, taken June 14, 1880.

46. Elbert A. Garcia, *Billy the Kid's Kid* (Los Products Press, 1999), pp 30, 32, 39.

47. 1880 Census for Fort Sumner, p 18.

48. Garcia, *Billy the Kid's Kid*, pp 38-39.

49. *Albuquerque Daily Journal*, July 18, 1881.

50. Burns, *The Saga of Billy the Kid*, pp 183-184.

51. Walter Noble Burns, "A Belle of Old Fort Sumner," manuscript chapter, Walter Noble Burns Papers, UA, p 217.

52. Burns, "A Belle of Old Fort Sumner," p 219.

53. James W. Southwick, "Letter to E. A. Brininstool," Sept. 18, 1920, E. A. Brininstool Collection, Briscoe Center for American History, UTA.

54. James W. Southwick, "Letter to E. A. Brininstool," Sept. 25, 1920, E. A. Brininstool Collection, Briscoe Center for American History, UTA.

55. Burns, *The Saga of Billy the Kid*, pp 184.

56. John N. Copeland to Pat F. Garrett, quit claim deed May 23, 1881, Transfer of property in Lincoln, NM (Wortley Hotel) to Pat Garrett for $275.00, Lincoln County Trust.

57. Thomas, *Killing Garrett*, pp 19, 21

58. Garrett, *Authentic Life*, p 143.

59. Garrett, *Authentic Life*, p 143.

60. Poe, *The Death of Billy the Kid*, pp 18-19.

61. Poe, *The Death of Billy the Kid*, pp 20-21.

62. Poe, *The Death of Billy the Kid*, p 23.

63. Poe, *The Death of Billy the Kid*, p 26.

64. Garrett, *Authentic Life*, p 144.

65. Poe, *The Death of Billy the Kid*, p 29.

66. Poe, *The Death of Billy the Kid*, p 28.

67. Garrett, *Authentic Life*, pp 144-145.

68. Poe, *The Death of Billy the Kid*, p 31.

69. Poe, *The Death of Billy the Kid*, p 31.

70. Poe, *The Death of Billy the Kid*, p 31.

71. *Las Vegas Gazette*, July 19, 1881.

72. *Las Vegas Gazette*, July 19, 1881.

73. *Rio Grande Republican*, July 23, 1881.

74. Poe, *The Death of Billy the Kid*, p 32.

75. Poe, *The Death of Billy the Kid*, pp 34-35.

76. *Rio Grande Republican*, July 23, 1881.

77. Poe, *The Death of Billy the Kid*, p 37.

78. Poe, *The Death of Billy the Kid*, p 37.

79. Poe, *The Death of Billy the Kid*, p 38.

80. Louis Leon Branch, *Los Bilitos: The Story of Billy the Kid and His Gang* (Carlton Press, 1980), p 251.

81. *Chicago Daily Tribune*, July 27, 1881; Anaya, *I Buried Billy*, pp 124-125, 127.

82. *Clovis Evening News Journal*, May 31, 1937; *Albuquerque Journal*, June 28, 1926.

83. Poe, *The Death of Billy the Kid*, p 40.

84. Garrett, *Authentic Life*, p 148.

85. Garrett, *Authentic Life*, pp 144-145.

86. Garrett, *Authentic Life*, p 145.

87. Garrett, *Authentic Life*, p 145.

88. Anaya, *I Buried Billy*, pp 124-125.

89. Anaya, *I Buried Billy*, p 125.

90. Anaya, *I Buried Billy*, p 126.

91. *Las Vegas Gazette*, July 19, 1881.

92. *Las Vegas Gazette*, July 19, 1881.

93. Garcia, *Billy the Kid's Kid*, p 33.

94. Garrett, *Authentic Life*, pp 151-152.

95. Garrett, *Authentic Life*, p 148.

96. Poe, *The Death of Billy the Kid*, p 44.

97. *Clovis News-Journal*, July 13, 1938.

98. *Clovis News-Journal*, July 13, 1938.

99. *Rio Grande Republican*, July 23, 1881.

100. Coroner's Jury Report on William Bonney, July 15, 1881, Lincoln County Records, New Mexico State Records Center and Archives.

101. Coroner's Jury Report on William Bonney, July 15, 1881.

102. *Daily New Mexican*, May 5, 1881.

103. *Daily New Mexican*, July 21, 1881.

104. *Golden Era*, July 21, 1881.

105. *Daily New Mexican*, July 21, 1881.

106. *Rio Grande Republican*, July 23, 1881

107. *Las Vegas Daily Optic*, July 19, 1881.

108. *Rio Grande Republican*, July 23, 1881.

109. *Daily New Mexican*, July 21, 1881.

110. Act For the Relief of Pat Garrett, July 18, 1882, Territorial Auditor Papers, New Mexico State Records Center and Archives.

111. *The Roanoke Times*, December 14, 1892.

112. Fred R. Schwartzberg, "Pat Garrett Badge Authentication," *The Outlaw Gazette*, November, 2001, Vol. 14, p 17.

113. Poe, *The Death of Billy the Kid*, p 47.

114. *London Times*, August 18, 1881.

115. *Grant County Herald*, July 28, 1881.

116. *Santa Fe Weekly Democrat*, July 21, 1881.

117. *Las Vegas Daily Optic*, July 18, 1881

118. *Lincoln County Leader*, undated clipping.

119. *Lincoln County Leader*, undated clipping.

120. Coroner's Jury Report on William Bonney, July 15, 1881.

121. Anaya, *I Buried Billy*, p 132.

122. Anaya, *I Buried Billy*, p 132.

123. *Clovis News-Journal*, July 13, 1938.

124. Jean M. Burroughs, *On the Trail, The Life and Tales of "Lead Steer" Potter* (Museum of New Mexico Press, 1980), p 138; Evetts Haley, Interview with Deluvina Maxwell, June 24, 1927, PPHMRC.

125. Burroughs, *On the Trail*, p 139.

126. *Clovis Evening News-Journal*, May 19, 1934.

127. *Las Vegas Gazette*, July 18, 1881, quoted in *The Daily Gazette* (Colorado Springs CO), July 22, 1881.

128. Robert J. Stahl, *"We Saw 'Billy the Kid' Dead,"* Wild West History Association Journal, Dec., 2019, pp 20-26.

10 – Epilogue

1. David G. Thomas, *Billy the Kid's Grave – A History of the Wild West's Most Famous Death Marker* (Doc45 Publishing, 2017), p 41

2. *Clovis Evening News-Journal*, May 19, 1934.

3. *El Paso Herald*, December 9, 1905

4. *El Paso Herald*, August 25, 1927.

5. Thomas, *Billy the Kid's Grave*, p 52

6. *The Fort Sumner Leader*, April 11, 1930.

7. https://www.ulib.niu.edu/badndp/constellano_illion.html, accessed Oct. 14, 2020.

8. https://www.ulib.niu.edu/badndp/lewis_leon.html, accessed Oct. 14, 2020.

9. https://www.ulib.niu.edu/badndp/lewis_
leon.html, accessed Oct. 14, 2020.

10. https://babel.hathitrust.org/cgi/
pt?id=coo.31924022189355, accessed Oct.
14, 2020.

11. https://babel.hathitrust.org/cgi/
pt?id=coo.31924022189355, accessed Oct.
14, 2020.

12. *Rio Grande Republican*, December 3,
1881.

13. *Rio Grande Republican*, April 8, 1882.

Appendix A – Tunstall's Murder Site

1. *Albuquerque Journal*, April 4, 1927; *Las
Vegas Daily Optic*, December 19, 1929.

2. *Santa Fe New Mexican*, Oct. 25, 1927.

3. *Santa Fe New Mexican*, Oct. 25, 1927.

4. *Santa Fe New Mexican*, Dec. 19, 1929.

5. *Santa Fe New Mexican*, Dec. 19, 1929.

6. This reconstruction of Tunstall's murder
is derived from the accounts of the event
given under oath by Billy, Albert Howe, and
Florencio Gonzales to U.S. Department of
Justice Special Investigator Frank Warner
Angel, supplemented by recollections of Mrs.
Ealy and Robert Widenmann. Angel Report,
Interior Department Papers 1850-1907,
NARA; "Mrs. Ealy's Own Account," *New
Mexico Sentinel*, Oct. 5, 1937; Account of
Tunstall Killing, undated, Herman B. Weisner
Papers, Archives and Special Collections,
NMSU.

**Appendix B – Graves of Roberts and
Brewer**

1. *Alamogordo News*, Aug. 4, 1932.

2. *Albuquerque Journal*, June 13, 1932.

3. *Albuquerque Journal*, June 13, 1932.

4. *Alamogordo Daily News*, June 16, 1932.

5. *Alamogordo Daily News*, June 16, 1932.

6. The Blazer's Mill Cemetery is also called
the Mescalero Cemetery. *Ruidoso News*, June
29, 1989.

7. *Albuquerque Journal*, July 19, 1992.

Appendix C – Cast of Characters

1. *Santa Fe Daily New Mexican*, Nov. 13,
1880; *Las Vegas Daily Gazette*, Feb. 26, 1881.

2. *Santa Fe New Mexican*, Aug. 12, 1889.

3. *Silver City Enterprise*, June 26, 1903.

4. *Las Vegas Daily Optic*, May 28, 1890.

5. Blazer, "Dr. J. H.Blazer."

6. Frederick Nolan, *Tascosa, Its Life and
Gaudy Times* (Texas Tech University Press,
2007), pp 196-198.

7. Rich Eastwood, *Nuestras Madres, A Story
of Lincoln County New Mexico* (Creative
Space Independent Publishing, no date), pp
89, 92

8. Burton, *They Fought for "The House,"* p
39.

9. Donald R. Lavash, *Sheriff William Brady,
Tragic Hero of the Lincoln County War*
(Sunstone Press, 1986).

10. Gomes, "Manuel Brazil, A Portuguese
Pioneer in New Mexico and Texas," *Outlaw
Gazette*, Jan., 1995.

11. Harry Leighton, "The Story of Richard M.
Brewer, 1850-1878, Frontier Fighter, Farmer,
Cowboy," *Billy the Kid Outlaw Gang*, 2016.

12. *Rio Grande Republican*, Jan. 13, 1883.

13. Bill O'Neal, *Henry Brown The Outlaw-
Marshal* (Creative Publishing Co, 1980).

14. *Santa Fe New Mexican*, Dec.23, 1876;
Weekly Arizona Miner (Prescott AZ), Sept.
9, 1881; Maurice Kildare, "Murder at Sunset
Crossing," *Oldtimers Wild West*, January
1975, p 38.

15. *Honolulu Star Bulletin*, June 8, 1917.

16. *Evening News* (Emporia, KS), Sept. 29,
1883; *Garden City Telegram* (Garden City,
KS), March 2, 1907.

17. *Newman's Thirty-Four*, March 5, 1879.

18. Clifford, *Deep Trails in the Old West*.

19. *Cavern City Chronicle* (Carlsbad, NM),
May 22, 1930; *Las Vegas Daily Optic*, Dec.
19, 1929.

20. *Santa Fe Weekly New Mexican*, Jan. 3,
1880.

21. *Las Vegas Gazette*, June 24, 1881; *Las
Vegas Daily Optic*, June 13, 1884; *Santa Fe
Daily New Mexican*, Feb. 19, 1889.

22. *Las Vegas Gazette*, July 18, 1881, quoted
in *The Daily Gazette* (Colorado Springs CO),
July 22, 1881; *Las Vegas Daily Optic*, Feb. 9,
1887.

23. *Tri-Weekly Herald* (Marshall, TX), May
25, 1880; *Galveston Daily News*, July 9, 1880.

24. *Santa Fe Weekly New Mexican*, July 26, 1879; *Santa Fe Daily New Mexican*, March 2, 1898.

25. E. Donald Kaye, *Nathan Augustus Monroe Dudley, Rogue, Hero, or Both?* (Outskirts Press, 2007).

26. Ruth R. Ealy, "Medical Missionary," *New Mexico Magazine*, March, 1954.

27. *Douglas Daily Dispatch*, May 14, 1930.

28. *Santa Fe New Mexican*, Oct. 17, 1877.

29. "Mrs. Ealy's Own Account," *New Mexico Sentinel*, Oct. 5, 1937.

30. *Kansas Daily Commonwealth* (Topeka, KS), Nov. 11, 1871; Grady E. McCright and James H. Powell, *Jesse Evans: Lincoln County Badman* (Creative Publishing Company, 1983); *Santa Fe Weekly New Mexican*, Feb. 1, 1876.

31. Don McAlavy, "Uncle Charley Foor," *Outlaw Gazette*, Vol. XII, No. 1, Nov., 1999.

32. A. M. Gibson, *The Life and Death of Colonel Albert Jennings Fountain* (University of Oklahoma Press, 1965).

33. Thomas, *Billy the Kid's Grave*.

34. David G. Thomas, *Killing Pat Garrett, the Wild West's Most Famous Lawman – Murder or Self-Defense?* (Doc45 Publishing, 2019).

35. Francisco Gomez Statement, Exhibit 11, Dudley Court of Inquiry Records.

36. Daniel Flores, *Alexander Grzelachowski, Puerto de Luna's Renaissance Man*, Vol I and II, no date, no publisher; Francis C. Kajencki, Alexander Grzelachowski, Pioneer Merchant of Puerto de Luna, New Mexico, *Arizona and the West*, Vol. 26, No. 3, Autumn, 1984, pp 243-260.

37. Thomas, *Billy the Kid's Grave*; Elbert A. Garcia, *Billy the Kid's Kid* (Los Products Press, 1999).

38. Eastwood, *Nuestras Madres*, p 88

39. Lily Klasner, *My Girlhood Among Outlaws* (University of Arizona Press, 1972), pp 153-154.

40. Sidney Leonard Gardner, *A Just and Determined Man, The Life and Times of Ira Leonard*, (iUniverse, 2007); Philip J. Rasch, The Would-Be Judge, Ira E. Leonard, *The Denver Westerners Monthly Roundup*, Vol. XX, No. 7, July 1964.

41. https://www.ulib.niu.edu/badndp/constellano_illion.html, accessed Oct. 14, 2020.

42. *Clovis News-Journal*, December 22, 1940; *Santa Fe New Mexican*, Feb. 27, 1890.

43. Elvis E. Fleming, *J. B. "Billy" Mathews, Biography of a Lincoln County Deputy* (Yucca Free Press, 1999); *Roswell Register*, June 10, 1904.

44. Thomas, *Billy the Kid's Grave*.

45. Thomas, *Billy the Kid's Grave*.

46. Robert J. Stahl, "No! Paula Maxwell Was Never Pregnant with Billy the Kid's Love Child: Let's Finally Get Her Story to Conform to What Really Happened," unpublished manuscript; *Fort Sumner Review*, July 24, 1909.

47. Thomas, *Billy the Kid's Grave*.

48. *Las Vegas Gazette*, May 17, 1881.

49. *Las Vegas Gazette*, Aug. 17, 1878.

50. Kathleen P. Chamberlain, *In the Shadow of Billy the Kid* (University of New Mexico Press, 2013); Frederick Nolan, *The Lincoln County War, A Documentary History*, (Sunstone Press, 2009).

51. *Silver City Enterprise*, Dec. 7, 1882.

52. *Las Vegas Gazette*, Jan. 23, 1880; *Las Vegas Gazette*, Jan. 16, 1881.

53. *Fort Smith News Record*, March 15, 1905.

54. *Rio Grande Republican*, May 24, 1901.

55. Simeon H. Newman, "The Santa Fe Ring, A Letter to the New York Sun," *Arizona and the West*, Vol. 12, No. 3, Autumn, 1970, pp 269-288.

56. *Santa Fe Weekly New Mexican*, Sept. 20, 1879.

57. Robert Olinger testimony, Dudley Court of Inquiry Records

58. George Olinger, "A Look at the Controversies Surrounding Ameredith Robert B. Olinger," unpublished manuscript, 2010; Robert Olinger testimony, Dudley Court of Inquiry Records; George Olinger, "John Wallace Olinger, His Life, His Ancestors, and His Descendents," unpublished manuscript, 2010; Sheila Blair, "Bob Olinger, Family History," *The Outlaw Gazette*, Vol. VIII, No., Dec., 1995.

59. *Albuquerque Journal*, Feb. 7, 1935.

60. Paul L. Tsompanas, *Juan Patron, A Fallen Star in the Days of Billy the Kid* (Belle Isle Books, 2013).

61. George W. Peppin statement, Exhibit 8, Dudley Court of Inquiry Records; *Lincoln County Leader* (White Oaks, NM), March 29, 1884; *White Oaks Eagle*, (White Oaks, NM), Jan. 20, 1898.

62. Don McAlary, "Alejandro Perea Found Living in Township of Rio Colorado" *Outlaw-Gazette*, Nov., 1997; *Clovis News-Journal*, May 29, 1938.

63. Don Cline, "Tom Pickett, Friend of Billy the Kid, *True West*," July, 1997, pp 40-49; *Santa Fe New Mexican Review*, Jan. 11, 1884; *Winslow Mail*, May 18, 1934.

64. *Roswell Daily Record*, July 18, 1923.

65. Ron Owens, *Oklahoma Heroes, The Oklahoma Peace Officers Memorial* (Turner Publishing Company, 2000), p 162.

66. *Clovis News-Journal*, May 29, 1938.

67. *Valley Republican* (Kinsley KS), Feb. 2, 1878; *Larned Eagle Optic*. Feb. 7, 1878; *Kansas Weekly Commonwealth* (Topeka KS), June 27, 1878.

68. *Galveston Daily News*, Oct. 14, 1879.

69. *Santa Fe Daily New Mexican*, Nov. 13, 1880.

70. *Santa Fe Daily New Mexican*, April 20, 1881.

71. *Las Vegas Daily Gazette*, Dec. 4, 1881.

72. *The Southwesterner* (Columbus NM), Aug. 1, 1962.

73. *Albuquerque Journal*, Oct. 16, 1885.

74. *Las Vegas Daily Opti*c, May 8, 1911.

75. *Las Vegas Gazette*, July 18, 1881, quoted in *The Daily Gazette* (Colorado Springs CO), July 22, 1881.

76. *Las Vegas Daily Optic*, Nov. 15, 1887; Doyle Davis, "Milnor Rudolph, Santa Fe Trader and Prominent Citizen of New Mexico," *Wagon Tracks*, Vol. 24, No. 4, Aug., 2010, pp 1, 17-20.

77. Gary L. Roberts, *Death Comes for the Chief Justice* (University Press of Colorado, 1990); Darlis A. Miller, William Logan Rynerson in New Mexico, 1862-1893, *New Mexico Historical Review*, Vol. 48, No. 2, April, 1973, 101-130.

78. Yginio Salazar, statement of events in McSween house, July 20, 1878, Letters Received by the Office of the Adjutant General, 1871-1880.

79. Philip J. Rasch, Joseph E. Buckbee, and Karl K. Kline, "'Doc' Scurlock, Man of Many Parts," *Outlaw Gazette*, Vol. XII, No. 1, Nov., 1999, pp 23-24.

80. *Newman's Thirty-Four*, July 2, 1879.

81. *Santa Fe New Mexican*, Feb. 19, 1884; *Cleveland Plain Dealer*, June 3, 1890.

82. *Illinois State Journal*, March 24, 1922; Joseph Wallace, P*ast and Present of Sangmon County* (S. J. Clarke Publishing Company, 1904), Vol. 2., pp 1627-1628; James W. Southwick, "Letter to E. A. Brininstool," Sept. 18, 1920, E. A. Brininstool Collection, Briscoe Center for American History, UTA.

83. *The Raton Range*, May 13, 1935.

84. Mike Tower, *The Outlaw Statesman, the Life and Times of Fred Tecumseh Waite* (Authorhouse, 2007).

85. William S. Speer and John Henry Brown, eds., *The Encyclopedia of the New West* (U.S. Biographical Publishing Company, 1881), New Mexico Volume, pp 34-36.

86. *Las Vegas Daily Optic*, Feb. 25, 1881; Jack Demattos, "Gunfighters of the Real West, John Joshua Webb," *Real West*, April, 1981, pp 32-34, 54; Joseph W. Snell, "Wretched Webb," *Frontier Times*, Feb-March, 1973, pp 26-29, 64-69.

87. Nolan, *The Lincoln County War*, pp 428-433.

88. *Las Vegas Gazette*, May 18, 1882.

89. Donald R. Lavash, *Wilson and the Kid*, (Creative Publishing Company, 1990); *Santa Fe New Mexican Review*, Jan. 11, 1884; *Santa Fe New Mexican*, Feb. 12, 1882; *Santa Fe New Mexican*, Sept. 15, 1882.

90. Jan. 4, 1875, *Santa Fe New Mexican*.

91. March 16, 1876, *Santa Fe New Mexican*; John B. Wilson testimony, Dudley Court of Inquiry Records.

Index

Killing Pat Garrett, The Wild West's Most Famous Lawman - Murder or Self-Defense?

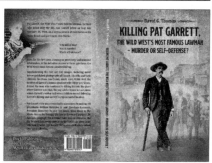

Pat Garrett, the Wild West's most famous lawman – the man who killed Billy the Kid – was himself killed on leap day, February 29, 1908, on a barren stretch of road between his Home Ranch and Las Cruces, New Mexico.

- Who killed him?

- Was it murder?

- Was it self-defense?

No biographer of Garrett has been able to answer these questions. All have expressed opinions. None have presented evidence that would stand up in a court of law. Here, for the first time, drawing on newly discovered information, is the definitive answer to the Wild West's most famous unsolved killing.

Supplementing the text are 102 images, including six of Garrett and his family which have never been published before. It has been 50 years since a new photo of Garrett was published, and no photos of his children have ever been published.

Garrett's life has been extensively researched. Yet, the author was able to uncover an enormous amount of new information. He had access to over 80 letters that Garrett wrote to his wife. He discovered a multitude of new documents and details concerning Garrett's killing, the events surrounding it, and the personal life of the man who was placed on trial for killing Garrett.

- The true actions of "Deacon Jim" Miller, a professional killer, who was in Las Cruces the day Garrett was killed.

- The place on the now abandoned old road to Las Cruces where Garrett was killed.

- The coroner's jury report on Garrett's death, lost for over 100 years.

- Garrett's original burial location.

- The sworn courtroom testimony of the only witness to Garrett's killing.

- The policeman who provided the decisive evidence in the trial of the man accused of murdering Garrett.

- The location of Garrett's Rock House and Home Ranches.

- New family details: Garrett had a four-month-old daughter the day he killed Billy the Kid. She died tragically at 15. Another daughter was blinded by a well-intended eye treatment; a son was paralyzed by childhood polio; and Pat Garrett, Jr., named after his father, lost his right leg to amputation at age 12.

Garrett's life was a remarkable adventure. He met two United States presidents: President William McKinley, Jr. and President Theodore Roosevelt. President Roosevelt he met five times, three times in the White House. He brought the law to hardened gunmen. He oversaw hangings. His national fame was so extensive the day he died that newspapers from the East to the West Coast only had to write "Pat Garrett" for readers to know to whom they were referring.

2020 Will Rogers Medallion Award Finalist for Excellence in Western Media
2020 Independent Press Award Distinguished Favorite, Historical Biography
2019 Best Book Awards Finalist, United States History
2019 Best Indie Book Notable 100 Award Winner.

Doc45 Publications

La Posta – From the Founding of Mesilla, to Corn Exchange Hotel, to Billy the Kid Museum, to Famous Landmark, David G. Thomas, paperback, 118 pages, 59 photos, e-book available.

"For someone who grew up in the area of Mesilla, it's nice to have a well-researched book about the area – and the giant photographs don't hurt either.... And the thing I was most excited to see is a photo of the hotel registry where the name of "William Bonney" is scrawled on the page.... There is some debate as to whether or not Billy the Kid really signed the book, which the author goes into, but what would Billy the Kid history be without a little controversy?" –Billy the Kid Outlaw Gang Newsletter, Winter, 2013.

Giovanni Maria de Agostini, Wonder of The Century – The Astonishing World Traveler Who Was A Hermit, David G. Thomas, paperback, 208 pages, 59 photos, 19 maps, e-book available.

"David G. Thomas has finally pulled back the veil of obscurity that long shrouded one of the most enduring mysteries in New Mexico's long history to reveal the true story of the Hermit, Giovanni Maria de Agostini. ...Thomas has once again proven himself a master history detective. Of particular interest is the information about the Hermit's life in Brazil, which closely parallels his remarkable experience in New Mexico, and required extensive research in Portuguese sources. Thomas's efforts make it possible to understand this deeply religious man." – Rick Hendricks, New Mexico State Historian

Screen With A Voice - A History of Moving Pictures in Las Cruces, New Mexico, David G. Thomas, paperback, 194 pages, 102 photos, e-book available.

The first projected moving pictures were shown in Las Cruces 110 years ago. Who exhibited those movies? What movies were shown? Since projected moving pictures were invented in 1896, why did it take ten years for the first movie exhibition to reach Las Cruces? Who opened the first theater in town? Where was it located? These questions began the history of moving pictures in Las Cruces, and they are answered in this book. But so are the events and stories that follow.

There have been 21 movie theaters in Las Cruces – all but three or four are forgotten. They are unremembered no longer. And one, especially, the Airdome Theater which opened in 1914, deserves to be known by all movie historians – it was an automobile drive-in theater, the invention of the concept, two decades before movie history declares the drive-in was invented.

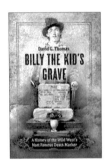

Billy the Kid's Grave – A History of the Wild West's Most Famous Death Marker, David G. Thomas, paperback, 154 pages, 65 photos.

"Quien es?"

The answer to this incautious question – "Who is it?" – was a bullet to the heart.

That bullet – fired by Lincoln County Sheriff Patrick F. Garrett from a .40-44 caliber single action Colt pistol – ended the life of Billy the Kid, real name William Henry McCarty.

But death – ordinarily so final – only fueled the public's fascination with Billy the Kid. What events led to Billy's killing? Was it inevitable? Was a woman involved? If so, who was she? Why has Billy's gravestone become the most famous – and most visited – Western death marker? Is Billy really buried in his grave? Is the grave in the right location?

These questions – and many others – are answered in this book.

Doc45 Publications

The Stolen Pinkerton Reports of the Colonel Albert J. Fountain Murder Investigation, David G. Thomas, editor, paperback, 194 pages, 28 photos.

The abduction and apparent murder of Colonel Albert J. and Henry Fountain on February 1, 1896, shocked and outraged the citizens of New Mexico. It was not the killing of Colonel Fountain, a Union Civil War veteran and a prominent New Mexico attorney, which roused the physical disgust of the citizenry - after all, it was not unknown for distinguished men to be killed. It was the cold-blooded murder of his eight-year-old son which provoked the public outcry and revulsion.

The evidence indicated that although Colonel Albert J. Fountain was killed during the ambush, his son was taken alive, and only killed the next day.

The public was left without answers to the questions:

- Who ambushed and killed Colonel Fountain?
- Who was willing to kill his young son in cold-blood after holding him captive for 24 hours?

The case was never solved. Two men were eventually tried for and acquitted of the crime.

The case file for the crime contains almost no information. There are no trial transcripts or witness testimonies. The only reports that exist today of the investigation of the case are these Pinkerton Reports, which were commissioned by the Territorial Governor, and then stolen from his office four months after the murders. These Reports, now recovered, are published here.

These Reports are important historical documents, not only for what they reveal about the Fountain murders, but also as a fascinating window into how the most famous professional detective agency in the United States in the 1890s - the Pinkerton Detective Agency - went about investigating a murder, at a time when scientific forensic evidence was virtually non-existent.

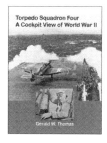

Torpedo Squadron Four – A Cockpit View of World War II, Gerald W. Thomas, paperback, 280 pages, 209 photos, e-book available.

"This book contains more first-person accounts than I have seen in several years. ...we can feel the emotion... tempered by the daily losses that characterized this final stage of the war in the Pacific. All in all, one of the best books on the Pacific War I have seen lately." – Naval Aviation News, Fall 2011.

Made in the USA
Monee, IL
30 November 2023

47123124R10164